T0305258

Aging and Working in the New Economy

Aging and Working in the New Economy

Changing Career Structures in Small IT Firms

Edited by

Julie Ann McMullin

University of Western Ontario, Canada

and

Victor W. Marshall

University of North Carolina at Chapel Hill, USA

Edward Elgar

Cheltenham, UK • Northampton, MA, USA

Published by
Edward Elgar Publishing Limited
The Lypiatts
15 Lansdown Road
Cheltenham
Glos GL50 2JA
UK

Edward Elgar Publishing, Inc.
William Pratt House
9 Dewey Court
Northampton
Massachusetts 01060
USA

A catalogue record for this book
is available from the British Library

Library of Congress Control Number: 2009937769

Mixed Sources
Product group from well-managed
forests and other controlled sources
www.fsc.org Cert no. SA-COC-1565
© 1996 Forest Stewardship Council
FSC

ISBN 978 1 84844 177 4

Printed and bound by MPG Books Group, UK

Contents

Contributors

Tracey L. Adams is an Associate Professor in the Department of Sociology at the University of Western Ontario, in London, Ontario, Canada. Her research focuses on the sociology of work, and especially the nature and development of professional work across time and place. Her current research projects focus on the formation and regulation of professions and inter-professional conflict in Canada.

Elizabeth Brooke is Associate Professor, Business Work and Ageing Centre for Research, Swinburne University, Melbourne, Australia. She is the Australian Chief Investigator within the Workforce Aging in the New Economy (WANE) project. She has been researching the effects of aging workforces by conducting organizational case studies since the late 1990s. Most recently she has undertaken projects applying the Finnish work ability approach to support retention. She was awarded a five-year VicHealth Fellowship to trial the construction of employment pathways into aged care work targeting older non-employed people. As Chief Investigator in an Australian Research Council research project, she examined the implementation of work ability in case study organizations.

Neil Charness is the William G. Chase Professor of Psychology and an Associate in the Pepper Institute on Aging and Public Policy at Florida State University in Tallahassee, Florida, USA. He received his BA (McGill University, 1969), MSc, and PhD (Carnegie Mellon University, 1971, 1974) in psychology. Charness was at Wilfrid Laurier University in Ontario, Canada (1974–1977), then University of Waterloo, Ontario, Canada (1977–1994), before joining the Psychology Department at Florida State University in 1994. His research interests include understanding relations between age and technology use, expert performance, and work performance. He has authored or co-authored over 100 journal articles and book chapters.

Martin Cooke is an Assistant Professor, jointly appointed in the Sociology Department and Department of Health Studies and Gerontology at the University of Waterloo, in Waterloo, Ontario, Canada, where he teaches in the Masters of Public Health program. His research interests are in welfare state policies and the life course and the social demography of aboriginal peoples.

Erin I. Demaiter is a PhD candidate in the Department of Sociology at the University of Toronto in Toronto, Ontario, Canada. Her research focuses on the sociology of work, occupations, and gender, with a special focus on information technology workers in the new economy. She is currently completing her dissertation, entitled 'The study of organizational structures and workers: behaviours in highly skilled, small sized information technology firms in Canada'.

Mark C. Fox graduated from Michigan State University in East Lansing, Michigan, USA, in 2003 while working in the memory and aging lab of Rose Zacks. Since 2005, he has worked with Neil Charness at Florida State University, studying age-related differences in higher-level cognition, focusing primarily on how individual and age group differences in top-down processes influence problem solving and fluid ability. His other interests are methodological concerns involving the use of process-tracing methods such as concurrent verbalization and eye-tracking. His more applied research has involved studying age-related differences in response to the stress of technology, and assisting in research aimed at improving the traffic safety of older adults.

Sara B. Haviland received her MA in sociology at the University of North Carolina at Chapel Hill, North Carolina, USA, under the direction of Arne Kalleberg, with a thesis entitled: 'The gender paradox in job satisfaction: an international perspective'. In addition to work and family, Sara is interested in issues of employer benefits, retirement timing, retention of the healthcare workforce in long-term care, risk and society, and the life course. She served as Research Manager at the Institute on Aging for the Jobs to Careers project, and also for the US Workforce Aging in the New Economy (WANE) component. She is completing her dissertation from WANE data, under the supervision of Victor Marshall.

Victor W. Marshall, Head of the US component of Workforce Aging in the New Economy (WANE), is Director of the UNC Institute on Aging and Professor of Sociology at the University of North Carolina at Chapel Hill, North Carolina, USA. His PhD in sociology is from Princeton University. As Director of CARNET, the Canadian Aging Research Network, he developed an extensive research program, Issues of an Aging Workforce, that gathered case study data from firms in Canada and the United States to investigate the impact of workforce aging on human resources policy.

He has held several executive positions in the field of aging, including Vice-President of the Canadian Association on Gerontology, Editor of *The Canadian Journal of Aging*, and member of the Executive Committee of the International Association on Gerontology. His previous books include *Restructuring Work and the Life Course* and *Social Dynamics of the Life Course*.

Julie Ann McMullin is a Professor in the Department of Sociology and Associate Dean in the Faculty of Social Science at the University of Western Ontario, London, Ontario, Canada. She received her BA and MA from the University of Western Ontario and her PhD from the University of Toronto. Her recent work examines social inequality in paid work, especially in relation to older workers, and in families. She was the principal investigator of the Workforce Aging in the New Economy (WANE) project. Her edited book, *Working in Information Technology Firms: Intersections of Gender and Aging* is forthcoming and a second edition of her book, *Understanding Social Inequality: Class, Age, Gender, Ethnicity, and Race in Canada* (2010), was recently published by Oxford University Press.

Jennifer Craft Morgan is a Research Scientist and Associate Director for Research at the UNC Institute on Aging. She was Research Coordinator of the US Workforce Aging in the New Economy (WANE) and Workforce Issues in Library and Information Science projects at the UNC Institute on Aging. She is a co-investigator on the Better Jobs, Better Care applied research project and the on-going long-term care intervention program 'Win A Step Up'. She received her MA and PhD (2005) from the Department of Sociology at the University of North Carolina at Chapel Hill, North Carolina, USA. Dr Morgan's substantive interests include medical sociology, gender stratification, work and occupations and life course and aging. She is particularly interested in the intersection of issues of gender, age, health and work.

Kerry Platman is a Senior Research Fellow at the Warwick Institute for Employment Research, one of Europe's leading centers for research in the labor market field. Based at the University of Warwick in Coventry, England, she specializes in the aging of the workforce and its impact on employment and retirement practices. Her current research examines management practices and career transitions in the information technology sector. She speaks and writes about a range of issues associated with workforce aging, including: the management of longer working lives; age discrimination in employment; the business impact of workforce aging;

flexible transitions into retirement; learning and training over the life course; age management and healthy working lives; and employment and care burdens in later life.

Gillian Ranson is an Associate Professor in the Department of Sociology at the University of Calgary in Calgary, Alberta, Canada. Her research and teaching interests are in the interwoven areas of gender, families and paid employment. Apart from her participation in the Workforce Aging in the New Economy (WANE) project, she has recently completed a study of non-traditional families, described in a forthcoming book published by UTP Higher Education, called *Against the Grain: Couples, Gender and the Reframing of Parenting*.

Kim M. Shuey is an Assistant Professor of sociology at the University of Western Ontario in London, Ontario, Canada. Her research focuses on inequality in life course health and issues related to aging within the context of changing labor markets. Current research projects include investigations of cumulative advantage processes in life course health, the relationship between work context and disability accommodations, and worker health and well-being in new economy sectors.

Heather Spiegel is a PhD student in Organizational Behavior at the Richard Ivey School of Business in London, Ontario, Canada. She studies how work-related stressors affect the health and well-being of individuals. In addition to examining burnout in the IT sector, she also investigates how incivility and work–home conflict affect employee and organizational outcomes.

Acknowledgments

This research was supported by a grant from the Initiative on the New Economy (INE) program of the Social Sciences and Humanities Research Council of Canada, Julie McMullin, Principal Investigator. Our thanks go to all of the Workforce Aging in the New Economy (WANE) project co-investigators, students, post-doctoral fellows and other project associates whose work over the last seven years made this book possible. Special thanks to Emily Jovic and Catherine Gordon, WANE researchers and doctoral students in the Department of Sociology at the University of Western Ontario, who proofread, reference checked and formatted the chapters in this book.

1. Introduction: aging and working in the New Economy

Julie Ann McMullin and Victor W. Marshall

This book is about aging and working in the New Economy. It is about how individuals manage their paid work within firms that are struggling to survive and compete in global economies. It is also about the tensions that arise as workers and owners struggle for personal and firm survival, two processes that are often contradictory and result in paradoxes that occasionally produce conflict. For centuries, of course, tension, contradiction, paradox, and conflict have been used to describe the employment relations that exist between employers and employees. Yet, as this book will show, the specific character of employment relations and the tension, contradiction, paradox, and conflict that ensue, take on a somewhat different character in the small, New Economy firms in this study.

Throughout the 1990s, the New Economy concept came to refer to the idea that old ways of doing business were waning, largely due to advances in information technology, the innovative implementation of these technologies in the workplace, and the commodification of knowledge (Castells, 1996; Ranson, 2003). Although there have been debates about how new the New Economy really is, the evolution of employment relations over the last several decades and the idea that 'business is not being conducted as usual' have policymakers, think tanks, and academics taking notice. Indeed, according to Chris Benner 'it is not at all an exaggeration to say that we are in the midst of an information revolution as significant for changing economic and social structures in the twenty-first century as the first and second industrial revolutions were for the nineteenth and twentieth centuries' (Benner, 2002: 1–2). Although it is difficult, and perhaps premature, to say for certain whether the changes in the use of information technology could be classified as a revolution of the same magnitude and scope as the first and second industrial revolutions, one need only consider the vast changes in manufacturing processes and the omnipresence of email and text messaging at work and at home to recognize that profound change is underway.

The transformation of employment relations in the New Economy has coincided with workforce aging. Over the next few decades, population

1

and workforce aging in industrialized nations will occur at unprecedented rates, reducing the indigenous supply of younger workers entering the labor force. Potential labor shortages in certain knowledge-based industrial sectors, along with concerns about financial support of retirees, and the need for companies in fast-paced industries to respond rapidly to market demands, have prompted commentators to argue that a critical issue facing industrialized countries is the retention and retraining of workers throughout the life course. This will require encouraging employers and governments to develop workplace and social policies that consider the changing needs and capacities of workers across the life course so that they can remain productive over a longer term.

Understanding the complexities associated with aging and working in new economies requires a multi-level analysis that takes into account processes of globalization as they are realized in local contexts, the place of firms within these processes, and the situation of individuals within these firms. The 'life course perspective' is well suited to such an analysis and guides our work by providing a conceptual framework for analysing the complex relationships between individual lives and social change. New economic realities mean that individuals face rapidly changing labor markets and these realities have ramifications that extend across the life course. Yet, research has not explicitly considered what it means to age and work in a New Economy industry from a life course perspective. Hence, the primary objective of this book is to contribute to our understanding of how careers take shape as workers age within the context of a changing labor market. In this chapter, we begin with a discussion of our study design and then briefly outline some of the key concepts of the life course perspective as they relate to aging and working in the New Economy. As we discuss these life course concepts we also introduce and provide brief overviews of the chapters in this book.

WANE: THE WORKFORCE AGING IN THE NEW ECONOMY STUDY

The chapters in this book draw on data from the project, 'Workforce Aging in the New Economy Project: A Comparative Study of Information Technology Firms,' an international study that was funded in 2002 by the Social Sciences and Humanities Research Council of Canada (for more details about the project see www.wane.ca). The broad objective of WANE was to study the intersection of workforce aging and the restructuring of work within information technology (IT), an industrial sector that may be considered a benchmark case of a New Economy. Because we were interested in highly skilled, knowledge work that is characteristic of New Economy employment, our primary focus in this study was with a subsector of IT firms, those that are classified as software and computer systems design and services under the North American Industry Classification 54151 (Duerden Comeau, 2004: 1).

The WANE project examined the nature of work within the IT industry and how employment relations and human resource practices shape and are shaped by the life course transitions of workers. To examine these issues, a team of researchers conducted case study research in small and mid-sized information technology sector firms located in four countries, Australia, Canada, England, and the United States.

To address our study objectives, we conducted in-depth assessments of IT employment from the perspective of both employers and employees. We used a case study research design which allowed us to consider multiple points of view that, when taken together, provide us with a more complete understanding of the relationships among members in a given organization (see Marshall, 1999; Ragin, 2000; see also Chapter 3). In the WANE study, a case is broadly defined as an IT firm and several criteria were established for firms to be eligible for participation in the study. Firms had to be in operation at least one year and have four or more staff. The conditions of participation could not compromise data collection. Thus, firms were required to support employee involvement in the study, provide access to HR documents, and in most cases, allow researchers to observe on site for a predetermined amount of time. A focus on smaller businesses was salient as very little research on IT work has considered small to medium-sized enterprises (SMEs), which are in fact quite prevalent in all of our study countries. For example, in 2001, 96 percent of IT firms in Canada and 93 percent of computer services businesses in the United Kingdom (UK) employed less than 10 people (Bjornsson, 2001; Da Pont, 2003). Similarly, in Australia, 88 percent of IT firms employ 0–4 workers and 29 percent of IT workers were employed in small firms in 2001 (Brooke et al., 2004). Data from the US show that 85.3 percent of IT firms employed fewer than 10 workers in 2006 (United States Census Bureau, 2006).

Within each country, IT firms were further targeted on criteria suited to the particular region and industry context. Geographical location was a primary and effective means of seeking participants, for convenience and cost effectiveness, and also because of the proximity, and in some cases, association of researcher post-secondary institutions with sector 'hot beds' – regions in which there is a relatively high concentration of IT activity. Table 1.1 outlines the cities and regions from which the case studies were selected in each country. In some regional contexts, particularly Australia and England, case firms were also monitored in order to maximize heterogeneity beyond the baseline conditions outlined above. Criteria in this

Table 1.1   City/regional representation of case study firms

Team	City/Region
Australia	Melbourne, Sydney, Brisbane, the Gold Coast
Canada	London, Ottawa, Calgary
England/United Kingdom	Cambridgeshire, West Midlands, London, South East England, South West England
United States	North Carolina (NC) – Research Triangle Region, Florida (FL) – Tallahassee

regard included IT sub-sector, firm ownership arrangements and management structure, and the demographic composition of staff (for example, gender, age).

Such variation in the selection of firms into the sample creates a potential for bias, as some may have been specifically targeted or are particularly sensitive to certain workforce issues. This would be problematic if the aim of the study was to illustrate broad, generalizable trends; however, the intent here is to use mixed methodology to document experiences and processes relating to the nature of IT work.

Case Study Selection

The processes through which case studies were selected varied somewhat from country to country. In Canada, a sampling frame was defined using city and IT business directories. Then short, sampling frame telephone surveys were conducted in spring 2004 to gain access to firms and to learn more about the local IT landscape. Data were collected at this stage to inform regional IT context and case firm eligibility. Sampling frame respondents, usually firm owners or senior management personnel, were asked basic questions about the firm (for example, how long the firm had been in business, what products or services they provided, and so forth), its workforce (for example, number of employees, demographic composition) and the IT field in general (for example, subcontracting, skilled worker shortages). They were also asked if they would be willing to be contacted again about involvement in case studies and/or key informant interviews. Virtually all of the Canadian case firms were recruited through this sampling frame interview process; one case came from a contact list provided by one of four key informants.

For North Carolina, the US team employed a similar sampling frame methodology, drawing on regional professional association directories. Those who completed a sampling frame survey and whose firms were eligible (see criteria above) were asked if they would participate in a key informant interview; snowball sampling was used to recruit additional key informants. In-person, key informant interviews ($n = 46$) were conducted with industry representatives and business executives in order to learn about their perspectives on IT employment and workforce aging issues. These interviews also aided in the identification of firms that might be suitable for, and amenable to, participation in case studies. Because there were many fewer IT firms in the Tallahassee region, in Florida the US team directly recruited from a regional listing of IT firms.

The Australian team took a different approach to recruitment, forgoing the sampling frame interview method. Instead, the team used print media releases to raise awareness about the study and also disseminated study information to local business councils and technology networks. A formal business information kit was created for distribution through these various channels and interested parties returned an enclosed 'expression of interest' form to the team, which initiated the case study process. Many Australian case firms were therefore self-selected into the project; additional firms were tapped through referrals and social contacts.

For their research in England, the UK-based team employed media releases and an information kit. They also enlisted the help of the UK employer organization for the IT sector, which circulated details of the study to its members. One firm was recruited in this way; the rest were approached directly, cold-calling using contact information from technical directories, listings and recommendations.

Negotiations with potential case study firms began in mid-2004 and field work continued through early 2006. In most cases, negotiations entailed a series of telephone conversations and eventually a meeting between the research team leader and the company executive – usually the firm owner(s) and/or senior management. Owners and managers who agreed to have their company participate in the study signed a case study agreement form on behalf of the firm, outlining mutually determined parameters of participation. Typically, firms agreed to supply employee contact information, access to HR policies and employee participation time. In return, the research teams pledged to provide the participating company with first access to international research reports. Feedback reports were also provided to each firm in Canada and the US, and also to the larger British firms.

Data Collection

Whenever researchers entered a firm, they took observational notes about the environment and how work is structured. These notes were recorded after most company visits, including negotiations and interviews. Archival data were also collected for each case study company from publicly available sources such as business trade journals, magazine or newspaper articles and company websites, as well as firm-specific newsletters, human resource policy documents, annual reports and collective agreements. Where applicable (not all firms had such information available), HR documents and policy related material were provided by the CEO or administrative/HR staff. Finally, we conducted both in-depth, qualitative interviews and self-administered web surveys with managers and employees at each case study firm.

In-depth interviews were conducted with company executives, human resource managers, and employees in various occupational groups. Respondents were asked about their personal histories and experiences with IT work, and for management, their views about the IT field in general. As well, demographic attributes (for example, gender, age, job title, tenure at firm, family status) were gathered from the interviews for each participant. The number of interviews targeted at each firm depended largely on characteristics of the organization, such as number of employees and occupational groups. For many of the firms, and particularly the smaller ones, all employees and managers were invited to take part. In some cases, however, research teams solicited a particular profile of respondents using characteristics such as age, gender, occupational role or length of tenure; in other cases, management made autonomous exclusions – such as those in certain roles (for example, non-IT positions) or contract workers.

The firm provided contact information for potential participants, usually most or all of their employees, and qualitative interview invitations were delivered to each person. Employees were then contacted by telephone or email to see if they might be interested in participating. If an individual declined the request, there was no further attempt to involve that person. For those who agreed, a convenient time was arranged for an interview. Most interviews took place in a private office or meeting room at the respondent's place of work; occasionally, they occurred off work premises or via telephone at the discretion or preference of the interviewee. In some cases, a company liaison facilitated the scheduling. Interviews were recorded on tape and/or digitally. They generally lasted for about one hour, but ranged from 30 minutes to upwards of three hours.

Managers and employees were invited to complete a self-administered web survey. This solicited information about demographic characteristics, work history, attitudes about older and younger workers, non-standard employment practices, and so on. Retrospective questions about life course transitions, using well-established procedures that map out the timing and sequencing of individual lives, were also included. Web surveys took approximately 40 to 60 minutes to complete and could be filled out at the discretion of respondents from any location with internet access. An

Table 1.2 Interview participation, survey response, and partial completion rates

Region	Interviews		Surveys			
	#	participation rate (%)[a]	#	response rate (%)[a]	# complete	partials (%)[b]
Australia	91	82	81	22	69	15
Canada	141	81	107	60	94	12
England	61	100	125	75	117	6
United States	106	90	139	50[c]	123	12
Total	**399**	**86**	**452**	**46**	**403**	**11**

Notes:
a. Participation and response rates are calculated using the number of interview transcripts/survey records out of the number of *eligible* respondents at each firm; eligible respondents are those who were invited to participate in the study
b. 'Partials' refers to the proportion of incomplete survey records (i.e., those who completed at least the first section, but did not complete the entire survey; does not include question non-responses)
c. One US case, a medium firm of 100+ staff, experienced complications with data collection as company officials had not fully bought into study participation and as such, the project never really took off in that location. Removing these cases from the US response rate yields a cleaned response rate of 67%. Responses from this company remain available for analysis.

important feature of the survey was the ability for respondents to complete it in stages, over days or weeks as required. The qualitative and quantitative components of this research are complementary, with the former providing information on meaning and process and the latter providing data that allows us to describe, contextualize and, to a limited extent, make generalizations about the nature of work in IT firms.

Management input and logistical considerations meant that not all employees in all firms were targeted for inclusion, particularly in larger companies. Across the 47 case study firms in four countries, there were 399 in-depth interviews and 452 web surveys (49 of those were partial completions). There was significant, but not perfect, overlap between the interviews and web surveys: 45 percent of respondents did both; 23 percent completed an interview but no survey; and 32 percent filled out a web survey only. This variation reflects both participant and researcher-initiated selection processes. Table 1.2 shows how the interviews and surveys are divided among the four countries.

The overall participation rate for the interviews is 86 percent, ranging from 81 percent in Canada to 100 percent in England. This figure represents the number of viable interview transcripts (i.e., electronic failures are excluded) out of the total number of eligible participants in each country. As noted previously, both researcher considerations and management dictates meant that not all employees at all firms were invited to participate. The participation rate reflects both direct and soft refusals from potential interviewees, as well as those who may have agreed but did not participate for whatever reason. The British team engaged in negotiations with managers and requested interviews once they were on site, which likely served to augment their participation rate.

The overall survey response rate is 46 percent and ranges from a low of 22 percent in Australia to 75 percent in England. These rates are influenced by lower participation in larger firms, where nearly all employees received a survey invitation, yet had little or no contact with the research team. In smaller firms, most or all employees were interviewed. Most respondents ($n = 403$, or 89 percent) completed the survey in full; regional partial completion rates were between 6 and 15 percent.

Sample Characteristics – Firms

From mid-2004 through early 2006, 47 firms took part in the study, with 586 unique individuals participating in interviews and/or web surveys, responding to questions on a wide range of topics. Table 1.3 presents characteristics of firms broken down by country. Keeping with the project's interest in understudied small and mid-sized businesses, the majority of case study firms ($n = 37$, or 79 percent) are quite small, employing just 4 to 20 people. Seven firms employed between 21 and 99 workers and three had between 100 and 250 staff.

Pinpointing how long these firms had been in business proved challenging because many had experienced an assortment of mergers, divisions, and name changes. Thus, the reported year of inception may vary on these terms. From the data on offer, firms were in operation on average 9.8 years; however, nearly half were less than 8 years old. Three-quarters of the firms were involved with software and/or web development. Six percent of the firms focused on systems analysis and support functions and 19 percent were involved in consulting, business or other endeavors.

Sample Characteristics – Participants

Table 1.4 contains a sample profile by country of select demographic characteristics of those who participated in the interviews (I) and web surveys (S).

Survey and interview samples overlap considerably so rather than

Table 1.3   Firm characteristics

	Region				Total	
	Australia	Canada	England	US	*n*	%
Firm size						
4–20	9	17	4	7	**37**	79
21–99	1	1	2	3	**7**	15
100–250	1	0	1	1	**3**	6
Firm age						
>5 years	2	4	3	2	**11**	24
5–10 years	5	6	2	6	**19**	40
11–20 years	2	7	1	3	**13**	28
21+ years	2	1	1	0	**4**	8
Firm specialization						
Software/web development	6	13	7	9	**35**	75
Systems analysis/ support	1	1	0	1	**3**	6
Consulting/business	4	4	0	0	**8**	17
other	0	0	0	1	**1**	2
# Case study firms	**11**	**18**	**7**	**11**	**47**	

discussing both, for illustrative purposes, the interview data will be discussed here. While we make no claim that the sample is representative of the IT industry as a whole, the profile is comparable to reports of industry and labor force composition (Duerden Comeau, 2004). In particular, our sample reflects industry trends in the distribution of gender (male-dominated) and age (generally younger than overall labor force averages).

Interview participants ranged in age from 19 to 63, with a mean of 38.4 years. In England and the US, respondents were, on average, slightly older (40 years) compared to Canada and Australia (approximately 37.4 years). Nearly three-quarters (71 percent) of the sample are men. A small proportion of respondents (12.6 percent) were identified as visible minorities. There were considerable regional differences in this designation, with Australia and the US having higher proportions of visible minorities in their samples, compared to Canada and England.

In addition to demographic characteristics, occupational data were collected in the surveys and through descriptive information contained in the in-depth interviews. From the surveys, 80 percent of respondents report working in one of 26 IT/technical roles, while 20 percent held non-IT

Table 1.4 Sample characteristics

Interview/Survey	Australia		Canada		England		US		All regions	
	I	S	I	S	I	S	I	S	I	S
N	*91*	*81*	*141*	*107*	*61*	*125*	*103*	*139*	*399*	*452*
Age (in years)[a]										
mean	37.6	38.1	37.2	37.4	40.0	37.8	40.0	38.7	38.4	38.0
median	37.0	35.0	37.0	38.0	39.0	36.0	41.0	38.5	38.0	37.0
range	21–61	23–62	19–62	20–63	22–63	21–64	23–63	20–63	19–63	20–64
% age 45+	27.6	27.9	24.8	19.8	33.3	27.4	33.3	28.7	28.9	25.8
Gender										
% female	40.7	34.8	23.4	23.4	26.2	23.1	26.4	30.6	28.6	27.5
% male	59.3	65.2	76.6	76.6	73.8	76.9	73.6	69.4	71.4	72.5
Minority status[b]										
% visible minority	17.6	5.8	6.4	9.6	6.0	5.1	20.7	15.4[b]	12.6	9.4

Notes:

a. For the interviews, 'age' was reported at the time of the interview; for the surveys, 'age' was calculated as @ 2005 using the respondent's birth year; this is reflected in discrepancies in age range

b. US survey respondents were asked a filter question 'Are you Spanish/Hispanic/Latino' followed by a 'select all that apply' race question; all other regions were asked 'Are you a member of an ethnic/visible minority group?'

Table 1.5   Interview sample characteristics – occupations

	Australia	Canada	England	US	all regions	*n*
Occupation						398
IT/technical role %	48.4	41.8	37.7	36.2	41.2	164
IT/other role %	14.3	14.2	14.8	34.3	19.6	78
IT/management role %	19.8	17.7	23.0	17.1	18.1	75
Non-IT role	9.9	13.5	13.1	6.7	10.8	43
CEOs/Presidents	7.7	12.8	11.5	5.7	9.5	38
% contractor	7.8	12.1	0	0	6.3	398
Job tenure (in years)						388
mean	5.2	5.3	7.5	3.3	5.1	
median	3.0	4.0	7.0	2.0	4.0	
range	0–29	0–21	0–30	0–19	0–30	
n	*91*	*141*	*61*	*103*	*399*	*399*

positions. Interview respondents were asked about their job and tasks and ten broad occupational categories were distilled from this more detailed qualitative data. These job groupings were further refined into IT/technical roles (programmers, engineers, technicians), IT/other roles (analysts, other), non-IT roles (administration, HR, sales/marketing), management (IT managers) and CEOs/presidents. By and large, most respondents (79 percent) work in positions that entail a considerable technical component – programmers, engineers, technicians, analysts and IT management. Table 1.5 contains a sample profile by country of occupation-related characteristics of the workers who were interviewed. Australia and Canada included some contract workers in their samples, while England and the US did not. In some cases, based on the nature of their employment relationship, these workers would have been excluded from the original contact list by firm management. Finally, for job tenure, respondents were employed with their firms for a mean of 5.1 years. There was some regional variation, with British employees more likely, on average, to have longer tenures (7.5 years) and American workers shorter ones (3.3 years).

Analysis

The vastness and richness of the WANE data are at once a curse and a blessing. A curse because it is very difficult to make full use of all of the different data sources across all the different countries and a blessing because the possibility of doing so is there. In this book, our use of the data is modest. Some chapters rely only on quantitative data, others only on the qualitative data, and still others combine both the qualitative and the quantitative data in the analysis. All chapters use data from at least two countries and some use data from all of our study countries. Some of the chapters use case study analyses; others rely on individual level data analysis. In each of the chapters, authors outline their specific use of the data and the methods of analyses they use. Although some may quibble with the eclectic nature of our approach, this book, and a second, that is being published (McMullin, forthcoming) represent some of our preliminary steps in understanding the data and our aim is that they will shed some theoretical insights into the nature of work in the IT sector.

THE LIFE COURSE PERSPECTIVE

All of the chapters in this book draw on the life course perspective at least to some extent. The significance of the life course perspective is that it guides research in terms of problem identification and formulation and that it has 'made time, context, and process more salient dimensions of theory and analysis' (Elder, 1995: 104). The concept of 'social structure' is linked to the notion of 'context' in the above quotation and refers to the idea that social life is organized and patterned so that individuals, quite often unconsciously, act in a certain way because 'that's the way it has always been done.' Social structures influence all aspects of behavior because they represent 'taken-for-granted mental assumptions or modes of procedure that actors normally apply without being aware that they are applying them' (Sewell, 1992: 22). With respect to the life course, researchers in the European tradition consider how nation states and labor systems organize the life course and argue that the life course itself is a social structure because patterns in the sequencing and timing of life course transitions (for example, school-to-work; work-to-retirement) can be identified in societies (Marshall and Mueller, 2003). Alternatively, life course researchers in the North American tradition focus more on age structure and the associated roles and status positions that are organized on the basis of age (Marshall and Mueller, 2003). From our perspective these views of social structure are interconnected. Hence, in this book we consider how age and the life course structure working in the New Economy and how institutions such as labor systems and nation states, influence the structure of individuals' lives.

Social structures influence individuals' choices and behavior but they do not fully determine them (McMullin and Marshall, 1999). Hence, when we consider context and process as we do in life course research we must also consider human agency. Human agency plays a role in 'how individuals construct their own life courses through the choices and actions they take within the opportunities and constraints of history and social circumstances' (Marshall and Mueller, 2003: 20). Furthermore, individuals actively attempt to manage their lives – they make decisions about the timing of their careers and their training and they negotiate and navigate the social structures that serve to constrain their choices (Marshall and Mueller, 2003).

'Social time' is a fundamental consideration in life course research and is examined in multiple ways. First, individuals begin the dynamic and contextual aging process at birth. Age is thus a relative concept and what is 'old' or 'older' in one context may not be in another. Second, the historical time in which individuals are born influences individuals' experiences and the aging process. As a result, the particular economic and social context into which one is born, goes to school, and begins paid work, shapes life experiences. Third, individuals make transitions from one life course stage to another (e.g. from education to paid work) and, in most societies, the timing and sequencing of these transitions is patterned. At the same time, aging processes and the patterning of life course transitions are shaped by social contexts and cultural meanings that lead to some diversity in the sequencing of life course events and social transitions (Elder and O'Rand, 1995; Hagestad, 1990; Heinz, 2001; Marshall and Mueller, 2003; Mayer, 1988). Hence, with its emphasis on time, context, and aging processes, the life course framework allows us to examine how individuals negotiate paid work within the New Economy. In particular, there are two principles of the life course paradigm related to time – 'lives in time and place' and 'the timing and sequencing of lives' (Elder 1994, 1995) – that are considered in most of the chapters in this book and require further discussion here.

The life course perspective provides a conceptual framework for analyzing the complex relationships between individual lives and social change (Elder, 1994; Marshall and Mueller, 2003; Heinz, 2001). It allows us to examine how individuals manage social change and how their past experiences affect their ability to cope with such change. Structural characteristics of work in the New Economy and their potential influence on individual lives are important contextual considerations that relate to the life course concept, lives in time and place. Studies of the progression of individuals through life course stages and life events, must always take into account the context of economic and social change (Leisering and Leibfried, 1999; Heinz, 1997). Related to the New Economy, the idea here is that individual experiences will be different depending on the life stage one is at when changes to the economic order ensue (McMullin et al., 2007). In other words, life course research begins with the characteristics of a particular event (for example changes associated with the New Economy) and then assesses how this event affects individual lives while taking into account the age of individuals at the time of the historical event that led to social change.

We know that we are facing a new era of work which is increasingly characterized by greater individualism, job insecurity, risk, and instability (Smith, 2001). Traditional economies are giving way to ones marked by the commodification of knowledge and technological change (Castells, 1996). Governments and employers are increasingly stressing the need for workers to manage their own careers and encourage them to engage in lifelong learning to keep up with changes in technology. Do these changes in the structure and organization of work influence career development? Do they influence the wage negotiations? Are there unique pressures associated with working in a New Economy firm? How do workers keep up with new technology? These are among the questions related to the lives in time and place principle that are addressed in this book.

Thus far this discussion has focused much more on the lives in time part of the lives in time and place concept. Yet, 'place' is a central element of the analyses that are presented in this book. All the chapters in this book examine, in one way or another, the extent to which changes in the organization of IT work vary across our study countries. On the one hand, because education, labor, and social welfare policies vary significantly across our study countries we might expect differences in this regard. Alternatively, the global nature of the IT industry or the fact that labor market policies may apply more readily to large firms than to small ones, may mitigate some of these expected variations.

In old industrial economies, and at a time when life expectancies were lower, the timing and sequencing of lives was thought to be standardized through school-to-work-to-retirement transitions with few job disruptions or changes. Of course, there was a lot of irregularity in life course sequencing with significant variations along class, gender, and ethnic and racial lines (Connidis, 2009; Marshall and Mueller, 2003; Ranson, 1998; Rindfuss et al., 1987). For all groups, however, organizational restructuring in new economies may lead to shifts in patterns of career transitions (Heinz, 1997) and in patterns of training and knowledge acquisition. With this in mind, this book considers the following questions: To what extent does the structure of work in new economies lead to variation in the timing and sequencing of lives? Do workers transition in and out of careers with time off to retrain? To what extent does formal versus informal training matter in these transitions? Do family transitions influence career and training transitions?

The importance of family transitions points to the notion of 'linked lives,' the final life course concept that is considered in several chapters in this book. Discontinuous work histories and non-standard employment are characteristics of new economies but, historically, they are issues that have been confronted by many women who take primary responsibility for family caring even when employed (Duxbury and Higgins, 1994; Fast and Da Pont, 1997; Ginn et al., 2001). The life course concept of linked lives underscores the fact that an individual's actions in the labor market are intricately influenced by that individual's connections to others, including family members. Hence, a life course view of the New Economy must also be applied to the trajectory of family transitions in order to examine their mutual influence (Connidis, 2009; Szinovacz et al., 1992). A multifaceted life course perspective that incorporates the timing, duration, and sequencing of education, training, work, family, and retirement (Elder, 1994; Heinz, 2001) captures the complexities of balancing work and family over an increasingly individuated life course (Henretta, 2000). It also enhances multilevel analysis in which the experiences of individuals are linked to their relationships in various social domains (for example work and family) and with broader social, economic, and political issues. Recognizing the importance of linked lives in the context of New Economy work, our book considers the following questions: Does the structure and organization of work in New Economy firms influence the timing and sequencing of life course transitions among employees and do life course transitions outside paid work influence careers? Does it make sense to think about employment policy from a life course perspective that takes into account linked lives?

CHAPTER OVERVIEWS

This book is organized in three parts. Chapters 2 to 5 consider the concept of career and how the structure of work influences career development among IT workers. Chapters 6 and 7 consider issues of training, education and credentials within the context of IT employment and Chapters 8 to 10 consider the implications of the structure of IT work for employees' health and issues related to public policy.

Making Careers in Changing Structures

There is an emerging distinction between work and employment in the New Economy.

> Work refers to the actual activities workers perform, the skills, information, and knowledge required to perform those activities and the social interaction

involved in the process of performing that work. Employment, on the other hand, refers to the contractual relationship between employer and employee, including compensation systems and management practices. (Benner, 2002: 4)

Another emerging distinction is between jobs and careers, an issue that Victor W. Marshall, Jennifer Craft Morgan, and Sara B. Haviland take up in Chapter 2. In this chapter, the authors consider the differences between tasks, jobs and careers and argue that the way careers are experienced by IT workers is rather unique. Taking into account both the structural features of work in the IT sector as well as issues related to human agency and subjective careers, Marshall and his colleagues ask 'what constitutes a career in IT?' They show that IT careers are characterized by a lack of stability and career progression and that the structural organization of work in IT firms leads to much individuation of career ownership. This stands in contrast to 'old economy' industries in which internal labor markets had much more influence on an individuals' career structures.

In Chapter 3, Haviland, Craft Morgan, and Marshall further discuss the complexity of a New Economy careers by considering individuals' perceptions of career success. If the barometer of success in traditionally organized firms was perceived as working one's way up the career ladder in an internal labor market, how do employees gauge their success in the New Economy and what management practices are related to individuals' perceptions of career rewards? To address this question, Haviland and her colleagues construct a career rewards scale and distinguish the IT companies that fall in the top quintile on this scale, 'high career reward firms,' from those who fall in the bottom quintile, 'low career reward firms.' In high career reward firms, employees felt that they gained career rewards by being included in business decisions, firm-based training and development, and being able to maintain a balance between work and life. Management practices in these firms focused on inclusion and on developing both the firm *and* human capital among its employees. These rewards were absent in low career reward firms largely because the management practices in these firms favored client concerns over providing an enriching work environment for employees.

Gillian Ranson, in Chapter 4, takes the analysis of New Economy careers still further through a discussion of the 'boundaryless career' and an analysis of the career trajectories of IT workers in small firms. Focusing on men's careers (recognizing that men comprise the majority of IT workers), Ranson asks: (1) 'What place do small firms, founded at different time periods and with different histories, have in the career trajectories of men working in IT? and, (2) What theoretical model of "career" best fits the career trajectories of the men in the study?' In response to the first question, Ranson convincingly shows that small, viable IT firms play a role in launching, stabilizing, building, and sometimes saving, careers within the industry. Ranson takes the lives in time and place specifically into account by distinguishing between firms established before 2000 and those established after 2000. She shows that there are some opportunities in the older, more well-established firms to build long-term, single-employer careers, adding further complexity to debates around the idea of boundaryless, New Economy careers.

The concept of risk in relation to New Economy careers is touched on in Chapters 2 through 4. Indeed, for many workers who are coming of age in the era of the New Economy, careers will be characterized by greater risk. The risks of doing business that were typically assumed by entrepreneurs and owners are increasingly being dispersed to workers (McMullin, et al., 2008). It seems then that a new category of employees has emerged, who like the entrepreneur of post-Fordist economic orders, must assume responsibility for risk without the possibility of deriving profit from the risk. This leads to matters related to the wage and how employees negotiate wages in an environment of instability and risk. Elizabeth Brooke examines these issues in Chapter 5 as she asks: 'What sets of distribution practices are in place?' and 'What are the implications for older workers and for women?' Brooke differentiates between two types of firms that are differentiated according to profitability and volatility. High-end, profitable firms linked remuneration strategies to productivity and a rational rewards system thereby removing individual agency from the wage negotiation process. These firms engaged in a 'chargeable hours' process which 'rationed time and money.' Wages were unstandardized and highly individualized in these firms and there was a focus on rewards and the ability to jump ahead of regular wage structures as a result. In theory, employees in more volatile firms could exercise their agency in the negotiation of the wage. Yet, in practice, the fragility of the firms left little room for owners to offer more. These firms were often limited in their capacity to make their payroll which heightened the risk for employees within these firms. Notably, older workers and women were more often employed in volatile firms and thus had fewer opportunities to achieve higher wages.

Knowledge and Training

In new economies, maintaining lifelong employment in one firm is increasingly rare (although possible as noted in Chapter 4) and there is a heightened emphasis on lifelong learning that enables workers to keep pace with technological change (Lowe, 2001). But how is lifelong learning achieved in New Economy employment? Do employees transition in and out of formal educational programs as they negotiate their employment in the New Economy and are certain workers better able to do this than others? What role do informal training mechanisms play in keeping workers' skills current? Do training patterns vary depending on age, gender or job status? Chapters 6 and 7 address these questions.

In Chapter 6, Tracey L. Adams and Erin I. Demaiter consider self-learning and skill acquisition drawing on Manuel Castell's idea of the 'self-programmable' worker – 'workers who are flexible, adaptable and quick to retrain.' They further examine the roles that formal education, credentials and self-learning play in developing 'self-programmable' employees. This chapter provides descriptive data on the types of skill acquisition process in which IT workers engage, and the various transitions that IT workers make from school or training programs to paid work. It also considers IT workers' perceptions of skill acquisition and its importance, and an examination of whether factors such as age or gender are influential in either regard. Although one might expect little variation in the extent to which IT workers engage in independent learning, Adams and Demaiter find some variation on that score especially with respect to credential attainment. In short, Adams and Demaiter conclude that today's flexible, self-programmable worker is also a credentialed worker, but not necessarily a credentialed worker in the traditional sense.

Neil Charness and Mark C. Fox consider the issue of training in relation to age, job status, and gender in Chapter 7. Although age did not influence the likelihood of receiving training in the past year, compared to younger workers, older workers engaged in fewer training days and among those who reported no training, older workers had lower levels of self-efficacy than younger workers. Men were more likely than women to view training as unnecessary, managers were more likely than non-managers to use the skills gained from formal training, and non-IT workers (sales and administrative staff) were less likely to report that training was available than IT workers within these firms. Finally, there was an overall perception that there was a lack of time for adequate training. And, as Chapter 8 shows, the lack of time for training is linked to stress.

Stress Outcomes – Policy Solutions

Chapters 8 to 10 consider the implications of working and aging in the New Economy for stress outcomes and policy matters. The stress associated with aging and working in the New Economy is taken up in Chapter 8. In this chapter, Kim M. Shuey and Heather Spiegel show how negotiating the need to keep skills current within the structural context of IT work is stressful for workers and is experienced differently by workers depending on their age and life course stage. Stress and burnout are often normalized among IT workers in firms that organize work around tight deadlines and long working hours and create workplace cultures that glorify 16-hour work days. Shuey and Spiegel show that life course transitions, particularly the transition to parenthood, heighten the work-related stress and burnout that workers experience (see also Connidis and Kemp, forthcoming) and that relationships with friends and family members are often strained because of the pressures associated with work. Employees and employers actively engage in strategies that help to reduce stress levels. Employers would sometimes attempt to create fun work atmospheres, encourage employees to take time off, or put in place flexible work hour options in an effort to alleviate employee stress. For their part, some employees would actively set boundaries between their work and personal lives in an effort to manage stress. But, often, escapist strategies that involve daydreams of lives outside of IT or in management positions served as a way for workers to manage their stress.

As the chapters in this book show, the pressures associated with aging and working in the New Economy are not insignificant. As we noted earlier, a critical issue facing industrialized countries is the retention and retraining of workers throughout the life course. The question that we face then is how policies can be transformed to consider the changing needs and capacities of workers across the life course so that they can remain productive over a longer term. Considering 'flexicurity' and transitional labor market (TLM) policy ideas from Europe that explicitly considered life course issues in their development, in Chapter 9, Martin Cooke and Kerry Platman examine 'how employees currently navigate insecure employment, and how policies might be formulated to better provide security.' Cooke and Platman show how labor market transitions are influenced by other life course transitions often having to do with family formation and development. They argue that life course informed policies such as flexicurity and TLM hold promise for enabling workers to better negotiation employment insecurity in the New Economy.

In our final chapter we conclude by considering the research contained in this book and how it has contributed to our understanding of working in the New Economy. We consider how employment relations and the structure of paid work in the New Economy may be unique and we show how the life course perspective enables us to shed light on the simultaneous processes of aging and working. Aging has generally been ignored in studies of paid work but, as the chapters in this book show, working and aging are interrelated, dynamic processes that influence career development and employees' well-being.

NOTES

1. Excerpts from this section are taken from E. Jovic, J.A. McMullin and T. Dureden Comeau (forthcoming). Chapter 2, Methods. In J.A. McMullin (ed.), *Gender, Age and Work in the New Economy: The Case of Information Technology Firms*. Kelowna: University of British Columbia Press.
2. Our focus is on one industry within IT or ICT services, namely the computer design and related services Industry. In Industry Canada data, Total ICT services typically includes the following: software publishers, telecommunications services, cable and other program distributors, internet service providers, data processing, hosting and related Services, and often, ICT wholesaling. Where possible in this report we utilize the term IT reflecting our interest in the computer design sector (NAICS 54151) of ICT services.

REFERENCES

Benner, C. (2002), *Work in the New Economy: Flexible Labor Markets in Silicon Valley*, Malden, MA: Blackwell Publishing.

Bjornsson, K. (2001), 'Computer services: strong employment growth and low labour productivity despite high labour costs and a highly-educated labour force', *Statistics in Focus: Industry, Trade and Services*, theme 4-11/2001, catalogue no. KS-NP-01-011-EN-I, Eurostat: European Communities.

Brooke, L., L. Rolland, E. Jones and C. Topple (2004), *Australian Country Report, WANE International Report No. 3*, London, ON: University of Western Ontario, Workforce Aging in the New Economy (WANE), available at www.wane.ca.

Castells, M. (1996), *The Rise of the Network Society*, Malden, MA: Blackwell Publishers.

Connidis, I.A. (2009), *Family Ties*, 2nd edn, Thousand Oaks, CA: Sage.

Connidis, I.A., and C. Kemp (forthcoming), 'Negotiating work and family in the information technology industry', in J.A. McMullin (ed.), *Working in Information Technology Firms: Intersections of Gender and Aging*, Kelowna, BC: University of British Columbia Press.

Da Pont, M. (2003), 'Building the perfect system: an analysis of the computer systems design and related services industry', in *Analytical Paper Series–Service Industries Division, Statistics Canada*, (catalogue no. 63F0002XIE-No. 45, Ottawa: Statistics Canada.

Duerden Comeau, T. (2004), *Cross-national Comparison of Information Technology Employment, WANE International Report No. 5*, London, ON: The University of Western Ontario, Workforce Aging in the New Economy (WANE), available at www.wane.ca.

Duxbury, L. and C. Higgins (1994), 'Families in the economy', in M. Baker (ed.), *Canada's Changing Families: Challenges to Public Policy*, Ottawa: Vanier Institute of the Family, pp. 29–40.

Elder, G.H., Jr. (1994), 'Time, human agency, and social change: perspectives on the life course', *Social Psychology Quarterly*, **51** (1), 4–15.

Elder, G.H., Jr. (1995), 'The life course paradigm: historical, comparative, and developmental perspectives', in P. Moen, G.H. Elder, Jr. and K. Luscher (eds), *Examining Lives and Context: Perspectives on the Ecology of Human Development*, Washington, DC: American Psychological Association Press, pp. 101–39.

Elder, G.H., Jr. and A. O'Rand (1995), 'Adult lives in a changing society', in K. Cook, G. Fine and J.S. House (eds), *Sociological Perspectives on Social Psychology*, New York: Allyn and Bacon, pp. 452–75.

Fast, J. and M. Da Pont (1997), 'Changes in women's work continuity', *Canadian Social Trends*, Catalogue no. 11-008- XPE, pp. 2–7, Ottawa: Statistics Canada.

Ginn, J., D. Street and S. Arber (2001), 'Cross-national trends in women's work', in J. Ginn, D. Street and S. Arber (eds), *Women, Work and Pensions: International Issues and Prospects*, Philadelphia, PA: Open University Press, pp. 11–30.

Hagestad, G. (1990), 'Social perspectives on the life course', in R.H. Binstock and L.K. George (eds), *Handbook of Aging and the Social Sciences*, 2nd edn, New York: Van Nostrand-Reinhold, pp. 36–61.

Heinz, W.R. (1997), 'Status passages, social risks, and the life course: a conceptual framework', in W.R. Heinz (ed.), *Theoretical Advances in Life-course Research. Vol. I of Status Passages and the Life Course*, 2nd edn, Weinheim, Germany: Deutscher Studien Verlag, pp. 9–21.

Heinz, W.R. (2001), 'Work and the life course: a cosmopolitan-local perspective', in V.W. Marshall, W.R. Heinz, H. Krüger and A. Verma (eds), *Restructuring Work and the Life Course*, Toronto, ON: University of Toronto Press, pp. 3–28.

Henretta, J.C. (2000), 'The future of age integration in employment', *The Gerontologist*, **40** (3), 286–92.

Jovic, E., J.A. McMullin and T. Dureden Comeau, (forthcoming), 'Appendix A: methods', in J.A. McMullin (ed.), *Working in Information Technology Firms: Intersections of Gender and Aging*, Kelowna, BC: University of British Columbia Press.

Leisering, L. and S. Leibfried (1999), *Time and Poverty in Western Welfare States*, Cambridge: Cambridge University Press.

Lowe, G.S. (2001), 'Youth, transitions, and the new world of work', in V.W. Marshall, W.R. Heinz, H. Krüger, and A. Verma (eds), *Restructuring Work and the Life Course*, Toronto, ON: University of Toronto Press, pp. 29–44.

Marshall, V.W. (1999), 'Reasoning with case studies: issues of an aging workforce', *Journal of Aging Studies*, **13** (4), 377–89.

Marshall, V.W. and M.M. Mueller (2003), 'Theoretical roots of the life-course perspective', in W.R. Heinz and V.W. Marshall (eds), *Social Dynamics of the Life Course: Transitions, Institutions, and Interrelations*, New York: Aldine De Gruyter, pp. 3–32.

Mayer, K.U. (1988), 'German survivors of World War II: the impact on the life course of the collective experience of birth cohorts', in M.W. Riley (ed.), in association with B.J. Huber and B.B. Hess, *Social Structures and Human Lives: Vol. 1. Social Change and the Life Course*, Newbury Park, CA: Sage, pp. 229–46.

McMullin, J.A. (ed.) (forthcoming), *Gender, Age and Work in the New Economy: The Case of Information Technology Firms*, Kelowna, BC: University of British Columbia Press.

McMullin, J.A. and V.W. Marshall (1999), 'Structure and agency in the retirement process: a case study of Montreal garment workers', in C. Ryff and V.W. Marshall (eds), *The Self and Society in Aging Processes*, New York: Springer, pp. 305–38.

McMullin, J.A., T. Duerden Comeau and E. Jovic (2007), 'Generational affinities and discourses of difference: a case study of highly skilled information technology workers', *British Journal of Sociology Volume*, **58** (2), 297–316.

McMullin, J.A., V.W. Marshall, T. Duerden Comeau and C. Gordon (2008), 'Aging and employment relations: dilemmas of owners and workers in a risk society', paper presented at the American Sociological Association Meetings, Boston, MA: August.

Ragin, C.C. (2000), *Fuzzy-set Social Science*, Chicago, IL and London: University of Chicago Press.

Ranson, G. (1998), 'Education, work and family decision-making: finding the "right time" to have a baby', *Canadian Review of Sociology and Anthropology*, **35** (4), 483–99.

Ranson, G. (2003), Understanding the 'New Economy': A Conceptual Journey, *WANE Working Paper No. 3*, London, ON: University of Western Ontario, Workforce Aging in the New Economy (WANE), available at www.wane.ca.

Rindfuss, R.R., C.G. Swicegood and R.A. Rosenfeld (1987), 'Disorder in the life course: how common and does it matter?', *American Sociological Review*, **52** (6), 785–801.

Sewell, W.H.J., Jr. (1992), 'A theory of structure: duality, agency, and transformation', *American Journal of Sociology*, **98**, 1–29.

Smith, V. (2001), *Crossing the Great Divide: Worker Risk and Opportunity in the New Economy*, Ithaca, NY: ILR Press.

Szinovacz, M., D. Ekerdt and B.H. Vinick (1992), 'Families and retirement: conceptual and methodological issues', in M. Szinovacz, D.J. Ekerdt and B.H. Vinick (eds), *Families and Retirement*, Newbury Park, CA: Sage, pp. 1–19.

United States Census Bureau (2006), '2006 county business patterns', accessed 23 March 2009 at www2.census.gov/csd/susb/2006/usalli06.xls.

2. Making a life in IT: jobs and careers in small and medium-sized information technology companies

Victor W. Marshall, Jennifer Craft Morgan and Sara B. Haviland

More than a dozen years ago, in an article on the software industry, sociologist and business guru Rosabeth Moss Kanter (1995: 52) opined that 'The requiem for jobs and careers as the American middle class has known them has already sounded. Some purveyors of career advice claim that "jobs" are increasingly obsolete; instead, people will perform tasks on a project-by-project basis under short-term contracts'. She went on to note that 'The software and related knowledge industries are inventing a new kind of career with profound implications for the way we work and live'. Kanter's observation covers only one aspect of IT sector work, where the concept of career, and its relationship to jobs, has developed a much broader meaning. In this chapter we explore these issues through a comparative study of IT workers in small and medium sized enterprises—the social location where traditional careers are probably at greatest risk. As Cappelli (1999: 14) has observed.

> much of contemporary American society has been built on stable employment relationships characterized by predictable career advancement and steady growth in wages. Long-term individual investments such as home ownership and college educations for children, community ties and the stability they bring, and quality of life outside of work have all been enhanced by reducing risk and uncertainty on the job. . . . How these characteristics may change with the new employment relationship is an open question.

In this chapter we focus on changes in the way careers are experienced in a New Economy sector.

To understand changes in the domain of careers and their implications, we need to understand the difference between a task, a job, and a career. These concepts will be defined in turn. Task work is piece work, in which people are paid for deliverables. People are paid for completing tasks rather than for the time they are contracted to work. In the IT sector of interest to us, tasks refer to specific projects that are often 'outsourced' (and often 'offshored'), with payment dependent on completing the project. Alternatively, tasks may be assigned to temporary workers brought into the firm but working on a project or deliverable basis rather than an hourly wage or salary. A job is work that is paid for time applied to it. If a worker or employer manage to keep a job going for a long period of time, that job could become a career. In the IT companies we studied, our main interest is in the circumstances in which the employees are working in jobs or careers – although some of the work of these companies is often performed as tasks.

In the world of work, tasks, jobs and careers have both individual and organizational dimensions. In traditional work settings, especially large ones, one can think of a career organizationally as a linked set of positions arranged hierarchically. As Wilensky (1961: 522) puts it, an 'orderly career' is one 'in which one job normally leads to another, related in function and higher in status.' Structurally, he defines career as 'a succession of related jobs, arranged in a hierarchy of prestige, through which persons move in an ordered (more-or-less predictable) sequence.' Corollaries are that the job pattern is instituted (socially-recognized and sanctioned within some social unit) and persists (the system is maintained over more than one generation of recruits). In a bank, for instance, one might find assistant or junior teller positions, senior teller, assistant manager, manager, vice president and president positions. In a university one finds lecturers, assistant professors, associate professors, full professors, department chairs, deans, vice provosts, associate provosts, provosts, and chancellors. In the military, one usually finds orderly progression through the ranks, although individuals might experience presumably downward career progression through demotion. These are all organizational positions or, sociologically, status positions that are properties of the work organization. An organization that links jobs in this way, offering an internal labor market, and providing security in both the position and the prospects of advancement for incumbents, can boast that it offers its employees careers in Wilensky's sense of the term.

Careers are thus properties of social structure but they are also pathways followed by individuals. At the individual level, one can imagine a person starting at the bottom of such a hierarchy and 'making a career' by progressively moving up through the ranks. People can have an idea that they have careers and are doing well (or not) in them. This confirms Hughes' distinction between objective and subjective careers, a distinction that underlies much of our thinking in this area. As Hughes (1971: 37) put it almost four decades ago:

However one's ambitions and accomplishments turn, they involve some sequence of relations to organized life. In a highly and rigidly structured society, a career consists, *objectively*, of a series of status [*sic*] and clearly defined offices. In a freer one, the individual has more latitude for creating his own position or choosing from a number of existing ones . . . but unless complete disorder reigns, there will be typical sequences of position, achievement, responsibility, and even of adventure. The social order will set limits upon the individual's orientation of his life, both as to direction of effort and as to interpretation of its meaning. *Subjectively*, a career is the moving perspective in which the person sees his life as a whole and interprets the meaning of his various attributes, actions, and the things which happen to him.

To add one more degree of complexity that is important for this chapter, individuals may find they can fashion a career over time by switching employers while retaining security and the prospects for advancement. They can structure careers that are not dependent on internal labor markets within individual firms.[1] Alternatively, if they do not have security of position and the prospects for advancement, they may feel that they have only jobs.

In this chapter, we draw on survey data from a study of information technology workers, in order to understand workers' views of the jobs and careers in that employment sector. We find that: career prospects are not terribly strong in the broader sense of careers that involve changing employers; the possibility to have careers within specific firms is less than for careers in the wider field; and, while retention of workers is problematical in the IT sector, it is even more problematical within the small and medium-sized firms that we studied. We will conclude the chapter by briefly addressing issues affecting retention within firms.

SOURCES OF DATA: THE US WANE PROJECT

The Workforce Aging in the New Economy study is an international research program examining small and medium-size IT firms in concentrated study regions in Canada, Australia, England, and the United States. The project is centered in a case study methodology, with individual IT firms serving as cases.

We have anchored this analysis to the US data, which come from seven case study firms in the Triangle region of North Carolina (Chapel Hill, Durham, Raleigh, the Research Triangle Park, and surrounding areas) and four in Tallahassee, Florida and surrounding areas. These US firms range in size from four to 104 employees, and altogether employed 284 persons at the time they were studied. For the other countries, the company size range and number of employees ranged from four to 21 in

Canada, five to 193 in Australia, and seven to 115 in England. All data were gathered between late 2004 and early 2006, well after the bursting of the 1990s IT bubble and the onset of economic downturn following the events of 9/11.

In addition to our analysis of US cases, we examined the survey data from Australia, Canada, and England to determine what, if any, significant differences there were between the countries in web survey responses. For all variables considered in this chapter, we ran ANOVA analyses comparing differences between the countries, and further tested the results using LSD and Tukey *post hoc* tests.[2] To simplify the presentation, the focus of this chapter is on the United States situation. Unless otherwise noted, the generalizations are based on US findings and we largely restrict our sample description to the US component of the study. There are instances where significant differences emerged among the countries, and we have noted them. Our findings indicate that the story developed from US data is largely a universal story across the study countries. No comprehensive competing story has emerged through the patterns of difference among the countries across variables, but there are some differences.

In the study, we collected archival data as well as two additional types of data. The first was based on semi-structured qualitative interviews with 108 employees in the American case firms.[3] While the qualitative data inform our interpretations, in this chapter we focus on the second source of data, namely, a web-based survey sent to all employees of the case study IT firms, as determined by employee rosters provided by company leadership. The web survey garnered 123 completed surveys from an eligible sample of 284 persons in the US case studies, for a response rate of 43.3 percent.[4] The web survey covered topics similar to the interviews, and took about an hour for respondents to complete.

As is the case for all our study countries, the US sample is dominated by men (69 percent; and exceeding 75 percent in six of the 11 companies). The age ranged from 20 to 63 years old, with a mean age of 38.7 years. More than half of the sample were under the age of 40 and 70 percent were under the age of 45. Given the timing of our data collection, many of the respondents had been in the IT field before and during the so-called 'bubble' at the end of the last century, the 'bursting of the bubble' with the economic downturn in the US in 2000 and following the terrorist events of 9/11. All respondents were in an industry in a process of recovery at the time of our data collection. This is confirmed by their work histories. Those who had held a previous job were asked why they left it, and 23 percent said that downsizing or their company closing down was a major reason, and another 8 percent said it was a minor reason.[5] Twenty percent listed layoff as a major reason, and 5 percent listed it as a minor reason.

Thus, the information technology sector, as least in North Carolina and Florida, was under considerable strain in the years just prior to our survey. This historical circumstance no doubt influenced respondents' subjective feelings of job security and other attitudes and cognitions they held concerning their jobs and careers. We focus on job security issues in another paper from this project (Haviland and Marshall, 2007).

Before leaving this section we caution that the story we tell with these data should be viewed as suggestive rather than definitive. We have chosen to focus, in this chapter, on understanding the story based mainly on the survey data rather than relying more heavily on the rich qualitative data. This strategy affords us the 'big picture' view of how careers are made across the study countries. Additional caution is recommended because our sample of case studies is quite opportunistic and does not necessarily represent the geographical areas from which the cases are drawn. The American cases on which we focus were drawn from just two small geographical areas, the Research Triangle of North Carolina and the area in and around Tallahassee, FL. The Canadian, Australian and English cases, while from different regions of those countries, were also selected opportunistically. Yet, the fact that the story is the same across countries and oceans is telling in itself.

JOBS IN IT

We asked many questions dealing with workers' experiences, expectations and opinions about their jobs and aspects of careers. We begin by describing the job situation of the respondents, setting aside for the moment the issue of whether these jobs form part of careers.

Of the 152 US respondents to the web-based survey, 132 provide information on their current employment status. Of these, 125, or 95 percent, said they were employed on a permanent or ongoing basis. Seven (5 percent) said they were either self-employed, or employed on a fixed contract, or employed on a casual basis. Post hoc tests confirm differences in self-employment between Canada as compared to England and US; this is unsurprising as Canada has more than double the rate of self-employment compared to the other countries in the WANE data, and its rate is around four to six times that of either England or the US. This likely reflects differences in country-level inclusion criteria for contract workers. *Post hoc* tests also confirm differences in permanent employment for England compared to Canada and Australia, and for the US compared to Canada and Australia (England and US both had over 90 percent of WANE respondents in this category, while Canada and Australia only had about seven out of ten). Finally, *post hoc* tests confirm differences between Australia and all other countries in owners and managers; Australia was the only country to have respondents self-select these categories to describe their employment relationships.[6]

The primary work location for 92 percent of the US sample was in an office onsite at the company, and another 3 percent were employed off-site at another office (no significant differences emerged between the US and other countries for working on-site versus other). Only one US employee claimed to work at home and six gave 'other' responses. The predominance of on-site workers is to some extent an artifact of our sampling, as we allowed company officials to exclude off-site workers if they wished. Despite this sample selectivity, the majority of firms in our study relied heavily or exclusively on onsite workers (with the exception of offshored IT tasks), and this sampling selectivity would likely bias the sample to those with more secure jobs and possibly careers.

WHAT CONSTITUTES CAREERS IN IT?

By definition, all our respondents have jobs. But do they have careers? In Wilensky's conceptualization of career, a career implies some progression, hopefully upward. The mean number of positions in the current company held by our respondents was 1.33, suggesting some mobility within the firm. Two-thirds (67 percent) of respondents reported having held just one position since beginning work in the company, and one-third (33 percent) reported holding two or more positions. Data on the nature of career progression within the current firm, for those who held more than one position, are given in Table 2.1. We asked, 'In general, thinking of the time you have worked at this company, would you describe your total job history as . . .: 1) Two or more positions, moving up the organization, 2) Two or more positions, moving both up and across the organization, 3) Two or more positions, moving across the organization, 4) Two or more positions, moving down and across the organization, or 5) Two or more positions, moving down the organization.'

Since two-thirds of respondents who had held just one job in the company are not considered in this table, we have within-company mobility data for just 42 US respondents. Because two-thirds experienced no job changes, the complete picture would include them as well. Just three of those who had held more than one position experienced downward mobility within the company. Fourteen experienced lateral mobility, and 24 experienced at least some upward mobility. There were differences between England and the US on within-firm mobility[7] (ANOVA significant at the

Table 2.1   Percentage of self-reported with-in firm mobility, by region

	Canada (*n* = 36)	Australia (*n* = 28)	England (*n* = 53)	US (*n* = 42)
Two or more positions, moving up in the organization	38.9	57.1	56.6	26.2
Two or more positions moving both up and across in the organization	30.6	25.0	26.4	31.0
Two or more positions, moving across the organization	19.4	10.7	11.3	33.3
Two or more positions moving down and across the organization	0	7.1	1.9	4.8
Two or more positions, moving down the organization	0	0	0	2.4
Don't know	11.1	0	3.8	2.4

0.05 level). The English sample had the highest proportion of respondents reporting an upward trajectory, nearly 83 percent (close to Australia, which had nearly 82 percent) while the US brought up the rear with only 57 percent reporting upward mobility (the closest comparison being Canada at 69 percent). Thus, the total picture is one of little upward career progression within firms in the US, and similarly in Canada, while the within-firm outlook is more positive in England and Australia.[8]

We also asked about job mobility more broadly, with the question, 'In general, thinking about all the years in your working life, from your first job until now, would you describe your total job history as (the same five options as above) but also "one or no job moves".' The question was answered by 125 respondents (27 chose not to answer). The data appear in Table 2.2. Over their working histories, over three-quarters of the US respondents (77 percent) reported at least some upward mobility, another 8 percent reported lateral mobility only, and 8 percent reported downward or no mobility. When comparing Table 2.1 to Table 2.2, the data pattern suggests less 'lateral only' mobility over a career than within a firm. This is perhaps indicative of the strategy of IT workers to gain clusters of different skills and then 'hop' to other firms to move up. Job-hopping is also a deliberate strategy of employees to ensure they acquire expertise in

Table 2.2　Percentage of self-reported job mobility over entire job history, by region

	Canada (n = 94)	Australia (n = 69)	England (n = 117)	US (n = 125)
Two or more positions, moving up	41.5	31.9	44.4	33.6
Two or more positions moving both laterally and up	39.4	50.7	37.6	43.2
Two or more positions, moving laterally only	5.3	7.2	5.1	8.0
Two or more positions moving laterally and down	1.1	0	2.6	1.6
Two or more positions, moving down	2.1	0	0	2.4
One or no job moves	4.3	5.8	8.5	5.6
Don't know	6.4	4.3	1.7	5.6

new technologies (for example, coding languages, platforms, web-based tools). This comparison between tables, however, is difficult to make as the window is likely much longer when a respondent is asked about their entire working history as compared to mobility within the current firm. Still, there is some evidence that lateral movers in the shorter window move into the 'lateral and up' or just 'up' category when individuals are asked to look over their whole career.

How do the workers feel about career development? We inquired about several dimensions of career development. Note that of these indicators, three refer to an evaluation of the career or career prospects in general terms, while two refer to the firm (see Table 2.3). Strong majorities of IT workers in the US companies express overall satisfaction with their career progress (60 percent agree and another 11 percent strongly agree with the statement). Almost two-thirds consider their chances for career development were good (55 percent agreed and 11 percent strongly agree). Strong majorities also agree, across country, that they have the opportunity to develop and apply the skills they need to enhance their career (78 percent agree or strongly agree in the US data). On the other hand, fewer than 60 percent of the respondents state that their firm does a good job in helping them develop their careers, and only 43 percent agree with the statement, 'My chances for promotion are good.' When these five items are summarized in a scale ($\alpha = 0.85$), no significant regional differences are found.

Table 2.3   Self-reported career rewards, by region* (percentage who
agree)

	Canada (n = 104)	Australia (n = 73)	England (n = 122)	US (n = 129)
I have the opportunity to develop and apply the skills I need to enhance my career	80.8	83.5	82.0	78.3
My firm does a good job of helping develop my career	59.6	67.1	71.3	58.9
My chances for career development are good	67.4	64.3	58.0	65.9
My chances for promotion are good	42.6	41.4	40.3	42.9
Overall, I am satisfied with my career progress	76.9	68.6	72.3	70.6

Note: * Measures were dichotomized into strongly agree and agree vs. disagree and strongly disagree.

It seems clear that firm level activities and other opportunities created through work contribute to overall career satisfaction, but that firm-specific dimensions like chances for promotion are weighed less heavily.

Further, the data suggest that satisfaction with one's career is tied more to the information technology field than to the specific firm. Two-thirds of the respondents agreed with the statement, 'I believe that I have opportunities within the IT field, given my education, skills and experience.' There are no significant differences among countries in responses to this question.

We also asked respondents what they planned to do when they left the company they currently worked for (see Table 2.4). This question was answered by 126 of our US respondents. Only 8 percent said they intended 'to retire completely from the workforce.' At the other extreme, 12 percent said, 'I intend never to leave this company.' A quarter (26 percent) intended 'to move to another firm in the IT sector,' 14 percent 'to start my own company,' and 8 percent 'to do consulting work.' Another 11 percent said they intended 'to move to another firm, not in the IT sector, and 7 percent said the intended 'to take time off.' Chi square tests arraying this variable by region indicated no significant differences.

The question of retirement deserves further comment. Fully 58 percent of US respondents asked, 'would you like to continue working after

Table 2.4   Plans for when respondent leaves current job, by region (percent)

When you leave the company you currently work for, you intent...	Canada ($n=94$)	Australia ($n=69$)	England ($n=117$)	US ($n=124$)
To retire completely from the workforce	9.6	14.5	15.4	7.9
To move to another firm in the IT sector	19.1	27.5	30.8	26.2
To move to another firm, not in the IT sector	6.4	10.1	7.7	11.1
To start you own company	14.9	11.6	4.3	13.5
To do consulting work	11.7	4.3	7.7	7.9
To take time off	5.3	7.2	6.8	7.1
I intend to never leave this company	12.8	7.2	12.0	11.9
Other	20.2	17.4	15.4	12.7

formally retiring?' said yes. Only 18 percent said no, and another 24 percent said they didn't know. Our sample is, of course, quite young, with seven in ten under the age of 45. Yet surprisingly, one-third had given a moderate amount of thought to retirement, and another quarter had given a lot of thought to retirement. This was significantly more thought than reported by respondents in Australia, Canada, and England, perhaps in part due to the comparatively weak social safety net in the US (for further discussion of this issue, see Haviland and Marshall, 2007). In only one country, England, were there significant differences from the US in respondent reports about plans to continue working after retirement. Retirement, then, rarely means a complete exit from the work force for US, Australian, and Canadian respondents. Many will continue working after they leave their current employer, and some of these will continue to work in the same field, as employees, consultants, or entrepreneurs starting their own firms.

Respondents other than those who said they would never leave the company they work for were asked how many more years they would work for the company before leaving. While many respondents did not answer this question, over one-third (35 percent) of the 51 US respondents who did answer said they would leave in one year or less, and almost half (47 percent) said they would leave in two years or less. If they exit as anticipated, 71 percent of these respondents will have left their current company within five years. These data suggest that, while retention of workers in the field of IT may not be highly problematic, retention of workers by individual firms could be a problem. We thus conclude by briefly addressing retention issues and strategies.

STRATEGIES TO RETAIN WORKERS IN IT

In the past few years, an increasing number of strategies to encourage job retention of older workers in general (that is, not specific to IT) have been proposed by organizations such as AARP (2004), IBM (Lesser et al., 2005), and the Pension Research Council (Mulvey and Nyce, 2004). These include recommendations to reduce economic subsidies to early retirement benefits; change the nature of medical benefits, including untying them from jobs (Sweet 2007), implement work life benefits such as eldercare and phased retirement (Mulvey and Nice, 2004), provide opportunities for workers to continually update their skills, facilitate the coexistence of multiple generations in the workforce (Lesser et al., 2005), offer career management and training programs, provide attractive economic security packages, offer workplace and worktime flexibility, and provide family-friendly policies and programs (AARP, 2004).

Our respondents shed some light on factors in their own IT-based work settings that make a difference for them. Since the respondents do seem to be interested in careers and career progression, yet do not evidence a great deal of it, it is not surprising that four in ten respondents report that their firm does not do a good job in developing their career and only about four in ten think their chances for promotion are good.

Salary seems less an issue than challenging opportunities. We infer this from responses given by those who had held a previous job as to their reasons for leaving that job. While, as noted above, some had no choice due to downsizings and layoffs, fully 61 percent of the 105 respondents who answered that question said that 'better salary' was not a factor, and only 31 percent gave it as a major reason. In contrast, half the respondents (51 percent) said that 'more challenging or interesting projects' was a major reason for leaving their last job. Better benefits were not a major factor, being listed as a major reason by only 10 percent of respondents and as 'not a factor' by 79 percent.

The question about reasons for leaving the previous job had several items that documented significant differences between countries. There were significant differences between Canada and Australia in how better opportunities for career development factored into the decision to leave the previous job; Australians more often reported it as a major factor while Canadians more often reported it as not a factor at all. Additionally, there were significant differences between Australia and England in how the opportunity to use leading edge technology factored into the decision to leave the previous job. Australians more often reported it as a minor or major factor while English respondents more often reported it as not a factor at all.

In addition, there were significant differences between the England and both Australia and the US in how seeking better management factored into the decision to leave the previous job; more than half of English respondents reported that it was not a factor while US and Australia respondents more often reported it as a minor or major factor. There were also significant differences between Australia and England in how better working hours factored into the decision to leave the previous job. Approximately half of Australians reported it as a minor or major factor while English respondents more often reported it as not a factor at all. There were significant differences between England and both Australian and the US in how seeking a better work environment factored into the decision to leave the previous job; more than half of English respondents reported that it was not a factor while US and Australian respondents more often reported it as a minor or major factor. All these differences suggest that further comparative study of these issues is warranted.

Creation of family-friendly workplaces was a stated goal of several CEOs of case study firms, and interview data suggest that once employees marry and have children, they are less receptive to working long hours and pulling the all-night work sessions that often occur as small IT firms strive to meet tight deadlines (Marshall et al., 2005). However, 39 percent of the employees in our survey said they were expected to work overtime some of the time, and an additional 27 percent said they were expected to work overtime hours most of the time. This was comparable in Australia and England but not Canada, where responses differed significantly from the US. Canadians did report working overtime hours, although the bulk of responses were in the 'some of the time' (46 percent) or 'rarely' (34 percent) categories.

While concerns about health benefits appear to be low, not all US firms in our study provide them. Both health benefits and the family-friendly workplaces are related to life course issues. As people live through young adulthood and pass into later years, they become more involved with their own families, and also more aware of the risks of not having adequate health insurance. Health benefits should be of the greatest concern to the US respondents because the United States does not provide universal medicare to persons under age 65, and private health insurance coverage is available to less than one in five workers (Hacker, 2006; see also Chapter 3). US WANE workers report receiving better incomes, benefits and job security at work than their Canadian counterparts, but also experience greater anxiety about the state of the economy and international stability. Despite the greater perceived outcomes revealed in survey data, interview data showed that US workers had greater concerns about maintaining employment to maintain basic levels of health benefits, while Canadian workers were more concerned with supplementing or replacing state plans with private health benefits such as prescriptions, dental, or vision (Haviland and Marshall, 2007).

DISCUSSION

The US version of the story of 'Making a Life in IT' appears to be similar to the career story for other WANE study countries. Individuation of career ownership (rather than firm influence on career through established internal labor markets) seems to be a trend in these data. In this context it makes sense that the data also point to a lack of formal retirement as many IT workers will continue working after they leave their current employer, and some of these will continue to work in the same field, as employees, consultants, or entrepreneurs starting their own firms. There is not much career progression within firms and not much career stability either. Generally, it also appeared that turnover in the US was more likely due to factors such as more challenging or interesting projects rather than to matters of compensation. For many workers in IT, framing their lives in terms of careers is no longer constrained by the internal labor markets of the firms they work for. There are practically no internal labor markets in these small and medium IT firms. Rather, IT workers tend to think of their careers in terms of the broader field of IT work.

In this, they are not alone, at least in the United States, where studies have shown increases in firm-based employment insecurity and a move to encourage employees to be more self-reliant in terms of career. In a sense, for the past two decades, human resources management policies suggest a move away from the career as a structural property of the firm to career as a property of the individual. An earlier study of a Canadian-based international company operating in the gas pipeline transmission and petrochemical manufacturing sectors found that management explicitly fostered such a view. An article in the company newsletter, with the title, 'Take charge of your career with the Career Resource Centers,' stated that continuing change at the company would make it unlikely that employees could depend on lifetime employment. Instead, employees were told to take responsibility for their own careers and make themselves as market-able as possible for the flexible workforce—whether at the company or elsewhere (Marshall and Marshall, 2003: 635). In the same comparative case study research (Marshall, 1996), human resources managers in a large health and life insurance company reported being forbidden to even use the term 'career,' as the company (which had been undergoing a series of large down-sizings) did not wish to foster a company-based career mentality in its employees (Marshall and Marshall, 1999).

Social scientists refer to the emergence of the 'risk society' in which social institutions provide less insurance and protection from risks to employment or to health, and individuals must assume more of the responsibility and thus bear more of the risk of navigating the life course (Giddens, 1991; Mendenhall et al., 2008; O'Rand, 2003). The IT employment sector, particularly with small and medium-sized firms such as those we studied, is perhaps among the more risky sectors of employment. In terms of feelings of security at work, we asked employees, 'Looking to your future, do you have a clear sense of how you would like your working life to unfold?' Over half our respondents (53.6 percent) answered yes to this question, but when asked, 'How confident are you that your future will unfold in this way?,' 14.9 percent said 'not at all,' 38.8 percent said, 'quite a bit,' and just 11.9 percent said, 'a great deal.'

De-institutionalizing the internal labor market version of the career throws the employee on his or her own resources for career management and is a major feature of the risk society. As Sweet (2007: 45) points out, 'While the problem of insecure jobs is not new to those in the lower-earning sectors of the economy, the extension of the problem into professional fields and to older workers in every sector is a recent phenomenon.' Mendenhall et al. (2008), with qualitative data from unemployed mid- and top-level managers in the Chicago area, find that most respondents attributed their unemployment to globalization, and that their coping strategies involve the adoption of a 'free-agent' mentality. Robson and Hansson (2007: 332), from the psychological perspective on career development, note that 'long-term development and the acquisition of skills and competencies necessary to compete in a rapidly changing and globalizing economy requires employees to be self-directed, motivated, and strategic in pursuing their opportunities.'

Our focus has been on the individual coping with a de-structuring or individualization of the life course. Building a career within an occupational field is very different than building a career within the prestructured hierarchy of the Fordist firm. Not all IT workers experience such radical de-structuring of the workplace-based occupational career. Large IT companies used to (for example, IBM) or still do (for example, SAS Institute) provide considerable occupational mobility opportunities, and career-supportive structures within the firm.[9] But the turbulent nature of the

IT industry, at least in the countries we have studied, leaves the struggle largely to the individual to make a life in IT.

NOTES

1. Internal labor markers were never the predominant form of working relationships and to the extent they existed, participation in them varied widely by gender, race and class. For a brief overview of their emergence see Chapter 2 in Cappelli (1999). See also Hacker (2006) and, for an extensive analysis, Levine et al. (2002).
2. ANOVA tests were performed directly on scalar and dichotomous variables. For variables with categorical responses, dummy variables were created either for each response category or for collapsed categories. The affected variables include employment arrangements (q7), primary work location (q8), job history (q24 and q119), and plans for when respondent leaves the company (q114).
3. These interviews were conducted by trained WANE study team members (including the authors) in 2005 and 2006, on-site in private spaces at the study companies. They typically lasted one hour. Topics covered included work histories and experiences, company practices, work/life balance, and respondent assessments of the IT industry. Additional information on interviews completed in the other study countries can be found in Chapter 1.
4. An additional 29 partially completed surveys were returned but are unusable for this analysis. For this reason, the number of cases for the data analysed below is 123.
5. To say layoff or company shutdown is a minor reason may reflect that the individual was ready or anxious to change jobs.
6. For testing purposes we collapsed this item (q7) into three variables; self-employed versus other, permanent employed versus other, and owners and managers versus other. All three variables showed differences between the countries (ANOVAs significant at the 0.001 level).
7. Job history questions q24 (at company) and q119 (over career) were recoded into upwardly mobile (including those who reported moving up and across organizations as well as those who simply moved up) and other. For the career question, no significant differences emerged.
8. The situation in the US and Canada may not be entirely dire as it is possible for lateral mobility, or even downward mobility, to ultimately prove career enhancing as it may lead to the on-the-job acquisition of new skills.
9. Even within the firms we studied, size matters. See Chapter 3 for an example.

REFERENCES

AARP (American Association of Retired People) (2004), *Staying Ahead of the Curve 2004: Employer Best Practices for Mature Workers*, Washington, DC: AARP.

Cappelli, P. (1999), *The New Deal at Work: Managing the Market-driven Workforce*, Boston, MA: Harvard Business School Press.

Giddens, A. (1991), *Modernity and Self-identity: Self and Society in the Late Modern Age*, Stanford, CA: Stanford University Press.

Hacker, J.S. (2006), *The Great Risk Shift. The Assault on American Jobs, Families, Health Care, and Retirement, and How you can Fight Back*, Oxford and New York: Oxford University Press.

Haviland, S.B., and V.W. Marshall (2007), 'Societal allocation of risk and individual feelings of stability: an analysis of US and Canadian information technology workers', paper presented at the Work, Employment and Society conference, Aberdeen, Scotland, September.

Hughes, E.C. (1971), *The Sociological Eye: Selected Papers*, Chicago, IL: Aldine, Atherton.

Kanter, R.M. (1995), 'Nice work if you can get it: the software industry as a model for tomorrow's jobs', *American Prospect*, **23** (Fall), 52–8.

Lesser, E., C. Hausmann and S. Feuerpeil (2005), 'Addressing the challenges of an aging workforce: a human capital perspective for companies operating in Europe', an IBM Institute for Business Value executive brief, Somers, NY: IBM Global Services.

Levine, D.I., D. Belman, G. Charness, E.L. Groshen and K.C. O'Shaughnessy (2002), *How New is the 'New Employment Contract'?*, Kalamazoo, MI: W.W. Upjohn Institute for Employment Research.

Marshall, V.W. (1996), *Issues of an Aging Workforce in a Changing Society: Cases and Comparisons*, Toronto: Canadian Aging Research Network and the University of Toronto Center for Studies of Aging, available at www.aging.unc.edu/infocenter/resources/1996/cases.pdf.

Marshall, V.W. and J.D. Marshall (1999), 'Age and changes in work: causes and contrasts', *Ageing International*, **25** (2), 46–68.

Marshall, V.W. and J.D. Marshall (2003), 'Ageing and work in Canada: firm policies', *Geneva Papers on Risk and Insurance*, **28** (4), 625–39.

Marshall, V.W., J.C. Morgan and J.D. Marshall (2005), 'Age designations in a demographically young industry: workforce aging in the New Economy', paper presented at International Association on Gerontology Conference, Rio de Janiero, June.

Mendenhall, R., A. Kalil, L.J. Spindel and C.M.D. Hart (2008), 'Job loss at midlife: managers and executives face the "new risk economy"', *Social Forces*, **87** (1), 185–209.

Mulvey, J., and S. Nyce (2004), 'Strategies to retain older workers', Pension Research Council working paper PRC WP 2004–13, Wharton School, University of Pennsylvania, Philadelphia.

O'Rand, A.M. (2003), 'The future of the life course: late modernity and life course risks', in J.T. Mortimer and M.J. Shanahan (eds), *Handbook of the Life Course*, New York: Kluwer Academic/Plenum Publishers, pp. 693–701.

Robson, S.M. and R.O. Hansson (2007), 'Strategic self-development for successful aging at work', *International Journal of Aging and Human Development*, **64** (4), 331–59.

Sweet. S. (2007), 'The older worker, job insecurity, and the new economy', *Generations*, **3** (1), 45–9.

Wilensky, H.L. (1961), 'Orderly careers and social participation: the impact of work history on social integration in the middle mass', *American Sociological Review*, **26** (4), 521–39.

3. New careers in the New Economy: redefining career development in a post-internal labor market industry

Sara B. Haviland, Jennifer Craft Morgan and Victor W. Marshall

INTRODUCTION

Traditional conceptualizations of career development do not comprehend the complexity of New Economy careers, particularly in small information technology (IT) firms. In the past, scholars of work often used internal labor markets of firms as models of ideal career development (Osterman, 1999) but today's IT firms face several factors that make it difficult to create internal labor markets for employees. IT is an industry with an accelerated pace of industrial evolution in which both the tools and the products are constantly changing. Small and medium-sized IT firms must respond to new opportunities and build niches in the market in order to grow and survive. Small IT firms do not necessarily strive for market longevity, but rather often seek a rapid ascent in the market followed by an Initial Public Offering (IPO) or sale to a larger company. In this context, individual career development differs from traditional models of careers that were characterized by ascension within a firm tied to increasing responsibility and increased pay and benefits. With fewer structural aids within firms, individuals navigate the new organizational landscape and attempt to create meaningful careers for themselves across organizations or through their own efforts at entrepreneurship (see also Chapter 2). The internal labor market ideal of individual career ascension up a corporate ladder within one firm is supplanted by new conceptualizations of career success. The central question for this chapter is: What firm management practices are related to perceived career rewards of employees in this dynamic marketplace?

BACKGROUND AND SIGNIFICANCE

The classic Fordist conceptualization of careers has been tied strongly to the structure of internal labor markets. With limited points of entry into a firm, employees came up from the bottom ranks and worked their way through a proliferation of job titles meant to suggest upward career movement (Baron and Bielby, 1986). The heyday of internal labor markets in the US began in the mid-twentieth century (Doeringer and Piore, 1971; Althauser and Kalleberg, 1981), a time when union organizing and collective bargaining were at their height, and the American Federation of Labor (AFL) and Congress of Industrial Organizations (CIO) were at their peak (Guillen, 1994). The general inflexibility of internal labor markets, coupled with historical context, led to a decline in their use in the late twentieth century. Labor laws became more protective of permanent employees in organizations, creating disincentives for employers to maintain internal labor markets; it became easier and cheaper to maintain a core of permanent employees that was supplemented by a periphery of non-standard workers (Atkinson, 1984; Cappelli et al., 1997; Kalleberg, 2003; Pollert, 1988; Hakim, 1990). Organizations began to compete on a global stage, the pace of technology increased, and firms began to seek arrangements that could respond to this environment (Piore and Sabel, 1984; Kalleberg, 2003), providing both functional and numerical flexibility (Atkinson, 1984).

The Rise of Flexible Firms and its Costs to Workers

The resulting organizations were lean, mean, productive machines, but not very stable for a large class of workers. While shifts towards functionally flexible arrangements such as high performance work operations (HPWOs) (Marsden, 1999) may have benefited individuals with scarce, valued skills, those who did not possess these skills often faced stagnant wages, layoffs, and inadequate benefits (Osterman, 1999; Capelli, 1999). Wages become increasingly linked to performance, resulting in growing inequality. It is important to note that the shift to more flexible arrangements like HPWOs was never fully complete, nor was the presence of internal labor markets in the mid-twentieth century ever universal. There are disagreements about the extent to which these flexible forms have been adopted, which have been made more difficult to resolve given the scarcity of longitudinal data and industry variations (Kalleberg, 2003).[1] Just as there is disagreement about the extent of the shift from internal labor markets to flexible arrangements, there is disagreement about extent to which nonstandard work arrangements actually represent a change in institutions underlying employment relations (Kalleberg, 2003; Cappelli, 1999). Novel or not, the reduction of internal labor markets poses difficulties for workers in most nation states, whose pension systems have assumed a standardized life course with individuals having stable occupational career histories, accumulating private pension and public pension credits (Guillemard, 1991; Kalleberg, 2000; Marshall, 2009). In addition, the US system, unlike that of most other western countries, has left much of the burden for health care to the employer (Kohli, 1991), but in recent years the US has seen a significant reduction in employer-based health insurance. Hacker (2006: 139) points out that firms providing full health care insurance coverage fell over the period 2000–6 from 29 percent to 17 percent for individual programs and from 11 to 6 percent for family coverage. The absence of universal health care for persons under age 65 clearly differentiates the United States from the other nations in our study, making its workers particularly vulnerable both in terms of health and finances.

DATA AND METHODS

The analysis that follows employs a mixed-methods case study methodology. IT, as a demographically young and technology-enabled sector, is at the vanguard of New Economy changes in the organization and implementation of work. The very nature of IT is epitomized by continual change at a rapid pace. Given the rapid evolution of the industry, case studies are particularly appropriate sources for in-depth, contextualized data (Marshall, 1999). As noted by Ragin '[c]ase studies, by their nature, are sensitive to complexity and historical specificity' (1987: ix) thus making them an ideal research approach in which to analyse this ever-shifting industry. Case studies using both qualitative and quantitative data collection methods are likely to produce richly detailed data resources for analysis. While case study data may be seen as highly interpretive, a consistent theoretical approach and thematic organization may provide a valuable comparative framework within which to structure findings (Marshall, 1999). Using this approach, this chapter triangulates web survey data and firm-based interview data to explore the relationships between firm management practices and individual perceived career rewards.

The analysis began by using the WANE web-based quantitative survey to develop a career rewards scale. This scale was developed using responses from web-survey participants in four study regions ($n = 409$, including 94 Canadian respondents, 70 Australian respondents, 119 English respondents, and 126 US respondents). The survey included four questions that offer insight into the nature of career development at IT firms. These questions asked respondents to agree or disagree with statements about their careers, using a four-point Likert scale where 1 = strongly disagree and 4 = strongly agree. The statements included, 'I have the opportunity to develop and apply the skills I need to enhance my career,' 'My firm does a good job of helping develop my career,' 'My chances for promotion are good,' and 'My chances for career development are good.' We constructed a career rewards scale using these four items (Cronbach's alpha of .83).

Using the scale, we first identified those firms that were in the top and bottom quartiles of distribution on the career rewards scale. In order to enable variation in management practices by country, we selected two firms from the top and bottom quartiles on this scale for each country, with the exception that, as only one English firm scored in the top quartile, we added the next-highest ranking English firm.

Having identified the best and worst performers on this scale, we turned our attentions to characterizing the management practices and employee perceptions of owners/managers of the selected firms. Our objective was to examine how individuals described careers and the companies they worked for, extrapolating a set of factors that appeared to be present in High Career Reward (HCR) firms and absent or poorly executed in Low Career Reward (LCR) firms. The organizational profile of each selected firm is offered in Table 3.1. We examined interview data from each company ($n = 102$ interviews) using codes developed by the international team. Codes were applied using NVivo software. These coding categories included our category of interest, 'Work practices/Ideals,' which encompassed 'flexibility, speed of work, work practices, hours, and definitions of successful IT employee.' In the process of coding, coders on each international team finished 'first pass' coding and then a second coder from the same team reviewed how each document was coded. When there were disagreements, the two coders discussed the code and reached a compromise. In the analysis of the codes, two chapter authors separately analysed the codes and then discussed findings and deviant cases in developing the argument.

FINDINGS

We selected the US firms as our anchors due to the great familiarity we had with these data as members of the US study team. Using a case study narrative approach, we organize the findings by two anchor cases in the US – the highest ranking US career reward firm (also the highest ranked career reward firm across countries) and the lowest ranked US firm. We use these two firms to illustrate the common themes in each of the firm

Table 3.1   Organizational profile for IT firms in sample for qualitative analysis

Firm	Founded	Industry	Size (no. employees)
		Low career reward firms (LCRs)	
114	1995	Internet management software, design and consulting	11
104	1992	Software for industry-specific companies	15
206	1984	Financial management software, IT solutions	8
208	1978	IT consulting, custom software	16
406	2002	Software development	6
403	1978	Software development and consultancy	16
509	1994	Website and registration services	4
503	2003	Web-based software for industry-specific companies	7
		High career reward firms (HCRs)	
103	1999	Web services	4
109	1988	Computer repair and software development	4
205	1996	Online marketing	12
204	2000	Content management web tool for home businesses	12
407	1998	Software for legal offices	7
404	1969	Supply solutions and global support services	65
510	1996	Web portals	7
507	1997	Network installation, tech support; software distribution	15

groups (high career rewards vs. low career rewards) and supplement the descriptions of these themes by invoking theme-relevant examples from England, Australia and Canadian firms within firm group. Where relevant we describe case firms that are exceptions to the themes and tease out potential country-level differences.

Companies were arrayed on average career rewards. Firms ranged from a low score of 5.67 to a high score of 14.0. Firms in the low career rewards category for the analysis had a mean career rewards scale of 8.5 (SD 1.7) and those in the high category had a mean score of 12.6 (SD 0.9). Despite the small number of firms available for comparison, the average career rewards score for high career reward firms was significantly higher when compared to those of the low career reward firms indicating that these groups of firms were indeed distinct given the small sample size ($n = 16$ firms). The firms ranged in size from four to 16 employees, indicating that surprisingly, none of the larger WANE firms (including firms with up to 69 employees) were particularly high or low on the career development scale, despite theoretically having greater structural opportunities (more available positions, more layers of authority).

High Career Development Firms

In the US, the firm that ranked the highest on the career development scale was Case 510, a small, stable company that had been in business for more than a decade at the time of study and had fewer than ten employees. Funded by a female CEO/owner, it was a family-led firm as the CEO's life partner had one of the top leadership positions. At first glance, the company has elements that might be considered limiting for employee careers: it is quite small, some intentionally cautious growth, and a couple occupies two of the three top positions. All three of these factors limit the number of and access to company leadership positions, effectively removing rungs from the company ladder. However, the company has overcome these factors and created a culture of development in many ways. We have specifically identified the following factors that emerged through qualitative interviews with Case 510 owners and employees, but also resonated with other high career rewards firms in the US and internationally: the creation of ownership through input, cautious growth to maintain lifestyle, protection for employees, firm-based training and development, teamwork and regular meetings, and overt management practices that demonstrate a high commitment to maintaining employment security for employees when possible. We will discuss each in turn.

Creating Ownership through Input

While firm 510 may not have many rungs in its ladder, everyone at the company has a role in its leadership. This is not to say that the organization is completely flat; there are three managers who comprise the leadership, though only the couple in charge has a financial stake in ownership. However, the leadership actively seeks input from employees through regular meetings, an open-door policy, and a human resource practice known as 360-degree reviews or multi-rater feedback (Bracken et al., 2001). This feedback system elicits the input not only of supervisors for employees, but also of co-workers and subordinates. Therefore, all individuals in a company can be reviewed, including those at the very top, and feedback can come from all members of a team. While there is some question surrounding the value of this feedback as a means of improving employee performance (cf Waldman et al., 1998; Beehr et al., 2001), this process of creating opportunities for, and valuing of, employee input creates a non-financial sense of ownership in the company for its employees and was discussed positively by many interview respondents. The 360-degree review process at this company was a fascinating tactic for overcoming personnel difficulties and ensuring all voices were heard at this firm. Initiated following a period of employee malaise, this process included reviews of the owners, who found that their employees were uncomfortable with some of their behavior as a couple. They had been too familiar in the workplace, most particularly in arguments, and it was uncomfortable for the employees. The couple responded by separating duties at work. The CEO and the non-couple manager began to take care of most human resource issues, while the other partner focused on management of the technical side. This process demonstrated a serious commitment not only to listening to employees, but actually following through and making appropriate changes based on their feedback. When employees come to them with requests, the managers speak seriously with them about the implications – for example, one employee revealed to the owners that he would like an opportunity to become an owner in the company. The request was taken seriously, but the owners were careful to ensure that the implications of ownership were known:

> One person, was interested in being a partner in the business. And the irony was that he had never brought this up to us. Now, also the irony is that if you want to be an owner in a small business, you cannot not step up. And so that's one of the things that I've had to work out with him is, ok, well, if you were an owner how would that change who you, what you do here? How would that change this company because to be an owner means you take more responsibility than if you're an employee. Not just that you get a say, because everyone gets a say. . .what you're saying to me that you want to be a partner. What does that mean to you? Does that mean, you know, that you get to have a say in business decisions. Well, do you really need to be a partner to do that? Do you understand the ramifications of being a partner? You're legally liable for every loan that we take out. You are responsible for everyone else's salary. These are things that you take on. And really, this is something this one person who this was an issue for, we're continuing to have conversations with him about what are his expectations really. And what will make him happy. Because what I find is that people get an idea in their head, this is what will make me happy. But they don't really know what that means. And it's my responsibility in the company to make sure that I'm only bringing in partners who know what they're getting into.

This response demonstrates the CEO's approach to employee feedback; careful consideration is applied, and discussions are ongoing if resolution is not immediately possible. The employee was not immediately given what he wanted, but through continued dialogue, the CEO was attempting to make sure that the employee was happy with whatever resolution was applied. While there is no immediate resolution in this approach, there is a level of engagement with the employee that demonstrates a commitment to taking concerns seriously and customizing solutions to meet employees' needs.

Similar management practices were utilized in Australian high career rewards firms. As one Australian manager in Case 205 noted, their firm sought to involve employees:

> just simply by giving them responsibility and making them feel as if they're, they're crucial to the on-going operation of the business. And the way you do that is by entrusting them with certain tasks and not looking over their shoulder. And, just asking them to, from a reporting mechanism, to report back. You know, at regular intervals. Just to keep you abreast of what's happening.

Ownership is created through valuing input and making employees feel crucial to the central functions of the business. From the employee's perspective, this practice allows individuals to be creative and creates a perception of the company as flexible rather than rigid and bureaucratic, as larger firms can often be. One employee in this Australian case stated:

> I guess the good side is we're really flexible in the company. Whereas in the job I had before was pretty . . . you have certain procedures you have to follow. Whereas here you can be creative and you always have to come up with new things to attract clients, which arrive in our brainstorming. And, achieving . . . creating, something that the client really appreciates our work, is sort of the driver behind keeping me going in this industry.

This creates a sense of ownership of the process but also ownership of the product, such that positive feedback is an affirmation not only for the product but also for the work of the team. A similar phenomenon was noted in US Case 507, where a uniform business ethic was echoed by managers and employees: 'Is it good for the long-term interest of the company and is it in the best interest of our customers?' Employees were basically given carte blanche to serve clients, so long as they kept those questions in mind. This gave employees a sense of ownership over their work and autonomy to do what they needed to do to get the job done in a way they could be proud of. As one employee remarked:

> They're less structured, really, but [pause], they have faith in us. The owners of this company have faith in us to do what we're here to do. I think that they

don't really watch what time we come to work. They don't watch what time we go home because it doesn't matter, because they know we're gonna handle stuff, and we're gonna be here and, and that things are taken care of.

The same employee later remarked:

I'm not really an employee as much as I am part owner. I mean, yes, I don't have the authority to do everything. I can't spend money and, you know. But, it is my business. I wanted to be here. I wanted it to grow. I want the customers to be happy. It is my business.

Careful Growth Maintains Lifestyle

This careful, reasonable approach of the anchor case defines not only communication and planning, but the general company approach to growth. Case 510 began in the mid-1990s, the heyday of the IT boom, and has since weathered the IT bust. While the bust had implications for them – the owners report that at times they had to personally finance payroll to avoid laying people off – they emerged on the other side relatively unscathed, and in fact continued to grow conservatively.

One reason for the cautious growth was that this company, like many in our study, defined itself as a 'lifestyle company.' One employee offered the following explanation:

Well, they call it a lifestyle company. It pretty much is. You know, people come in and out, work from home. You know, it's pretty much when there's something to do we all work hard. When there's not a lot to do, you know kind of, loosens up a bit. And, you know, people come and go as they need to come and go. I really like that. And, the people you know, there seems to be a lot of dialogue. It's very team-oriented. We meet every week as a team. And, it's not a real stodgy, silly meeting. We pass around the responsibility for leading the meeting, for taking the minutes. And you're expected to add humor to the minutes, things like that. So, I think that's what makes it a lot more fun.

While the lifestyle company model allows for growth, in many companies we found that it motivated owners to keep things small – rather than constantly push for new contracts and a rapidly expanding employee roster, owners try to strike a balance somewhere between enough growth to maintain payroll, and not so much growth that people are forced to work around the clock on a regular basis.

Time and Workload Protection

Lifestyle was protected for employees as well as the owners. The management team created weekly schedules for their employees, outlining key tasks and including built-in time for learning. Additionally, the owners pushed back on clients when needed. One employee explained:

> The owner does an exceptional job, risk managing and scheduling and that sort of thing and that's one of the real perks of – I haven't mentioned it up until now. . .You know Monday morning I get my schedule, and that's what I'm going to be working on for the week. That's all laid out and I know there's no questions and that sort of thing. Of course it's all subject to change if something happens. . . It's not a big deal and can be ironed out. I've never had to work more than a couple of hours overtime in a week in the time that I've been here just because it's all very well managed and things are very well balanced. They're not the least bit reluctant to push back on a client. . . . They're always willing to push back and say yeah, you can have that but it's going to be – here are the implications. That's not always been the case for where I've worked.

Just as the owners discussed implications with their employee who wanted ownership, they discussed implications with clients who made difficult requests. This insulates employees from meeting outrageous demands and prevents the company from doing too much work for free (for a stark contrast, see the discussion of Case 509 in the Low Career Development section below).

In one England high career rewards firm, Case 407, the owners felt strongly about protecting the work–life balance, acknowledging that, 'you're not just the person you are while you're in the office, you have a whole life, and that we wished to be more accommodating of people.' In this firm, employees choose their own working hours within 'regular' business hours. (for example, 10 a.m. – 6 p.m.). This choice accommodated employee needs from avoiding traffic congestion to managing child care arrangements. This time and workload protection was also characterized by a moderate amount of client push-back in this firm. If the owner/ managers find that employees are working over, they negotiate more time from clients, explaining the process and renegotiating the time. As they put it, 'you find, well in fact everything can be negotiated, it's really down to your approach.' Employees in this firm are also encouraged to take at least one day off a month and to keep nights and weekends work-free.

Firm-based Training and Development
One might expect a strong support for certifications and formal education in high career rewards firms. However, the opposite was often the case; skepticism of formal education was quite commonplace in many WANE firms (see Chapter 6 for a detailed discussion of credentials). What set our high career rewards firms apart was their willingness to create their own opportunities for company-based education and development, often as a substitute for formal certifications and education. Some companies

managed to use company-based development as a supplement for formal education. One such example, Australian Case 205, recruited employees straight out of college and began implementing supplemental training in the company that complemented formal education.

Basically, the high career rewards firms tended to structure learning one way or another. In US Case 510 there was little push for formal certification, but employees were regularly given time on their schedules for learning and development. By scheduling this time, on company time, the management sent a clear message that learning was valued and important (and, essentially, mandatory). Additionally, the company occasionally held 'lunch and learn' sessions, where participants brought in their lunches and one employee or manager would teach the others about a new skill or technique. Similarly, US Case 507, another high performer, practiced strong mentoring for new employees during a probationary phase, with more experienced 'techs' mentoring the new recruits. While this was not a large-group assembly, it gave newer technicians one-on-one development and reinforced the management's approval of the skill set of more senior technicians. Similarly, in England Case 407, another high career rewards firm, peer-to-peer learning was emphasized. Each employee knew the others' strengths and sought to share knowledge in working through project and client-centered challenges.

Teamwork and Meetings

One other way that employees were given a voice in Case 510 was through regular, weekly meetings with the entire staff. This was possible given its small size, which allowed all players to gather in a single conference room on a regular basis. All employees were able to contribute, and the meetings helped create a sense of cohesion among the group. It also kept the lines of communication open between the managers and the employees, and helped everyone understand what each others' roles were. Weekly communication strategies (conference calls among employees or weekly meetings) were also present in the Australian high career rewards firms and the lone English high career rewards firm. These meetings were described as times where other team members were consulted or where brainstorming occurred.

Management Commitment to Employees and Team

The owners of US Case 510 demonstrated a high level of commitment to their employees. As mentioned before, they had personally taken on meeting payroll in the past when the company itself did not have the money for it. They were driven to keep the team together, as they felt a sense of commitment to the group as a whole.

The managers also worked very hard to maintain a pleasant team, and have had their mettle tested in this area before. They describe an 'instigator' who previously worked for the company, someone who they felt was responsible for creating a culture of bitterness and complaint. They felt that this person was not meeting her objectives at work, and they worked with her through a formal system of planning and documentation to see if they could improve her as an employee. Finally this person quit, and the managers felt there was an air of dissatisfaction they wanted to clear after she went. They called all employees in for a meeting and had an open session to discuss problems at the company, and this was instrumental in installing the previously discussed 360-degree performance review process at the company.

Another firm, US Case 507, demonstrated management commitment to employees through a quarterly bonus program. This program rewarded good performance and any instances of overwork, and was very positively viewed by employees. In addition to bonus pay, managers were known to go to great lengths to keep employees they liked – they had even added a nursery when one employee had a baby, so that she could keep coming to work and bring the baby along when it was young.

Low Career Development Firms

Rather than possessing unique weaknesses, the low career development firms were characterized by the lack of the characteristics identified in high career development firms. For example, for every factor that made US Case 510 a high career rewards firm, the opposite was present in US Case 509, and that appeared to be what drove Case 509 to the bottom of the spectrum. Consisting of fewer than five employees, Case 509 had a very similar organizational profile to Case 510, which we just discussed: it was an older firm, with over a decade of experience at the time of our study. One manager at high-rewards Case 510 noted that he was not 'really sure what it would mean to be promoted,' and at low-rewards Case 509 a similar lack of positions was present. As the owner of Case 509 noted, 'there's really no place to jump up. It's not like they're going to be the boss, you know. It's not like they're going to be in charge of something different than they're already in charge of.' Case 509 was a player in a niche market, and was related to a hands-off business in another state. However, the owner of this firm was local, and the employees all worked together in a small office.

In contrast to Case 510, Case 509 offered fewer opportunities for employee input, made few efforts at growth, and did not offer employees a great deal of protection, training and development, or regular meetings. It was not clear what the relationship was between the owner and the employees, though it appeared to be quite hands-off. Factors that appeared to contribute to this low career reward environment were centered on the absence of development in general, not only for the employees but also for the company as a whole.

Low Firm Development and Difficult Client Relations

There were no discernible efforts at actively growing Case 509, which operated in a fairly small niche. Instead, the company was under pressure to keep current clients happy so they would become repeat customers. The owner at Case 509 felt a great deal of pressure to do things cheaply for the clients, and speculated that many were using them not so much for the quality as they were for the bottom line. He described the changing dynamics of client demands following the IT bust:

> In mean I remember, I remember doing projects for people where you, you wouldn't blink saying, 'This is going to cost you 10K.' And now you could say, 'Please, maybe $2,000 for this'. . . they need something like one of our registration systems, which would be, which would cost a lot of money for someone to build themselves, but they'll balk if you say this is going to cost you six or seven thousand dollars.

In essence, the owner was always saying 'yes' to clients, even when the demands would involve a great deal of work beyond the original contract and that work would be unpaid. He felt great pressure to perform in this way for clients to maintain their business.

More than one employee fretted a great deal about these client relations in interviews. One noted, 'cash flow is the lifeblood of a small company. . . . And so that, that does get a little frustrating when you realize that we just don't have that much revenues, and we probably could.' In essence, employees felt the customers were not paying for what they were getting, and should pay extra when their requests went far beyond the scope of the original contracts. This was perhaps aggravated by their assessment of their own pay as quite low, even compared to the region (which has a lower cost of living than the US in general). The one protection that was provided was a built-in buffer they made standard in all of their contracts: the company had 48 hours to respond to any requests made by clients. This may be one reason that the employees worked fairly regular hours, despite high demands from clients.

Low Personnel Development and Few Expectations

Employees at US Case 509 reported that there were no real expectations for skill improvement or upgrading, and as such, there were also no real company-sponsored opportunities for it. The owner had few expectations in general, and maintained a quite casual environment for the employees. One employee explained it as such:

> . . . I wouldn't say there was any kind of impetus or expectation to constantly be on the edge and, and finding new technologies. It's more like as long as it keeps working, it's good kind of thing, you know.

In many ways this suited the employees, most of whom had worked in larger firms and did not like the faster pace; one lauded the great hours and atmosphere, stating that:

> If Google were a four-man show, it would be [this company]. You know, we don't have the funds to put in huge cafeterias and you know, an exercise room and, and game rooms and stuff like that, but the people would prefer to work here because you have defined hours. You can go beyond them if you want to. It's up to you. And the expectations are what they should be, they're not overblown.

This employee appreciated the laid-back environment, and did not want to work at a larger firm where the demands might be higher. The employees of Case 509 had a high level of autonomy: they were only loosely tethered to the office and free to work remotely if they liked, even though many came to the office anyway. There was very little in the way of project management, which one employee complained 'hurts from a quality standpoint . . . it puts too much burden on developers to do everything.' The firm operated on a simple level of control (Edwards, 1979) with employees working directly under the owner. There appeared to be little professional interaction between employees. The casual approach in many ways mimics that of lifestyle firms in that there is little direction from company leadership about how exactly tasks must be accomplished; however, these firms take it one step further and put few expectations at all on the employees. While lifestyle firms emphasize quality work projects and employee development at a comfortable working pace, these low demand firms have little expectation of employee development, and little support for it.

A similar situation was found at US Case 503, which was barely surviving financially. One manager noted that he didn't really understand what his IT workers did:

> I can't possibly program what our programmers do. I can only challenge them to do it faster, cheaper, sometimes better. But, I can't possibly do what they do. Now, I do have a better understanding of the science side of the other company. . . . I've got a background for that. On the IT side, I get curve balls all the time and I say that's not logical. I don't understand what you're doing. I don't understand how you're doing it, but [pause] I know that in my analytical mind that what you just said to me doesn't make sense.

This manager was able to push on elements of the work (do it faster, cheaper, better) but unfamiliar with what that process might look like. This leaves the manager at a disadvantage when it comes to developing talent, and the subordinates at a disadvantage when it comes to the managers' ability to create reasonable expectations and protect their time and workloads.

The managers of a different company, Canadian Case 114, noted that they were willing to help employees develop their skills – but they also noted that they didn't go out of their way to point out opportunities. One stated, 'we're somewhat laissez faire in our employee relations. . .. In general people are, ask for a lot less than we're prepared to give in terms of time and tuition and things like that.' Another partner noted that information-sharing in general was poor between management and the employees:

> [Some employees] could insult the management at will. It was even though they had really great morale on one side because they hired a lot of friends and they have really good coffee and they give them lots of little perks and there's that fun chit chat, when it gets down to business they can be very resistant to change and resistant to taking orders. . . . I told [the other owners] before why don't we just get [employees] you know, get them involved in the decision making so that they can understand what they're up against. . . . You know we're all in it together, we're all in the boat but it's almost like we're on a small boat buffeted by big waves and the management puts blindfolds on them all and they don't know where they're rowing and they don't know what they're up against, you know. How can you get through a storm like that?

Low Career Reward Firms that Masquerade as High Career Reward Firms

While Case 510 and Case 509 are clearly opposites in their management and general level of company development, more muddy cases also appeared in the data that were enlightening. One strong example is Canadian Case 104, a firm with 15 employees that appeared to be doing everything right: there were efforts to allow employee input, and to provide protection for employees, firm-based training and development, teamwork and regular meetings; also, management described efforts at maintaining positive, open door relationships with employees and expressed an interest in greatly growing the size of the company in the near future. At first glance, it was unclear why such a firm would be in our low career rewards group; however, further analysis pointed to several factors that were causing misfires on these attempts at positive management practices. These misfires illuminated the contextual nature of positive management practices.

Scattershot Meetings and Inconsistent Management
Canadian Case 104 utilized an online communication system both for
intra-company communication and for communication with clients.
Nearly all communication occurred through this system. This is not to
say that there were no meetings; employees and the owners both described
numerous meetings, including a monthly staff meeting where, according
to an owner:

> Everybody stays involved, everybody has an opportunity to voice their opinion,
> um, everybody has an opportunity to communicate with the customer. . . . Once
> a month we actually hold staff meetings just to kind of give a sales perspective
> where we're at, where some of the new development directions that we might
> be looking towards.

The staff meetings were described by more than one person as a joking,
casual affair that offered some insight into the direction of the company.
One employee noted that 'you do feel like you are getting heard.' This
employee appreciated the regular performance bonuses the owners doled
out, stating 'that is a good motivator when your boss is behind you that
way, that if you are doing a good job, you will be told so.'

Despite these regular all-team meetings, there were issues with smaller
meetings for project managers. The company management consisted of
two owners and two managers, and these managers were supposed to
be on similar footing in terms of authority. However, the owners often
held informal or sudden meetings, where one manager would run into the
owners and get brought into their offices to talk shop. This meant that
both managers were not present and therefore the meeting did not have
all stakeholders.

Several employees felt that management by both the owners and the
project managers was not consistent; one employee even felt that one
project manager was more competent in management than the other. This
employee was concerned that the management had a tendency to take new
employees more seriously than older ones, ignoring the opinions of those
with more seniority in favor of those who had just joined the company.
He described a particularly frustrating experience where a new employee
offered an idea that he'd suggested previously that was dismissed by the
group, but was suddenly taken seriously because, he felt, a newer person
had said it. This concern was echoed by a project manager, who also
noted that the owners involve everyone in the interview process for new
employees and for that reason, many are aware of salary inequities in the
company. The manager estimated that 'there are variances of literally
two to three times in salary for people who do similar work.' The key to
a high salary was having worked for someone else prior to coming to the

company; in that situation the salary would be higher to compete with other companies, but might make the new recruit out of step with the pay rates for the rest of the company.

The owners did not always follow through on promises, such as promising employees more office space since physical space was tight. The owners had promised to remedy the situation, but with no real follow-through. One employee complained that he thought the company would pay for courses but had since been told otherwise. Another employee complained that management was not consistent in following its own HR policies, stating that '[HR policies] will be implemented but [are] not followed. The employees will follow it but management doesn't.' It was clear that there was frustration at both the employee and project management level with consistency in company management.

Spousal Team Lacks Self-awareness

In US Case 510, a high career rewards firm, the spousal team in charge of the company utilized a 360-review process to prevent some of the pitfalls of running a company as a couple. No similar process was in place at Canadian Case 104, and the couple demonstrated many of the pitfalls, though it seemed they were unaware of it. Some employees viewed them as removed and ineffective, they were known to put subordinates in awkward positions, and they created meaningless positions with little authority.

The remote and ineffectual nature of the owners was complained about by one person, who noted:

> I think probably the biggest one is the owners are very nice people, personally very nice, and in their effort to be nice they try to make everybody happy in whatever way they can but they don't actually look at the real issues. . . . They don't conduct one-on-one reviews except at raise time. So it's often very insulting when somebody sits down because they think you don't talk to me for six months and then you tell me all the things that you think are a problem, but you haven't talked to me for six months.

While the owners touted their open door policies, it was not the case that all employees felt connected to the owners or comfortable with them. This was in part exacerbated by the difficulty of the power dynamics in working for couples, as described by one manager in the following exchange:

> R: . . . I think the biggest political difficulty that we face is the fact that it is a husband and wife team that have 50–50 not 49–51. So when one comes and says "I want you to do this", and the other one comes and says, "I want you to do this", and they conflict, especially when they're in an area where they're actually asking for exactly the opposite thing to be done. You don't know which person to go back to and there is no chain of command so the only people that

you can turn to are the very people who are asking for this. And when you go to one and say your spouse has asked me to do it this way, 'oh but don't listen to that person do it this way' and then you get exactly the flip when you go on the opposite side so . . .

I: What are you supposed to do?

R: The solution is you get them both in the room and say, you know you're both presenting two different sides, you're going to have to duke it out between the two of you and come back with a unified response. The result would be an hour later one of them will come out and say okay this is what we decided. Five minutes later the next one will come and say this is what we decided and it's a different story. So it's . . . a bit difficult, but we have to play that game somehow and it's a . . . it changes from day to day as to how we actually handle it politically to satisfy both sides without getting in the middle of the conflict.

Another employee felt that the spouses rarely questioned each other, and the decision-making process was not as open or logical as you might find at a larger company. In addition to complaints about the owners' decision-making process, we encountered several complaints about the project management position at the company. One noted the owners' difficulty with really ceding authority to their managers:

Yeah, there are control issues because it is owned by two people. They have ultimate authority, so even when they say this is your title and this is your responsibility, and even if you're not sure of the title you'll go and look it up and say okay what does that entail? What exactly are my responsibilities what should I do, what should I be providing, what am I authorized to do, that sort of thing. . . . in a company of this size, 15 people and two owners where really everybody does work on the same level even though they're trying to get structure in place, everybody does still answer only to the owners. So the difficulty that you have is you're on the same level as people but you're also working on a level above them so there should be a chain of command but it doesn't always exist. So the result is after accepting that full-time when I looked at what the job should be and what that role defines and what project manager's responsibilities are supposed to be in that capacity, a lot of the control that I should have wasn't given to me. And it's superseded often by other decisions that shouldn't be made by senior level management, should be made by somebody who is specifically either trained in the field or who has been designated with that title. And when you pass authority on you're basically saying okay you're now in charge and responsible for this area but you can't make someone responsible for an area within the company if you overrule the decisions that are made because then that person's responsible for someone else's decision, which is politically a bit of a problem. Because you then end with someone else making the decision without all the information, overruling your own, and then you end up having to deal with the people below as a result of that. So it's been kind of back and forth, it goes up and down with the weather in a way as to whether that control is relinquished like it will be passed off for a couple of weeks and say it's your area, you're in charge of it. But then after two or three weeks 'oh no we want that back' and 'we'll just take the control back again' so it goes up and down frequently.

Prior to the two-manager system, one employee was serving as project manager, but was too prone to challenging the owners. This employee had ceded the management position due to this conflict. The new managers were selected, in the estimation of one, to set a good example of the type of teamwork the company was striving for. However, it was less clear what exactly that team was supposed to be doing, especially as the owners frequently overrode their decisions. In general, it appears that even though this firm pays lip service to many similar practices to US Case 510, there is no real culture of development; the owners are in charge, always will be in charge, and only wish to develop staff to the point that they do not interfere with the current company leadership.

High Career Reward Firms that Masquerade as Low Career Reward Firms

Also instructive with regard to the contextual nature of career rewards were a few high career reward firms that, on the surface, looked like they had more in common with low career reward firms. A prime example was Canadian Case 103, a very small firm where everyone was an owner and the company was barely solvent enough to allow all the partners to work there full time; the group still ranked into the top of career development companies. In this case, it appeared that the firm was a labor of love for the owners, and as everyone had an ownership stake they were achieving their career goals simply by running the company, itself in an initial growth period with little extra money (though it had been in business for more than five years at the time of study, this was how the employees characterized it). The founding team had left other companies to form this one, so being able to form a company that ran as they liked was a great reward for them. Canadian Case 109 was in a similar situation; with fewer than five employees, it was a small team where everyone had a major role. One employee fretted that this group relied too much on a certain brand of computer technology and that was limiting, both to business and to the transferability of his skill set. However, the group comprised some misfits from bigger companies – as one worker stated:

> I'm the kind of person that'll piss on anything just for effect so, you know, yeah again it gets back to you don't, in large corporations it's definitely not, I, I wouldn't work, I wouldn't, I wouldn't fit in even if I was young, you know, and desperately in need of a job so I've never been that way. And the world's full of

people who are willing to do that stuff so, hey, they can have those jobs. And I'll find something that isn't so personally restricting, I guess we'll call it.

In these firms it appeared that even if the more traditional markers of career development were not in place, there was something of a character match between the employees and the companies. Mavericks performed well in environments that encouraged them to be mavericks, and that may have led them to view the career development opportunities in their company positively, even when the company was small and struggling or didn't demonstrate many other efforts at training individuals.

DISCUSSION AND CONCLUSIONS

In the present study, we have identified several positive attributes that were present in top-performing high career reward firms that were absent in low career reward firms. In our most extreme US cases, the active solicitation of employee involvement, regular meetings, cautious company growth to maintain lifestyle and protection for employees, firm-based training and development, and the use of collaborative relationships both among employees themselves and managers and subordinates helped Case 510 create a culture of development where the emphasis was both on developing the company as a whole and on developing individuals within the company. There was much energy at this company; even though it emphasized cautious growth, there was a sense that the group as a whole was evolving and emphasizing continuous quality improvement not only in product, but in the operations of the business. Employees felt ownership in the business, even though they did not have formal shares in the company (and even in the face of some resistance from the owners at bringing on employees as partners). At Case 507, it was quite the opposite: there was little energy expended on quality improvement or employee development. Rather than attempting to actively grow the business, it appeared that the owner was happy to meet the demands of current customers and stay afloat by delivering a low-cost product. Employees felt disenfranchised and quite frustrated at the relationship between the owner and clients; they wanted more advocacy from the owner.

It is one thing to demonstrate two obvious cases at polar opposites on the development continuum. However, greater nuance emerged as we examined some interesting exceptions – cases where it appeared that the owners were doing everything right or wrong, and yet employees identified with the opposite levels of development than one might think. Case 104 offered a glimpse into the contextual nature of management practices; it was not enough for the owners simply to have meetings; they needed to have meetings with the right people. It was not enough for them to create layers of positional authority workers could aspire to; they needed to imbue these positions with real authority. Policies on paper were only frustrating when the owners themselves were inconsistent in following them. And unlike US Case 510, where the spousal team at the helm of the company noted the issues that might arise from their relationship at work and took steps to actively address these issues, the spousal owners of Canadian Case 104 demonstrated little awareness of the toll their relationship took on employees.

Canadian Case 114, on the other hand, offered little to indicate that employees should be satisfied with their career development; the company was tiny and had financial woes, someone had to scale back hours to make the budget work, all talked about getting other jobs and carrying on the company part-time or even putting it on hiatus while they figured out the money. However, in this company everyone was a partner; the group was working as a team to realize their own dreams of starting a company from scratch, and as such each team member felt a sense of ownership in the enterprise.

The firms that perform the highest on the career rewards scale appear to structure opportunities to build human capital rather than to build within-firm careers. Emphasis is placed on educating and developing workers, not necessarily through official credentialing programs but often through intra-firm training. Some of these training methods allowed employees to be experts, mentoring others one-on-one or through staff meeting presentations and 'lunch and learns.' These informal moments of leadership allowed employees to develop not only in their technical skills, but also in their interpersonal and leadership skills. This development in human capital, strengthening both technical and interpersonal skills largely through engagement in different work tasks and teams, allowed employees the opportunity to not only succeed in the jobs they currently held, but also to prepare for jobs with more managerial responsibility in the future. As IT, like many other industries, continues to experience outsourcing and the pressures of globalization, the acquisition of scarce skills is the only real protection for these workers from job insecurity. While the firms are not necessarily providing intra-firm opportunities for positional advancement, the precarious nature of small, young firms themselves means that the ability to resell one's skills may be the greatest career development of all. Imbuing current employees with managerial skills will also ensure that, should the current employing companies grow in the future, these employees will be eligible to compete for positions of greater responsibility in the more hierarchical arrangements of a larger company. Indeed, in some of our companies, employees spoke of the possibility that they could become managers if the company grew and more people were brought in.

The cases we have described demonstrate the contextual nature of career development in IT firms. We do have several limitations on our findings. The first is the difficulty in assessing the effect of firm size. The small size of WANE firms makes it possible for all employees to meet in a single room, thus easier to create a unified, roundtable culture where all employees have input and can have audience with the owners. This practice is likely unsustainable as firms grow in size, or for firms that are already medium or large in size. Also, it is unclear what the role of country differences played, if any, in the companies that emerged as high or low performers on the career reward scale. The WANE study does not offer a representative sample from each country and as such, it is difficult to determine the exact impact of country differences. However, we have highlighted several parallels between the countries and believe the role the state plays in employee satisfaction with firm-based career rewards to be a promising area for future research. The fact that the firms' stories largely echo one another across the study countries contributes to the likelihood, however, that these lessons can be applied quite broadly.

In this chapter, we have demonstrated that the most successful small and medium IT enterprises for career development have managed to create cultures of development, where the development of both the company and the individuals within it are emphasized. It is difficult to prescribe a list of best practices, for our exceptional cases demonstrated that some companies could appear to do everything right without creating strong opportunities for career development, while others could appear to do everything wrong and yet still create strong opportunities for career development. In the end, it appears that there are some usual markers for high career reward firms: they tend to actively solicit employee involvement, grow cautiously enough that they can maintain lifestyle and protection for employees, and feature collaborative relationships among employees, especially between managers and subordinates. These factors alone were not enough to make firms sufficiently rewarding from a career development standpoint. However, in firms where the owners and managers were truly committed to developing not only the firm itself but the individuals within the firm, these factors appear to combine with that favorable attitude to create a culture of development that was quite powerful and well-received by company employees.

NOTE

1. However, as Kalleberg (2003) also discovered using data from the Second National Organizations Survey, between a third and half of organizations use elements of

both numerical and functional flexibility. This is consistent with an earlier finding by Osterman (1994) that 35 percent of firms with 50 or more employees used two or more flexible firm practices.

REFERENCES

Althauser, R. and A.L. Kalleberg (1981), *Firms, Occupations, and the Structure of Labor Markets: A Conceptual Analysis*, New York: Academic Press.

Atkinson, J. (1984), 'Manpower strategies for flexible organizations', *Personnel Management*, **16** (8), 28–31.

Baron, J.N. and W.T. Bielby (1986), 'The proliferation of job titles in organizations', *Administrative Science Quarterly*, **31** (4), 561–86.

Beehr, T.A., L. Ivanitskaya, C.P. Hansen, D. Erofeev and D.M. Gudanowski (2001), 'Evaluation of 360 degree feedback ratings: relationships with each other and with performance and selection predictors', *Journal of Organizational Behavior*, **22** (7), 775–88.

Bracken, D., C.W. Timmreck and A.H. Church (2001), *The Handbook of Multisource Feedback: The Comprehensive Resource for Designing and Implementing MSF Processes*, San Francisco, CA: Jossey Bass.

Cappelli, P. (1999), *The New Deal at Work: Managing the Market-driven Workforce*, Boston, MA: Harvard Business School Press.

Cappelli, P., L. Bassi, H. Katz, D. Knoke, P. Osterman and M. Useem (1997), *Change at Work*, New York: Oxford University Press.

Doeringer, P. and M. Piore (1971), *Internal Labor Markets and Manpower Analysis*, Lexington, MA: Heath Lexington Books.

Edwards, R. (1979), *Contested Terrain: The Transformation of the Workplace in the Twentieth Century*, New York: Basic Books.

Guillemard, A.M. (1991), 'International perspectives on early withdrawal from the labor force', in J. Myles and J. Quadagno (eds), *States, Labor markets, and the Future of Old Age Policy*, Philadelphia, PA: Temple University Press, pp. 209–26.

Guillen, M. (1994), *Models of Management: Work, Authority, and Organization in a Comparative Perspective*, Chicago, IL: University of Chicago Press.

Hacker, J.S. (2006), *The Great Risk Shift. The Assault on American Jobs, Families, Health Care, and Retirement, and How you can Fight Back*, Oxford and New York: Oxford University Press.

Hakim, C. (1990), 'Core and periphery in employers' workforce strategies: evidence from the 1987 ELUS survey', *Work, Employment and Society*, **4** (June), 157–88.

Kalleberg, A.L. (2000), 'Non-standard employment relations: part-time, temporary, and contract work', *Annual Review of Sociology*, **26**, 341–65.

Kalleberg, A.L. (2003), 'Flexible firms and labor market segmentation: effects of workplace restructuring on jobs and workers', *Work and Occupations*, **30** (May), 154–75.

Kohli, M. (1991), *Time for Retirement: Comparative Studies of Early Exit from the Labor Force*, Cambridge: Cambridge University Press.

Marsden, D. (1999), *A Theory of Employment Systems*, Oxford: Oxford University Press.

Marshall, V.W. (1999), 'Reasoning with case studies: issues of an aging workforce', *Journal of Aging Studies*, **13** (4), 377–89.

Marshall, V.W. (2009), 'Theory informing public policy: the life course perspective as a policy tool', in V.L. Bengtson, D. Gans, N.M. Putney, and M. Silverstein (eds), *Handbook of Theories of Aging*, 2nd edn, New York: Springer, pp. 573–93.

Osterman, P. (1994), 'How common is workplace transformation and who adopts it?', *Industrial and Labor Relations Review*, **47** (2), 173–88.

Osterman, P. (1999), *Securing Prosperity: The American Labor Market: How it has Changed and What to do About it*, Princeton, NJ: Princeton University Press.

Piore, M. and C. Sabel (1984), *The Second Industrial Divide: Possibilities for Prosperity*, New York: Basic Books.

Pollert, A. (1988), 'The "flexible firm": fixation or fact?', *Work, Employment & Society*, **2**, 281–316.

Ragin, C.C. (1987), *The Comparative Method: Moving Beyond Qualitative and Quantitative Strategies'*, Berkeley, CA: University of California Press.

Waldman, D.A., L.E. Atwater and D. Antonioni (1998), 'Has 360 degree feedback gone amok?', *Academy of Management Executive* **12** (2), 86–94.

4. Shifting down or gearing up? A comparative study of career transitions among men in information technology employment

Gillian Ranson

INTRODUCTION

Men in their 30s are at an interesting stage in their work and family lives. This is the decade when, typically several years past the end of full-time formal education, their work experience begins to take a particular shape, and to accumulate as a particular 'work history.' At this age, too, many men establish long-term intimate partner relationships and become fathers. For the current cohort of 30- to 40-year-olds, work experience is being accumulated in a globalizing New Economy which is changing conventional understandings of work and career. This is also an era when traditional ideas about men's place in family life are being contested. So from a life course perspective, men in this age group may be challenged on more than one front.

For men working in information technology, most of whom are young, career transitions are particularly interesting. Information technology work both epitomizes and underpins the New Economy. It is also subject to employment arrangements that are often unconventional. Significant numbers of IT workers are in small, new firms, rather than large established ones; sometimes they are working in short-term contractual arrangements, negotiated directly with clients, or indirectly though placement firms. They are, in short, outside the environment of large, stable bureaucratic organizations on which traditional theorizing about careers has concentrated.

As a group, these men are well placed to address many of the questions emerging from more recent scholarly research which is interrogating this traditional theorizing, and moving the study of working life and career transitions to the New Economy employment situations in which many of them are located. This is the group whose experiences are explored in this chapter. Specifically, the chapter focuses on the career transitions of men aged between 30 and 40, employed in small IT firms selected as case studies in Canada, Australia and the US as part of the WANE project.

CAREERS IN THE NEW ECONOMY

Much of the theorizing on the New Economy (see for example Beck, 1992; Castells, 2000; Giddens, 1991; Heinz, 2001; Webb, 2004) assumes that work careers, considered in the broad sense of segments of paid employment accumulated over time, are taking a different shape in the new economic order. One school of organizational theorists claims that careers have now become 'boundaryless,' the antithesis of the 'bounded,' hierarchical organizational career which unfolded over time in a single firm or organization (Arthur and Rousseau, 1996). According to its chief proponents, there are several ways boundaryless careers can take shape – for example, they can emerge as employees move through several employers, or in situations where careers are regulated and validated by broader occupational mechanisms, rather than by processes within individual oranizations. However, '[a] common factor in the occurrence of all these meanings is one of independence from, rather than dependence on, traditional organizational career arrangements' (Arthur and Rousseau, 1996: 6).

The boundaryless career concept has served as a focus for a considerable body of research and theorizing. In some cases (for example, Jones, 1996; Saxenian, 1996; Valcour and Tolbert, 2003) it is uncritically taken up in studies which seek to elaborate particular aspects, or test the dimensions, of 'boundaryless careers' in specific occupational, organizational or other contexts. Other research in the area has a more critical edge. For example, the study by Bagdadli et al. (2003) on careers of managers in New Economy firms (usually small, start-up and Internet-related) in Italy established that boundaries of a different sort (based on competence, and professional networks) exist even in multi-firm careers which breach the more conventionally understood 'boundaries' of a single organizational workplace. Research by King et al. (2005) on IT professionals' experiences using placement agencies also found that 'bounded,' rather than 'boundaryless,' was a better descriptor of their careers. Cohen and Mallon (1999: 346), in their study of professionals who moved from organizational careers to set up in business on their own, found that their study participants often sought to reconstruct, rather than break free from boundaries, for example by seeking long-term contracts with formal organizations in order to 're-embed themselves within organisational worlds.'

For Barley and Kunda (2001) the abstract 'boundaryless career' is an example of conceptual inversion, which occurs when theorists try to move beyond images of traditional bureaucratic organizing by conceptualizing what they assume to be its opposite. They claim that the 'boundaryless career' has come to stand for all careers in which people move between organizations, in shorter periods of employment. But '[t]o argue that fewer people are playing out their careers within the confines of an organization or that employment relations are changing is different . . . from saying that careers no longer have boundaries.' For one thing, significant numbers of people have always constructed careers outside formal bureaucratic structures. For another, 'the boundaries of a career are partially determined by the sense that individuals make of the flows, sequences, and locations of their work activities' (Barley and Kunda, 2001: 78). In this context, Barley and Kunda cite research by Zabusky and Barley (1996) on the careers of technicians, most of which defied conventional expectations about vertical mobility over time. However the technicians themselves measured their careers in 'increments of technical expertise and challenge.' These 'careers of achievement' lacked coherence from an organizational perspective, but made sense from the perspective of an occupational community. The authors note that engineers, scientists and other professionals frequently speak in a similar way about their careers. Thus 'with the growth of knowledge-based work, careers of achievement may become increasingly common' (Barley and Kunda, 2001: 87).

INFORMATION TECHNOLOGY CAREERS IN THE NEW ECONOMY

From the foregoing, it is evident that some useful theoretical discussion of careers in the New Economy has focused explicitly on information technology employment. This work helps to show the distinctiveness of IT employment – a distinctiveness which is only now coming to be acknowledged. For example, IT workers, in many ways at the forefront of developments in the New Economy, were also at the forefront of employment restructuring in the wake of the dramatic crash of 'dot.com' technology stocks and the decline of the NASDAQ index in the spring of 2000. While the high-tech boom and bust had implications in many workplaces and labor markets, IT employers were particularly affected, and as a consequence IT workers were particularly vulnerable. The shift towards short-term, part-time or contingent work already seen to characterize the New Economy was exacerbated for IT workers as a consequence of the 2000 high-tech downturn. How IT workers experienced this downturn depended on factors such as the region where they worked, and the nature of their IT skills. But there were also cohort effects; for example, workers with experience were differently placed to find work in 2000 than new college or university graduates seeking their first IT jobs. Another consequence of the downturn was the proliferation of new, small firms, as large organizations laid off their IT workers and outsourced their IT functions. Small firms had always been a distinctive feature of IT employment – another reason why IT careers did not always follow the large-organization, bureaucratic routes of traditional career theorizing. However the firms formed as start-ups in the wake of the 2000 downturn were likely to be different, in terms of what they demanded and what they could offer, from older firms that weathered the downturn.

From a career perspective, this reinforces the significant position of small firms as employers of IT workers, and as entrepreneurial opportunities for high-tech innovators. Yet there appear to be no examples in the scholarly literature of work that examines career trajectories of IT workers with attention to the small firms where so many of them work. Much of the empirical research on IT workers (for example, Barley and Kunda, 2004; Benner, 2002; Kunda et al., 2002) focuses on the individual, regional or labor market dimensions of IT work, or (in the case of Perlow, 1995, 1998) software development work in a large US high-tech corporation. Barrett (2001, 2004), in her analyses of the labor process in two small Australian software development firms, provides a rare example of research on IT work in the small-firm environment.

One other aspect of IT careers also needs to be noted. These are primarily men's careers – and more specifically young men's careers. The place of men's work in the construction of their masculinity has been extensively documented. But as Barrett and others have suggested, the nature of IT work, in particular software development, seems to have invoked a labor process in which employees, often working in firms without much hierarchy or formal organization, internalize control mechanisms and push themselves to work long hours in order to show their dedication and technical skill. Cooper's (2000: 381) study of Silicon Valley knowledge workers who were also fathers contains a vivid portrayal of this 'new masculinity for the New Economy.' At the same time, most IT workers – especially those who are self-employed, or working in small firms – are operating in an economic environment of considerable uncertainty and risk. Portraying oneself as adventurous, rather than cautious, in the face of risk also conforms to hegemonic forms of masculinity (Connell, 1995, 2002). Many of the male engineers in Ranson's (2001) study who had been laid off in the wake of economic restructuring in the Western Canadian energy industry spoke disparagingly of those who remained in the sheltered world of large organizations, and framed their own multi-employer careers as signs of their own enterprise, marketability and confidence. The laid off IBM workers referred to by Sennett (1998) similarly regretted not having taken more risks. The paradox however, is that for men with families, risk-taking has to be balanced against a widely held belief that they are ultimately responsible for their families' financial support. The breadwinner role continues to be paramount, even in an era of heightened expectations about men's more direct involvement in family life (Christiansen and Palkowitz, 2001; Townsend, 2002). For men in IT, it may perhaps be used to justify the sort of heroic attachment to work described by Cooper (2000). In short, it seems safe to assume that however the careers of men in IT unfold, in the context of changing needs, interests and opportunities, they will be linked to individual men's understandings of masculinity, and themselves as men.

All of the foregoing establishes a picture of individual men, balancing often conflicting expectations of themselves as men, accumulating IT work experience over time in a variable number of workplaces. They are, in other words, establishing career trajectories. Their experiences are shaped by their age, both in terms of cohort effects with respect to large-scale economic change, and in terms of their family status and other responsibilities outside the workplace. They are also shaped by the history of the specific workplaces through which their career paths lead them. This chapter acknowledges these converging influences in an examination of the career trajectories of a group of Canadian, Australian and US men working in small IT firms. The men described here were in the same age cohort, but they differed in terms of their training, and their employment history in IT. Those who started their careers before the downturn, in firms that weathered the crisis, had different experiences from those whose first jobs were in more vulnerable firms. The chapter thus addresses two main questions: (1) What place do small firms, founded at different time periods and with different histories, have in the career trajectories of men working in IT? and, (2) What theoretical model of 'career' best fits the career trajectories of the men in the study?

THE STUDY

This chapter draws on data gathered during WANE case study fieldwork from men aged between 30 and 40, who participated in face-to-face interviews while working (either as employees, contract workers, managers or owners) for the small case-study firms in Canada, Australia and the US The only other selection criteria imposed were that they were current, not former employees, and that they had been employed in the firm for a minimum of three months at the time they were interviewed. In all, 51 men (30 in Canada, nine in Australia and 12 in the US) representing 25 case study firms (14 in Canada, five in Australia and six in the US) were eligible for inclusion. Overall, the average age of the respondents was 34.9. Of the 51 participants, 38 were married or in permanent relationships, two were separated or divorced, and nine were single. Twenty-eight of the men had children. Information about marital status or children was missing in four cases. Considered by study country, the average age of the Canadian men was 35. Twenty of the 30 Canadians were married or in permanent relationships, two were separated or divorced, and eight were single. Eighteen of the Canadian men had children. Information about children was missing for one of the Canadian men. The average age of the Australian men was 34.6; seven of the nine Australians were married, and four had children. Information about marital status was missing for two of the Australian men. The average age of the 12 US men was 35; 11 were married, and six had children. Information about children was missing for one of the US men. (More detailed demographic data on study participants is available in Chapter 1.)

In addition, the case study reports (produced from field notes, interview data and survey information from informants in every case study firm) were used to provide background information. This meant that material provided by individual men could be read in the context of in-depth information about the firms that employed them – in all their social and economic diversity. So the key analytic strategy used in this chapter to address the research questions noted above was to ask, for each individual, 'How does he come to be in this firm, at this time in his life?' This approach made it possible to contextualize career information at the individual level, while also helping to build up a picture of the role of small firms in career development and life-course transitions.

FINDINGS

Asking this question of the data on individual men, read in the context of case study information on the firm, revealed several key ways in which the study firms appeared to function for the individual study participants. For example:

- in some cases, they were temporary stopping places for men who were self-employed contractors;
- in some cases, they provided the opportunity for men to *launch* careers in IT;

- in some cases, they provided stable and relatively long-term employment, and/or the opportunity to build or stabilize IT careers; and
- in some cases, especially for casualties of prior restructuring and layoffs, they were opportunities to rescue or revitalize careers, and (for owners) to become entrepreneurs.

In fact, individual firms often fulfilled more than one of these functions simultaneously for a single employee. And they did not work in the same way for all employees. The age of the employee and the age of the firm were obviously highly relevant: 30-year-olds were unlikely to have accumulated ten-year histories in their present firm; but neither were 40-year-olds, if the firm in question was a recent start-up.

The history of the firm was significant particularly when considered in connection with the high-tech downturn of 2000. As noted earlier, this downturn served as a watershed for many individuals and firms. Firms established before 2000, and that weathered the crisis, were the ones able to offer longer-term, stable employment; as survivors, they were also able, in 2000 and later, to take in IT workers whose previous employers had floundered. But the downturn also produced in its wake a wide array of new firms, often formed out of the ashes of old ones and in the aftermath of the restructuring and layoffs noted earlier. Of the 39 men whose tenure in the workplaces in which they were interviewed started in 2000 or later, 20 had moved into these survivor firms. The remaining 19 started work in firms that were also new.

Because of its clear significance, both for individuals and firms, the year 2000 is used as an organizing device for the findings. The next section discusses the experience of the 39 men who joined their present firms in 2000 or later. The discussion then moves to the 12 men whose longer tenure, in firms formed before the downturn, shed a different light on IT careers.

2000 or Later

A focus on the 30–40-year-old men whose employment in the case study firms had begun in 2000 or later shows clearly the multiple functions that the firms were playing for IT workers bringing diverse employment histories to their current workplaces.

Firms as Non-permanent Stopping Places
An important category of post-2000 employees in the case study firms were those working on short-term contracts; they were the quintessential 'contingent workers' widely acknowledged as characteristic of New Economy workplaces. Yet the contractors interviewed for this study[1] were very

differently placed in terms of the nature of their work, their relationship to their clients, and their remuneration.

Three of the Canadian contractors were technically employees of placement agencies which mediated their access to the case study firms. These agencies, commonly known (in Canada at least) as 'body shops,' supply short-term contract labor to client firms in exchange for a percentage of the salary paid to the contractor. In some cases, they provide a bridge back to appropriate employment after a lay-off or voluntary resignation following organizational restructuring. This was the case for Alex Lagasse;[2] a 35-year-old single, childless programmer who was doing contract work brokered by Firm 113, after having been laid off from the company for which he had worked for 10 years. Julian Pascu, another 'employee' of Firm 113, was an immigrant from Eastern Europe. Aged 37, and with university degrees in computer science and electrical engineering from his home country, he was still trying to break into permanent employment.

A mediated relationship of yet another kind was experienced by Neil Kennedy, a 30-year-old database administrator working through a small body-shop (Firm 118) for a major telecommunications company. Neil had trained as a land surveyor, but found he was spending too much time away from home. So he took an IT college diploma program and distributed his résumé around recruiting companies in the city where he lived. Firm 118 gave him his present contract – his first formal IT job, which he had held for the two years prior to his interview. His view of Firm 118, however, was 'a means of finding employment.' He saw himself as working for the client, not Firm 118. When he was interviewed, his partner was expecting their first baby. As he put it: 'Now that I'm going to have a family to support, it does definitely change the views on what I should be doing as the father-figure.' The change he was anticipating was to permanent employment, possibly with his current client, in order to acquire the health and other benefits he lacked as a contractor.

The experiences just noted provide an interesting contrast to those of the men in the study working, not through placement agencies, but as independent contract workers or consultants – two in Canada, one in Australia. For example, the Canadian contractors, the oldest of the group at 37 and 40, were working as consultants on relatively long-term contracts for a high-end, technologically advanced consulting company (Firm 107). The 37-year-old, James Thayer, who was single and childless, had a university degree in computer science, and had worked as an employee in several companies before becoming an 'independent.' The 40-year-old, Kevin Vance, who was married with one child, worked his way up from the stock room of a major oil company. Over the 11 years of his employment with the company, he took advantage of its training support program, and completed a college IT diploma, along with several university courses. He moved from the large company to a series of smaller ones before becoming an independent seven years earlier. Both these men expressed considerable satisfaction with their working arrangements – for which each had earned in the $150,000–$200,000 range in the previous year. The Australian contractor, Bill Reyes, married, with no children, aged 34, was in a similar situation in a similar firm – Firm 202, a high-end, technologically advanced consulting company. Like his Canadian counterparts, he had a university IT degree. He had been laid off during the restructuring of his first employer, and turned to consulting after working as a permanent employee in three firms (interspersed with travel along the way). He had worked under contract in his present firm for two years, since it was formed, and was earning an above-market salary.

These examples of contractors' experiences – all of them working in established rather than post-downturn firms – illuminate many paradoxes about the 'short-termism' (Webb, 2004) or the transience of contract-type employment in IT, and the way it links to other dimensions of young men's lives. For those with few formal skills, poorly paid contract work may be all they can get. But at the other end of the skill and salary scale, contract workers are in a very different position, often able to choose their contracts – and also able to choose whether or not they wanted permanent employment. In these cases, another paradox emerged: these contractors were much less 'transient' than their employment arrangements might suggest. The high-earners were actually surprisingly loyal pseudo-employees, in good and often long-standing personal relationships with their 'clients.'

Firms as Launch-pads for Careers

Among permanent employees, good examples of the career-launching capacity of small firms came from two visible minority immigrants to Canada, who settled in two different cities. Both came to Canada with foreign IT-related university degrees, and both were working as programmers in software development firms. Larry Chung, aged 40, married with one child, found a permanent job in Firm 110 in 2003, after some 13 years' experience in his home country, and two years of short-term contract work and some time without a job in Canada. He noted the advantages for immigrants like himself, for whom English was a second language, to work in a small firm; in his view, fewer people meant fewer communication demands. He planned to stay in the firm for the long term. Seddik Benslimane, aged 30, and newly married, took a college diploma program as a refresher, was placed in Firm 108 on a practicum, and was then hired on full-time in 2003.

Another example came from Firm 507, a 14-employee firm offering mainly computer, network and server installation and support in the US, which 32-year-old Eliot Fowler had joined a year before he was interviewed. After an employment history that included work in convenience stores, and cab-driving, he completed a technical certificate that opened the doors to the kind of technical support work offered by Firm 507. He had some reservations about the long-term need for this kind of support, on the basis that the need for technicians would decrease as technology improved over time. But he spoke in strongly positive terms about Firm 507 as his launch pad. There was, he said, a 'serious level of trust' placed in employees, which they repaid in a serious commitment to the firm:

> I think they like the fact that we pretty well think of it as, as our company . . . We run it. We're here day-to-day. We're the front lines, yes, but we're trying to do everything to make it better because it really does mean something to us. This isn't a 9-to-5 . . . This is not, 'I forget about it when I go home.' It's, it's kind of like my company, too.

In all three cases, IT careers were being launched in stable well-established firms. But the individuals' ages, family circumstances, and the kind of work experience available to them within the firm were likely to influence their length of tenure and future career trajectories.

Firms as Places to Stabilize and Build Careers
Several of the men hired as permanent employees in 2000 or later had checkered, multi-employer work histories laughingly described by one highly mobile worker as 'young men's careers' in IT. The case study firms where they were interviewed, however, seemed to mark a shift. Their past experience, however random it may have seemed, could be pulled together to meet the firm's needs. Or the sort of stability that had eluded them in firms that were themselves unstable seemed to become available in the new situation. These firms seemed to be places in which they could make plans for the future.

In Canada, Sam Gibson, aged 37, joined Firm 112 when he was faced by a classic New Economy employment situation. His former employer, a major corporation for whom he had worked for 12 years, had decided to sell – in effect outsource – his client services department. He had the choice to go with the new company, but was approached directly about working for Firm 112, a 14-person software development firm formed in 1991, by its CEO, a former classmate and children's soccer contact. He chose Firm 112 instead, citing as his major reasons a higher salary, and the chance to work with leading edge technology. He indicated on his survey that he would like to start his own business, but wanted a few more years earning an income first.

Craig Hirsch came to work in Firm 117, a 14-person Canadian software development company, when he was 29 and the firm had been established two years. With an eclectic educational background, which included graduate work in engineering, he had accumulated several years of short-term contracts and permanent employment when he started. After less than two years in the firm, and shortly before he was interviewed, he had been promoted to a team lead position in his specialty, web development. His views on the place of the firm in his own career development were clear:

> There aren't other places . . . where I would have the opportunities to do what I do here. I wouldn't be able to move into another technical lead position where I would also have the kind of management responsibilities I have. Precisely because this company is at this really interesting, slightly bigger than tiny but not big, not even really medium-sized size yet. So I'm growing with the company and that's great. And that's working for me. So . . . in terms of my longevity in this position, the answer is as long as this continues to be cool and fun I will continue to find it cool and fun. As soon as it's not cool and fun anymore or as soon as I reach the point where I can no longer make my mortgage payments doing it, which will happen in the Fall if there isn't a raise soon . . . those are the things that would push me out of this job.

One of the Australian participants, 30-year-old Curtis Novak, brought a similar educational and work experience background to Firm 202, a 13-person high-end software development firm founded in 2000 (the firm in which Bill Reyes worked as a contractor). When Curtis joined it in 2003, he had had multiple employers, and had also completed contracts during travelling in Europe. He commented:

> This is my fourth job since coming back [in 2001], and this job is one I feel I could stay in for quite a while. I think I've been quite fortunate to finally land myself. This job to me sort of vindicates why I kept moving because I realized – I kept thinking, there has to be something better than – that more fits me, and this job I think is it.

The 'fit' involved being challenged, and included the opportunity to get more involved with all aspects of the business, so he was not 'pigeon-holed as a programmer.' There was also the opportunity to learn from the company's founders, his direct employers, who were 'great role models and mentors.' Unlike Craig Hirsch, his enthusiasm was not tempered by financial concerns. Firm 202 hired highly skilled, university-educated and experienced staff, paid higher than average salaries, and was growing. In the US, Firm 502 offered Alan Bridges a similar experience. He had graduate-level training in computer engineering, and came to the firm after two years in another company. He too was attracted by the firm's potential:

> I was pretty much sure that this is the place I want to be, this is the environment. And and I haven't thought about moving. And I don't think I will for a while. [There are] good, smart people. The resources are here. The other thing, the other reason is probably I see the potential for growth, and I believe in what we're doing. And, if it makes it, you know, it's like an accomplishment.

Michael Boyd had worked for Firm 110 in Canada for five years at the time he was interviewed – the longest he had worked anywhere. Aged 37, with a university degree in computer science, he had been laid off after four years with his first employer, a major financial institution undergoing restructuring of its IT functions. He then had a series of jobs in firms which went out of business, or were taken over, or merged – including the predecessor to Firm 110. As he put it, in the course of 14 years he had three job changes, but worked for six companies. The fact that five of his 14 years were spent in Firm 110 suggested he too had found some stability. He commented: 'I guess it means I like the place.'

But stability may not have been the way he would have classified his Firm 110 experience to himself. Like many small companies, Firm 110 was dependent on lucrative projects from dependable clients. When projects fell through or didn't materialize, instability was more likely to be the case. Perhaps because of his past experience, Boyd was much less sanguine about the firm's finances than the other long-term employees seemed to be, and he had a strategy for managing this uncertainty:

> I just make sure I keep my résumé current and my head hunters handy, and . . . if things are looking bad I just make some phone calls and see if there's anything out there. And, I'd have no problem if something fell in my lap along the way, I'd jump ship . . . without question.

The firms that served to stabilize and build the careers described here were a mix of more established and newer enterprises. In some of these examples, a combination of relatively short tenure on the job, and uncertainty about the firm's long-term economic prospects, meant that career plans were provisional. In these cases, the individuals might settle in for a (relatively) long term, or move on if the firm failed to live up to its promise. On the other hand, as with Curtis Novak, a stabilizing job with a growing firm could finally give an individual the sense, after many stops along the way, of having 'arrived,' at least for a while.

Firms as Places to Rescue or Revitalize Careers

For some of the men who had experienced firm and industry instability like that already mentioned, the case study firms were places where careers could be retrieved and potentially turned around after prior job losses. For example, Colin Navarro first started work for Firm 102, a five-person Canadian software development company founded in 2001, under the terms of a federal government employment insurance program, after he was laid off from a previous employer. Firm 102 then hired him on permanently more than a year before he was interviewed. Though according to his survey he worried about the financial security of Firm 102, he had no thought of changing jobs.

Brad Gerber joined Firm 115, a 10-person Canadian consulting company, after a seven-year stint with a large IT company which underwent major restructuring in 2002. Firm 115 was established in 2000 by individuals in the department where he worked, after they too were downsized. The firm provided him the opportunity to rejoin his former team, and continue the work he had been doing for his previous employer. He spoke positively about the benefits of working with a cohesive team who shared a history. But like many other employees in start-up firms, he voiced concern about his salary, which had already made him think about looking elsewhere for work.

In Australia, 30-year-old Mark Coutts joined Firm 204 in 2001. (The firm itself, a 16-person web development firm, had been established in the late 1990s.) With incomplete post-secondary qualifications, and self-taught in IT, he worked as a web developer for a year, until the company employing him folded. He then did some contract work, including a term in Firm 204, where he was then hired full-time. He shared concerns about firm finances, and wished his own salary was higher. But, as he added, 'I love what I'm doing.' And he spoke of a commitment to the firm that he anticipated would keep him there long-term: 'It feels a little bit like my business as well. I feel that connection to it.'

At 40, Russell Abbott's 'rescue' came at a later stage in his career. He joined Firm 210, an Australian company founded in 1989 and specializing in billing systems, in 2004, after multiple positions in firms where he balanced his business background and practical IT experience. Firm 210 did not rescue him from unemployment, but rather from a job he had taken to give himself some breathing space from work that was proving too stressful and demanding. He applied for a billing analyst job at Firm 210, but was asked to be operations manager instead – a job that closely matched his skills and background experience. He commented:

> I now work in a company which is a lot smaller. I know everybody, everything's upfront, there is none of this backstabbing, carry-on. If you're not happy with something you voice it, and you know someone will listen.

At 40, he said he had not envisaged retirement, but 'long-term' would mean at least another five years with Firm 210, followed by a review. In the meantime, he said he was not looking to climb any corporate ladder: 'I'm happy in the role I'm in.'

In the US, Keith Leishman joined Firm 510 in 2001 after a lay-off from a 'dot com' firm – the last in a series of start-ups for which he had worked. With only two years of college, and no formal IT training, he had taught himself, and apprenticed himself to mentors (one of whom was his brother). When he was interviewed, he had worked for Firm 510 for four years, so rescue was at the point of turning into stability. The firm, established in 1995 and specializing in building websites, was stable and salaries were good, his work (some technical consulting with clients, some programming) was interesting, and the explicit 'lifestyle' focus of the firm made for considerable flexibility. This was important in helping him adjust to another major life transition with the birth of his son 18 months earlier. But stability was a two-edged sword. It gave him the time he needed to be with his family, something that was 'more important' than it had been four or five years earlier; but there was less time for skill development and keeping up with new technology, and he worried about stagnating. 'I'm probably a little more interested in stability, I would say,' he commented. 'Although, I mean, I have a real problem with getting bored. So that's the line there . . . It's like, okay, I'm doing the same thing over and over again or what have you, um, and not getting anywhere.' He looked back on past job changes as a chance to 'reboot or refresh.' It was not hard to detect the possibility of another one coming. There were also family reasons why he might leave Firm 510; now they were parents, he and his wife were contemplating a move back to their home city in another state.

Firm 509, a US micro-firm formed in 1995 and offering website and registration services for conferences, had rescued all three of its permanent employees, at almost yearly intervals since 2001. All three, in their early- to mid-thirties, had been laid off from other firms. Two of the three had university degrees in non-technical fields, and were self-taught IT workers. The most recent arrival, Earl Johnson, was full of praise for the firm after a year as an employee. 'I would love to stay here,' he said. 'This is the epitome of a stress-free environment. . . . Put it like this, if Google were a four-man show, it would be Firm 509.' He added: 'The only reason why I would ever look for another job would be compensation . . . If I could have the compensation that I wanted, I would stay here until I retired.' Stephen Ingram, a three-year employee and the only one with formal university-level IT qualifications, echoed Earl Johnson's satisfaction with the working environment, and noted the opportunity working in a small firm gave him to acquire new skills. In the absence of a database specialist, he said he was 'sort of steering myself towards becoming a database administrator,' which was 'where my interest lies now.' But he too raised concerns about his salary, which in his estimation was about '75 percent of the low end.' Tied to that were concerns about the way the firm did its billing – 'we bill like boxed software, but we do custom work.' He would like to stay on, but for financial reasons was looking elsewhere. The most senior of the three, Richard Harris, was also wanting a change after four years in the firm:

> I would say right now, if I could find something outside of information technology, I would do that . . . because I'm kind of tired of it. The stuff that we do now, five years ago was valued and somewhat respected. Now it's just not.

But 'nothing has come along that has pulled me away;' a change was not on the immediate horizon. With a large family, he appreciated the stability Firm 509 offered, but like Keith Leishman he had experienced the stagnation – his word was the 'calcification' – that was its down side. At the same time, he lacked the range of skills that would make him employable in many other IT firms.

As these examples demonstrate, 'rescue' can take several forms, in both established and new firms. In some cases, it has the effect of providing a stable home, like the one Curtis Novak found in Firm 202. In other cases, it offers a reprieve, satisfactory sometimes only for a short time, a necessary resting place on what might be a continuing career journey. Less positively, a rescue may also derail a career over the long term.

Firms as Entrepreneurial Opportunities

Firms provided opportunities to build, or stabilize, or revitalize careers for their founders, as well as their employees. In these cases they were entrepreneurial opportunities, allowing men who had once been employees elsewhere to develop their ideas (often their passions) at a new level. In these cases, the investment in the firm, both psychic and financial, was often significant. So were the risks, especially in new firms.

Firm 102, the Canadian firm that rescued Colin Navarro, was actually formed when its much larger predecessor went into receivership. Three former employees got together with a venture capital firm to launch the new company in 2001. The key player was the 27-year-old who became president. The individual included in this study was David Osler, who as one of the three principals was also a minority shareholder. Sharing the ownership, he explained, was a way to compensate him for his role in the 'blood, sweat and tears' of the company's start-up, and 'all the different things we had done to maintain the company.' Though he was working more like a manager than an owner, shares in the company gave him more of an investment in its success.

Matthew Johnson and Sanjay Joshi, working for practical purposes as joint heads of Firm 117, a small Canadian software development company working more or less uncontested in a unique product niche, provided good, though different examples of entrepreneurial careers taking shape. The company (the same one in which Craig Hirsch was working as a technical team lead) was actually founded in 2001 by Johnson, when he was 29. The firm niche built on a solid base of experience and interest he had developed over the preceding 10 years. He had a degree in systems engineering, several high-end co-op positions in major IT firms while he was still a student, and five years as an employee in a major software company. He moved to a smaller company because he 'wanted his contributions to have a more immediate impact.' He says:

> It really gave me a good opportunity to see the ins and outs of how a young entrepreneurial organization operates. And you see some great stuff, you see some not so great stuff. And so I was there for less than a year and . . . decided I could do this a lot better myself.

Firm 117 began in his basement, but grew quickly to its present 14 employees, and is set to grow much bigger. In the early stages, Johnson was introduced to Sanjay Joshi, who a mutual acquaintance thought could bring some needed business acumen to the new firm. Joshi had parlayed a science degree with a minor in computer science into co-op opportunities in high tech firms, and by the time he was 30 had developed, grown and sold his own small high tech firm to its chief competitor. He was persuaded to join the firm full-time in 2001, as president and CEO, with a mandate to 'grow the company.'

In the US, Barry Collins and Carter Davis also broke away from their former employer to start out (with two other co-workers) on their own, persuaded that they could work more efficiently outside of the constraints of a large organization ('I've always been kind of entrepreneurial and wanted to do things kind of my way,' Collins commented). University-trained in computer and electrical engineering, and with large-firm work experience behind them, they founded Firm 504, a 13-person software development and support company, in 2001. The firm was taking a shape that both men found intensely satisfying. 'These are some of the best people I've ever worked with,' said Davis. 'There's no other company that I have worked for that has even approached the level of camaraderie and job satisfaction that we have here.' Both men wanted it to be the last place they worked. As Collins put it:

This is kind of the end game for all of us. We've been in different industries, and we're trying to grow a business so that it can be a stable business [so] that we can eventually work here a long time . . . and kind of retire there.

For some entrepreneurs, risk-taking did not always pay off. Firm 201, the Australian web development firm founded by Tony Phillips in 2000 was struggling at the end of 2004 when the case study was conducted, reduced to five people with the loss of several other staff members. The firm was under-capitalized, and wages were low. The future seemed very uncertain. Phillips isolated one problem his firm, and many similar firms, were facing:

> I know it sounds like an excuse but most small businesses, you're working *in* the business, not *on* the business, and that's a major failure.

Lack of capital, and lack of time, were chronic concerns. Business meetings often ended up in discussions about 'what the hell's going on and what are we going to do.' Phillips was willing also to blame his own lack of managerial skills. Selling out profitably, and moving on to other ventures characterized many of the career and life plans of the more recent entrepreneurs. But success was sometimes difficult to achieve.

In these examples, Phillips' experience stands out. For the other entrepreneurs, the future seemed brighter. The new, post-downturn firms they had created, drawing on a combination of confidence, past experience and expertise, were likely to be the successful culmination of their work careers.

Summing Up

The previous section focused on the 39 men whose histories in the case study firms where they were interviewed dated from 2000 or later. In some cases, the firms in which they worked had similarly short histories; in other cases their places of employment were well established by the time they arrived. The temporal history of the firm did not, however, seem to affect the function each served, for individual employees – launching, building, stabilizing and rescuing was done by newer and older firms. Many of the men were casualties of the restructuring and layoffs of the 2000 high-tech downturn, and in both the newer and the older firms they were building up the kind of careers (characterized by short stints with multiple employers) often theorized to characterize the New Economy.

Before 2000

The career trajectories of the men described above offer an interesting backdrop for the discussion to follow, which focuses on the theoretically interesting group of 12 men whose careers were following a markedly different path. These were the men (six working as employees or managers, and six with owner interests of various kinds) in case study firms established before 2000, whose tenure in these firms predated the downturn. In other words, their employment relationships were both stable and much longer term. The experiences of these men seemed to invite a different way of thinking about careers in small firms.

Employees and Managers
The men whose tenure in the case study firms began before 2000 were working for firms, founded usually in the early 1990s, that had themselves weathered the technology boom and bust a decade later, and established a track record for survival. They became places in which careers over the long term were viable. These were not careers marked by advancement up a conventional career ladder; small firms were seldom in a position to offer much upward mobility. But they could often offer something else that employees valued more highly: the opportunity to participate in building or growing the firm. For the six men working as employees and managers, their close involvement in this development, and the sense that their participation was closely tied to the firm's success, often – though not always – trumped other concerns.

For example, Firm 108, the eight-person software development company which gave Seddik Benslimane his first Canadian IT job in 2003, gave a similar development job to Ken Feng some four years earlier. He too was an immigrant, with foreign IT qualifications and a Canadian college IT diploma, and he too successfully served a practicum in the company. In this sense he had established a 'career path' of sorts which was available for Seddik to follow. Both Feng and Benslimane had another model in Mohinder Gill, who joined the company in 1990, four years after it had been launched, and straight after he had finished a degree in computer science. In his 11 years in the company, he had been promoted to manager, a position which made him the administrative and technical support person to the founder and president. Gill cited as small firm advantages the fact that he could play multiple roles, in a work culture that was like a 'family unit.' He had no thoughts of leaving on his own account, but was aware of another possible transition looming with the eventual retirement of the firm's owner-president. If it turned out that he needed to look elsewhere, he suggested that he would look in the direction of a company – either large or small – that could provide the income, pension and benefits package he was missing at Firm 108.

Lucas Anderson and Nick Cramer both worked for Firm 110, a Canadian company formed in 2005 from the merger of two separate software development companies, one established in the mid-1980s, one in the early 1990s. The original companies catered to two distinct and highly specialized niches which remained the focus of the merged company. As a science graduate student in the field served by one of the companies, Anderson was persuaded by the two principals to join them as they got the company going. His eclectic educational background and interests were a good fit for the company's product and market. Aged 40 when interviewed, he had worked for the company for 10 years. In a highly specialized field, as he commented,

> I love what I do and I love the company so I've never really wanted to go [else-where]. I've finally sort of found a niche that I really enjoy, where I can explore my interest in technology, but also stick with my true love [the specialized science interests].

This, in spite of the fact that his household income was less than $60,000, and he was working up to 20 hours a week at a second consulting job. Cramer's background was different, but his extended and loyal commitment to the second company in the merger echoed Anderson's. With a college IT diploma, he started work for Firm 110's predecessor in 1991, and had been there ever since. He spoke about the possibility in a small company of taking pride in building something. Responding to a survey question about future plans, he said he intended to retire after leaving Firm 110.

In the US, Jay Pierce had supported his life partner as she established Firm 510, the web design firm that had rescued Keith Leishman. Self-taught in IT, and with wide-ranging interests and a varied work history in IT behind him, he joined Firm 510 formally in 1998, when he was 29. When he was interviewed, the firm was seven-strong, and he was its CTO. He saw an important part of his role as 'helping to evaluate new technologies and figure out what the direction is for the company.' Though his personal relationship to the CEO differentiated his career path from that of a conventional employee, in his interview he clearly positioned himself as an employee – but one with considerable latitude to explore new technology and continue to challenge himself intellectually.

The sort of stability suggested in these longer-tenure career trajectories may be linked to the timing of the individual's arrival in the firm. All the men described above arrived in the case study firm early in their careers. Presumably, the firm's survival, and their own intimate participation in that survival, were enough to keep them invested on an ongoing basis.

'Founding fathers'

Men who made a career investment in starting a new firm, and then managed to grow it successfully over the long term, were in many ways the stereotypical New Economy entrepreneurs – autonomous, enterprising and risk-taking. But those in our study who seemed to have been most successful hedged their bets with a background of relevant experience and/ or training they could then apply in the new setting.

For example, the idea for Firm 105 in Canada came out of an association – and a friendship – between Fraser Quinn and Greg Reber, while they worked together in the IT department of a large organization. Quinn, aged 38, had a college diploma and training as an IT technician, and a corporate career which had provided him with extensive training in business and project management. Reber, aged 40, had a math degree, university-level computer science courses, co-op terms in an IT department, and a career in software development that ranged from programming to management. Both had been working on a major internet project for their former employer. Quinn described the background to their decision to start Firm 105:

> We saw the power of internet technologies, we had the knowledge and the background of developing software, we were . . . basically at the end of that project, which was a three-year project, it was more so turning into a maintenance program now versus a pioneering, developing, so just basically getting a little boring for us, and and we saw that we had an opportunity to get into a marketplace where there was a need.

They started Firm 105 in 1998, shrank it dramatically with the downturn of 2000 and 2001, and took the time to develop a business management software product, which allowed them to transform from a service-based to a product-oriented company. At the time of the case study, the company had six employees and was holding its own.

Robert Epp's history as the founder of Firm 112, also a Canadian firm, was actually the history of his own technical wizardry, and of a product, developed while he was working for the company which prompted its initial development, through time in a consulting firm run by a friend, into the emergence of Firm 112 as an independent entity – and, most recently, its friendly take-over by one of its largest clients. The buy-out in fact changed the financial arrangements, leaving Epp, aged 37, as one of three owners, with exclusive executive control.

In Australia, Jason Ferraro was not so much a 'founding father' as a 'founding son' in a family business established in 1997, when he finished a post-secondary IT course. The company (Firm 203) provided scalable enterprise technology which delivered server and applications over the Internet. Ferraro was the chief architect and CTO; at 30, he had spent his entire career in the company. His aspirations seemed similar to those of Sanjay Joshi at Firm 117, who had grown a company, sold it, and moved on to another company. His personal goal was either to sell Firm 203 at sufficient profit to leave family members and investors 'quite well off' (in which case he would start his own gaming company) or to make the company too successful to sell – in which case the gaming company would be one of its subdivisions.

In the US, Paul Green was not a 'founding son,' but the start of his company, Firm 509, was the result of a generous gesture by his previous employer, in a firm that among other things produced registration and other services for conferences and trade shows. He wanted to move inter-state to be with his girlfriend, who later became his wife. So he proposed to do his job at a distance. His employer, another young entrepreneur, sug-gested he take over the conference-trade show side of the business. That was the start, in 1995. This firm was the firm that 'rescued' Earl Johnson, Stephen Ingram and Richard Harris. Though they had some concerns about the firm's finances and its long-term viability as improved technol-ogy lessened their clients' need for their services, the fact remained that the company was still a going concern, and its founder at 38 could see himself eventually retiring from it.

These apparent success stories involved entrepreneurs who either pos-sessed or had access to appropriate background experience, business acumen, and some kind of financial backing. In all but one (Firm 509) of the cases just described, the most likely outcome was the profitable sale of the company, and, depending on the ages of the entrepreneurs in ques-tion, retirement, or new entrepreneurial challenge. Another pre-2000 small company founder who did not fill this bill was 30-year-old Eric Paterson, whose tiny Canadian home-based software development company Firm 103 had none of the necessary foundations and did not look much like a business. He admitted that, after six years of struggle, he was likely to abandon the company and become an employee. Eric's experience, echoed by that of Tony Phillips at Firm 201 in Australia, described earlier, is a reminder that small firms also fail. These failures represent significant career transitions for everyone affected by them.

Summing Up
The 12 men whose tenure in the case study firms where they were inter-viewed began before 2000 had career trajectories markedly different from the men who were post-downturn arrivals. Those among the 12 who were employers and managers had arrived early in their careers – perhaps quite fortuitously – in firms that, as it turned out, were firmly enough established to weather the high-tech downturn of 2000 and offer the opportunity for long-term employment. This long-term employment, as noted earlier, was not of the kind more typical of large enterprises, offering mobility up a

career ladder. But it did offer other inducements to longer tenure, which worked for the men in the study. The 'founding fathers' of these longer-established firms tended to be at the older end of the 30–40-year age range, but in other ways were not noticeably different from the men described earlier, who established firms after the downturn. What the more seasoned owners did have, though, was a demonstrable track record of successful entrepreneurship that the owners of the newer firms still had to build.

DISCUSSION AND CONCLUSIONS

This chapter proposed to address two key questions: the role of small firms, founded at different time periods and with different histories, in the career trajectories of men working in IT; and the theoretical model of 'career' that best fits these career trajectories. The preceding sections have covered the first question at some length. Small firms, when they are viable, fulfill multiple functions for their employees and occasionally their entrepreneurial founders as well: they launch, stabilize, build and occasionally rescue careers – whether or not the firms themselves are well established or recent arrivals. The older firms in the study – those established before the 2000 downturn – also demonstrated their ability to offer employees the opportunity to build stable single-employer careers. While many of the men in the study had joined these older firms too recently for long-term career conclusions to be drawn, those who joined them before the downturn had significantly different career histories.

The second question, however, is more complex, and returns us to the theoretical debate about careers and career trajectories introduced earlier in the chapter. That debate suggested that the traditional organizational career, marked by movement up an internal career ladder through a large organizational bureaucracy, is disappearing in the wake of organizational restructuring, flattened hierarchies and work increasingly organized as 'flexible.' The suggested (theoretical) replacement for the organizationally bounded career was the 'boundaryless' career, marked by episodes of employment with multiple employers, and 'independence from traditional organizational career arrangements' (Arthur and Rousseau, 1996: 6). Critics of the boundaryless career concept have suggested that it greatly oversimplifies the case; that even careers across multiple employers may have a pattern (Tolbert, 1996), or boundaries of another kind (Bagdadli et al., 2003; King et al, 2005); and that other models (for example the 'careers of achievement' described by Barley and Kunda, 2001) may better capture individuals' own sense of their working lives over time.

The experiences of the participants in this study speak to many issues raised in the debate. First, it is clear that for some, long-term careers within a single organization,– even a small one – are possible. A small but significant number of IT workers in the study – notably those who had joined their current firms before 2000 – had already spent a good proportion of their working lives in a single firm, and others seemed set to stay in the firms they had reached after prior experience elsewhere. These careers were certainly subject to organizational boundaries, though as noted earlier, they were not marked by mobility up career ladders. But there were other perceived rewards; men in this category spoke of their pride in having made a contribution to the firm and helping to build something, and/or the opportunity to find a niche exactly suited to their talents and interests. In this context, the 'careers of achievement' described by Barley and Kunda (2001) may be a more appropriate model.

That model, describing careers built up of increasing challenge and expertise, may also be a better model to apply to many of the men working as contractors, or those whose career trajectories were made up of many short-term appointments. In these cases too, though careers were not constrained by the boundaries of a single organization, they were certainly subject to constraints. Boundaries linked to individual competence, and to professional networks, applied here as they did in the study by Bagdadli et al. (2003). So in the very general sense proposed by Arthur and Rousseau (1996) these were not boundaryless careers. But neither were they invariably patternless.

Discovering patterns in careers that span multiple employers and multiple forms of work arrangements (permanent employment, short- and long-term contracts, individual entrepreneurship) is challenging. It is also important to bear in mind that patterns in career trajectories, the appearance of coherence, and the existence of an underlying logic or organization, depend on the perspective from which the career is viewed. That said, the preliminary analysis of career trajectories undertaken here does suggest the emergence of at least one pattern. The launching, stabilizing and building, and movement to entrepreneurship described as functions of small firms also in many cases represented a series of temporal transitions made by individuals, often through several small firms, with one firm playing a key role in integrating past career history and serving as the launch pad for a new enterprise, or new developments within the same firm. These are 'careers of achievement,' but there is a sense of upward progress as well.

As Barley and Kunda (2001) were earlier cited as suggesting, careers of achievement may become increasingly common with the increase in knowledge-based work like the software development characteristic of so many small IT firms. They also note the importance of acknowledging the subjective dimension of career (see also Chapter 3). Much of the work done in IT firms is routine, but much of it is intensely creative. The work is a passion, almost a calling in the Weberian sense, for those at the creative end. Subjectively, then, careers may have an internal coherence and meaning not always visible from the outside.

NOTES

1. Contractors were included if they were working full-time on contract. One US participant, 'moonlighting' in one of the case study firms while a full-time employee in another firm, was not included.
2. All names are pseudonyms. Except in cases where individuals were identified as representing a visible minority, or as immigrants from non-English speaking countries (where an attempt was made to match the surname to the ethnic origin) surnames of generally Anglo/European origin were chosen. These names were randomly distributed, and do not necessarily reflect individuals' heritage.

REFERENCES

Arthur, M. and D. Rousseau (1996), 'Introduction: the boundaryless career as a new employment principle', in M. Arthur and D. Rousseau (eds), *The Boundaryless Career: A New Employment Principle for a New Organizational Era*, New York: Oxford University Press, pp. 3–20.

Bagdadli, S., L. Solari, A. Usai and A. Grandori (2003), 'The emergence of career boundaries in unbounded industries: career odysseys in the Italian new economy', *International Journal of Human Resource Management*, 14, 788–808.

Barley, S. and G. Kunda (2001), 'Bringing work back in', *Organization Science*, 12, 76–95.

Barley, S. and G. Kunda (2004), *Gurus, Hired Guns and Warm Bodies: Itinerant Experts in a Knowledge Economy*, Princeton, NJ: Princeton University Press.

Barrett, R. (2001), 'Labouring under an illusion? The labour process of software development in the Australian information industry', *New Technology, Work and Employment*, 16, 18–34.

Barrett, R. (2004), 'Working at webboyz: an analysis of control over the software development labour process', *Sociology*, 38, 777–94.

Beck, U. (1992), *Risk Society: Towards a New Modernity*, London: Sage.

Benner, C. (2002), *Work in the New Economy: Flexible Labor Markets in Silicon Valley*, Malden, MA: Blackwell Publishing.

Castells, M. (2000), 'Materials for an exploratory theory of the network society', *British Journal of Sociology*, 51, 5–24.

Christiansen, S. and R. Palkovitz (2001), 'Why the "good provider" role still matters: providing as a form of paternal involvement', *Journal of Family Issues*, 22, 84–106.

Cohen, L. and M. Mallon (1999), 'The transition from organisational employment to portfolio working: perceptions of "boundarylessness"', *Work, Employment and Society*, 13, 329–52.

Connell, R. (1995), *Masculinities*, Cambridge: Polity.

Connell, R. (2002), *Gender*, Cambridge: Polity.

Cooper, M. (2000), 'Being the "go-to guy": fatherhood, masculinity and the organization of work in Silicon Valley', *Qualitative Sociology*, **23**, 379–405.

Giddens, A. (1991), *Modernity and Self-identity*, Stanford, CA: Stanford University Press.

Heinz, W. (2001), 'Work and the life course: a cosmopolitan-local perspective', in V. Marshall, W. Heinz, H. Krüger, and A. Verma (eds), *Restructuring Work and the Life Course*, Toronto, ON: University of Toronto Press, pp. 3–22.

Jones, C. (1996), 'Careers in project networks: the case of the film industry', in M. Arthur and D. Rousseau (eds), *The Boundaryless Career: A New Employment Principle for a New Organizational Era*, New York: Oxford University Press, pp. 58–75.

King, Z., S. Burke and J. Pemberton (2005), 'The "bounded" career: an empirical study of human capital, career mobility and employment outcomes in a mediated labour market', *Human Relations*, **58**, 981–1007.

Kunda, G., S. Barley and J. Evans (2002), 'Why do contractors contract? The experience of highly skilled technical professionals in a contingent labor market', *Industrial and Labor Relations Review*, **55** (2), 234–61.

Perlow, L. (1995), 'Putting the work back into work/family', *Group and Organization Management*, **20**, 227–39.

Perlow, L. (1998), 'Boundary control: the social ordering of work and family time in a high-tech corporation', *Administrative Science Quarterly*, **43**, 328–57.

Ranson, G. (2001), 'Engineers and the Western Canadian oil industry: work and life changes in a boom-and-bust decade', in V. Marshall, W. Heinz, H. Krüger and A. Verma (eds), *Restructuring Work and the Life Course*, Toronto, ON: University of Toronto Press, pp. 462–72.

Saxenian, A. (1996), 'Beyond boundaries: open labour markets and learning in Silicon Valley', in M. Arthur and D. Rousseau (eds), *The Boundaryless Career: A New Employment Principle for a New Organizational Era*, New York: Oxford University Press, pp. 23–39.

Sennett, R. (1998), '*The Corrosion of Character: the Personal Consequences of Work in the New Capitalism*, New York: W.W. Norton.

Tolbert, P. (1996), 'Occupations, organizations, and boundaryless careers', in M. Arthur and D. Rousseau (eds), *The Boundaryless Career: A New Employment Principle for a New Organizational Era*, New York: Oxford University Press, pp. 331–49.

Townsend, N. (2002), *The Package Deal: Marriage, Work and Fatherhood in Men's Lives*, Philadelphia, PA: Temple University Press.

Valcour, P. and P. Tolbert (2003), 'Gender, family and career in the era of boundarylessness: determinants and effects of intra- and inter-organizational mobility', *International Journal of Human Resource Management*, **14**, 768–87.

Webb, J. (2004), 'Organizations, self-identities and the new economy', *Sociology*, **38**, 719–38.

Zabusky, S. and S. Barley (1996), 'Redefining success: ethnographic observations on the careers of technicians', in P. Osterman (ed.), *Broken Ladders*, Cambridge: Cambridge University Press, pp. 185–214.

5. Employment relations and the wage: how gender and age influence the negotiating power of IT workers

Elizabeth Brooke

NEW ECONOMY EMPLOYMENT RELATIONS AND BACKGROUND

Introduction

This chapter is concerned with how the wage is negotiated in New Economy information technology (IT) firms. It examines processes of negotiation of compensation embedded within the employment relationship between employers and IT workers and compares case study firms across three countries: Australia, Canada and the United States. Within the information economy, the employment relationship is shaped by factors intrinsic to firms, including how knowledge-intensive work is performed and rewarded within labor processes, firms' organizational practices and extrinsic institutional factors, including legal and regulatory frameworks and the global context of the IT labor market. As Benner (2002: 29) notes: 'The implications of the employment relationship have a much more visible, immediate and direct impact on the livelihoods of workers, since it fundamentally shapes compensation.'

Macro-level processes linking globalization, deregulation and individualization have repercussions on employment relationships at the firm level. Employment relationships in IT firms are shaped by globalization imperatives for constant skills transformations (see Chapters 6 and 7 for more detail on the upgrading skills demands in the industry) and stepped-up demands for productivity (Beck, 2006; Benner, 2002; Castells, 2000). IT firms are restructuring due to globally driven market forces which consequently demand rapid accommodations by labor forces. New forms of labor processes and working time are influencing compensation in ways that are little understood.

Deregulation is a characteristic of New Economy employment relations and entails devolution of wage negotiation from the jurisdiction of collective bargaining to the firm level. The shift to post-industrial workplaces is evident in the proportion of non-unionized workplaces in the IT sector in the United States, where only 2 percent of computer workers engaged in collective bargaining (see Duerden Comeau, 2004). Over the last few decades, employment relations trends in liberal market democracies have devolved wage negotiation to the level of the individual situated in the firm. As Castells (1999: 8) states:

> The first process characterizing the information age as a result of its networking form of organization, is the growing individualization of labor: I refer to the process by which labor's contribution to production is defined specifically for each individual, with little reference to collective bargaining or regulated conditions.

Individualized employment relationships have emerged as adaptations to the dynamic of rapid commercialization of knowledge and its transformation into products. While new forms of flexibility have arisen in response to the chameleon forces of IT markets, workers are also experiencing downsides of wage losses. At the global level, supra-national firms are commonly pursuing deregulation of safety and union approved standardizations, trends which are perpetuating social inequalities within the new information economy (see Beck, 2006; Castells, 1999).

Remuneration is a crucial measure of the value of work in New Economy firms. It is embedded within labor processes, defined as the way work is performed and rewarded in these IT firms. Examining the practices distributing remuneration can show how IT workers managed to secure their wages amidst global marketplace pressures. However, little work has specifically considered how age and gender structure processes of distribution in non-unionized small firms with these unique New Economy employment relations. This chapter asks: What sets of distribution practices are in place? What are the implications for older workers and for women?

The argument is built section by section. I identify two sets of remuneration practices: The first set characterizes remuneration practices in high-end, high-growth firms while the second set of practices characterizes labor processes in small, fragile firms. Each section is based on a set of remuneration practices and analyses in one firm case study in each of three WANE study countries, Australia, Canada and the United States. These sections initially discuss the firms' organizational contexts and then address the implications of these arrangements for age and gender relations within firms. A summarizing discussion integrates the findings of the cross-country comparisons for each set of remuneration practices. The chapter concludes with a discussion of the implications for older workers and women negotiating the wage in New Economy IT firms.

Employment Relationships in the WANE Study Countries

The WANE study countries of Australia, Canada and the United States are typified by high levels of deregulation and a shift in the employment relationship from centralized wage fixing to devolved individualized models of determining work value. The restructuring of labor/capital relations within the Australian industrial relations structure occurred through the 1996 Workplace Relations Act, which signified a radical shift from collective bargaining to agreements on an individual level (Watson et al., 2003: 112). Benner (2002: 29) points out the significant mismatch between the conception of employment embodied in the regulatory system and employment relations currently practiced by United States firms (for example, the National Labor Relations Act and the Taft–Hartley Act) and the shift toward destandardized forms of employment. The Canadian industrial relations system, historically underpinned by collective agreements, is transforming to deregulate employment relations at the level of individual workplace agreements (see Human Resources and Skills Development Act Canada, 2008; Godard, 1997). Commonalities across the WANE study countries, characterized by capitalist marketplace dominance and reliance on the autonomy of individuals, typify liberal welfare capitalist countries (see Esping-Andersen, 1990).

The common shift from centralized wage fixing to devolved individualized models of determining work value in wage setting processes in these countries has been accompanied by a shift from industrial relations jurisdictions to individualized human resources management and performance management systems. The individualization and devolution of wage setting at the level of worker and firm can exclude bargaining by occupational groups. As Castells (2000: 255) states: 'The new model of global production and management is tantamount to the simultaneous integration of work process and disintegration of the workforce.'

The union density of IT workers is low across the WANE study countries. Australian national data show that only 15 percent of IT workers had trade union membership (Australian Bureau of Statistics, 2001). Duerden Comeau (2004) quotes Wolfson's Canadian report, which indicates that while 20 percent of IT workers were covered by a collective bargaining agreement, only 17 percent were active union members (Wolfson, 2003: 21, cited in Duerden Comeau, 2004). WANE data on United States levels of unionization similarly reveals that in the computer systems design and related services industry, less than 2 percent of workers were unionized or covered by union contracts (see Duerden Comeau, 2004). The WANE quantitative survey data on all the firms in WANE study countries (including the European Union countries) indicates the dominance of deunionization, as 98 percent of respondents did not belong to unions. This low proportion of unionized workplaces may be due to the fact that the WANE case study sample consisted of small- and medium-sized enterprises which are less likely to unionize in the first instance.

Analyses based on the cross-country WANE quantitative survey data indicate that employment arrangements are predominantly defined as permanent employment (86.4 percent) compared with other forms of temporary employment, such as employed on a fixed term or casual basis. Despite the 'permanent' label, large variations existed in remuneration outcomes attached to permanent employment. The quantitative survey data on wage earnings across all the study countries shows modest proportions of IT workers fell into in the highest income brackets: 23.7 percent earned under $40,000 a majority of 59.6 percent, $40,000–$99,999, while the smallest percentage, 16.5 percent earned $100,000 and over. (Responses are not standardized to a particular currency.)

DATA SOURCES AND ANALYTICAL APPROACH

The chapter analyses patterns of remuneration which emerged from the case studies of IT firms in three WANE study countries (Australia, Canada and the United States). The case study approach enabled processes of negotiating remuneration to be identified, which were based in the labor processes and characteristics of the firms using whole firms as units of analysis (see Marshall, 1999). Data sources utilized in the analysis were based on semi-structured in-depth qualitative interviews with firms' respondents, which were purposefully varied by position, level, age and gender. The data were analysed and stored using NVivo software. A further consideration in selection of the data that were included in the analysis was the quality of the NVivo data, particularly data on wages and older and female respondents.

The central research question asks how mechanisms of distribution of the wage operate in New Economy IT firms and how age and gender structure distribution. Therefore, the initial selection factor for analysing the population of cases in the three WANE country sites was the level of wages. Firms which were selected from the population of cases as cases for analysis illustrated sets of remuneration practices at the high and low ends of the range of wages. By selecting contrasting cases at the highest and lowest ends of wages the intent was to maximize differences and compare cases on the basis of elements of diversities and similarities (see Glaser and Strauss, 1967). I also hoped that further evidence could be collected to inform the issue of divergent and 'dual track' patterns of remuneration, an inference commonly reached in New Economy literature (see Benner, 2002; Carnoy, 2000; Castells, 2000).

The means used to select cases involved a preliminary review of the population of WANE cases produced by the three WANE country teams to identify patterns associated with firms' wage levels. From this review, a pattern of association between the size of firms and wage levels was recognized. This pattern also led to the size of firms together with the wage being used as decision criteria in the selection process. The preliminary scan of the population of firms based on the country case studies was followed by a search of the NVivo data on selected firms to confirm these patterns and to collect further data in the prospective firms selected for the analysis on wage negotiation, age and gender.

A set of interrelated structure dimensions connected with high wages and size emerged from the preliminary analysis, which included high skills, growth, marketability and productivity. The country sets which emerged, however, contained differences rather than being identical. US Case 507 was selected although it had slightly lower wage levels, and differed from the two other countries' high-wage firms as it produced both hardware and software technologies. Size was more clearly related to wage levels among the three low-wage micro-firms selected, as the size of the firms was interconnected with their fragility and low growth. Yet in the only US micro-firm, the age of respondents was in the 30s and inferences about older workers had to be drawn from interviews with these respondents.

Two types formed from sets of remuneration practices were identified consisting of labor processes and the firms' structure dimensions. Labor processes refer to how knowledge-intensive work is performed and rewarded in firms. The firms' structure dimensions consist of major underpinning characteristics, such as size, skills levels, profitability and market positioning. These characteristics are collected by national statistics agencies and are discussed in WANE Phase 1 Country Reports (see www.wane.ca). The two types are:

1. Chargeable hours remuneration practices, and;
2. Low-road remuneration practices.

The first type of remuneration practice is exemplified in firms at the high-end of wages which contained 12–15 people. The type consists of a set of remuneration practices characterized by the labor process of chargeable hours and includes the firms' structure dimensions of size, high skills, marketability and profitability. These firms are positioned at the high-growth end of the innovative IT marketplace.

The second type of remuneration practice was identified in low-road, fragile firms of five people and under with poor levels of remuneration, which were positioned at the least profitable end of the market. A set of remuneration practices connected the firms' labor processes with the structure dimensions of size, low-end skills, low marketability and profitability.

1. CHARGEABLE HOURS REMUNERATION PRACTICES

This set of remuneration practices was recognized in firms in the three WANE country sites and shows the close relationship between the employment relationship and the labor process. The process of setting chargeable hours reveals the connections between the labor process and remuneration, which was tightly calibrated to workers' productivity.

Australian Case Study 202

I begin the discussion of the first typology by taking an Australian high performance firm as an exemplar. This high-end firm produced 'state of the art' business processes, advanced transport system logistics and was moving into exporting global technologies in new areas, such as robotics. High margins and standardized overtime payments were paid for work in this high performance and high-end skills company that had been in existence since 2001. Employing around 12 people, including the two owner-directors, the remuneration was high and tautly ratcheted to performance. This firm positioned itself at the innovative frontier of new customized IT knowledge creation. The control structure was highly centralized in two directors, who employed recently skilled IT specialists working at the leading-edge of global invention.

This firm's high market positioning was associated with high wages paid for high performance within tight working time constraints. The wage was set by chargeable hours based on highly geared margins between the workers' performance and productivity targets. This effectively benchmarked employees' outputs to working time measured by remuneration, limiting the ambit of negotiation as the wage was technically measured. The high-level knowledge workers were able to command high wage rates between AUS$60 000 and AUS$150 000 as they produced globally competitive technologies. One director, a male in his 50s, commented:

> We just pay these guys I think bloody good money. They get paid about what they could earn anywhere else. And we also pay them overtime. The quality of the work is bringing in high paying, high margin work. That's what the whole company is about, and that's the fit with the new technologies, with doing things different to everyone else, that we can charge a premium for doing that, and you need really smart people to do that and smart people should be paid really well.

The firm operated as an extremely 'tight ship' that carried out performance audits measuring individual productivity. When people's performance was judged as lacking, according to a director, 'they are managed out,' meaning that they were encouraged to leave the firm. The director also explained that a culture of peer pressure to perform existed. New recruits were selected by their peers, suggesting that in this New Economy firm the traditional labor/capital distinction was masked by IT interdependencies:

> I don't think that we have any employees here that we wouldn't be satisfied with the productivity rates. But it doesn't take us long to find out . . . There's almost a peer pressure amongst people because what happens when somebody doesn't pull their weight is that everybody else suffers.

Job insecurity was a direct casualty of poor performance at the other end of high performance tightly calibrated to pay. Smith (2001: 7) defines risk and risk taking 'as the different chances workers take, whether in workplaces in relation to their employment contracts, that may or may not lead to a tangible pay off.' In this high-end firm, the risk for high fliers was to receive premium rewards within a high-performance environment monitored by peers, or risk toppling from an ascendant position to job insecurity.

The above arrangements have implications for age and gender relations within the firm. In this firm, labor value was reflected in performance-based wage setting which stringently constrained the time and labor costs of outputs, which were benchmarked to global competitors. Individual workers were caught in transforming work environments which could lower their marketability in the case of older workers, while younger workers could be advantaged for value-adding innovative products. Younger workers were commonly rewarded for inventiveness and 'self-programmable' skills which added market value to existing intellectual property, in contrast with their 'generic' skills as programmers (Castells, 2000).

This high-end firm benchmarked wages according to external marketability, and consequently, IT originators and developers who demonstrably augmented the firm's commercial value were well remunerated. The negotiation of high salary rates required the development of a commercial entrepreneurial venture, attracting rewards surpassing the value accorded to standard wage increments. A software developer in his early 30s who designed new technologies commented, 'you sort of get first dibs at the more interesting jobs.' The firm accordingly rewarded the development of new intellectual property and paid well for this:

> Yeah, they're very much not ones to delegate things but rather to say hey, we're looking for people willing to take this on and then the people that are willing to take it on get rewarded. The people that did the bare minimum, when they come to ask for a salary review, it's like, well, you know, you're just doing the bare minimum.

He commented on the direct relationship between remuneration and the value accorded to marketable inventions. This type of relationship could also lead to a destandardized and informal wage based on incentives rather than a standardized rate. He contrasted high-value entrepreneurial contributions in firms with incremental salaries perceived to be owed as an entitlement:

> There is a sort of natural hierarchy, and it's not necessarily related to experience either, it's more relating to the ability, the value of somebody to the company, and I would say my remuneration here is quite good, with the ability to earn more because my bosses recognize that I can help their business make money, and I know how to help make their business make money, so when it comes to asking for remuneration you've got a good business case for it, whereas some people just say oh, well, I'm a programmer, and the market should command this much, and so therefore what are you going to pay me?

By contrast, an older worker was less likely to command bargaining power relative to the external marketplace. A male worker in his late 40s downshifted from his previous employment status to learn new technologies in this firm after he had survived a second round of downsizing in his previous firm. He commented that 'the company was such that you're never sure when you're going to get kicked off.' His turning point was the realization that downshifting his position from a project manager to programmer would increase his skills levels and income security: 'Right, so I guess you could say a little bit about security, kind of make sure that you stay . . . employable.'

The stringent demands of his daily work schedule meant that he needed to study at home beyond standard working hours. He found it difficult to reconcile his study time with his parental role at this stage of his life course, despite his perception of the necessity to improve his external marketability: 'I've got demands of family, they need my time, so I might try and spend time with them, but some people might say, well hang on, I'm a real techhead, I'm just going to learn about this [and not] care so much about family.'

Similarly, for a highly-skilled female Vietnamese software designer in her mid-40s, her ability to meet the high-performance benchmarks expected in the firm was compromised by her life course gendered responsibilities. She underestimated her working time to meet competitive productivity outputs, thus undercutting her chargeable wage. As a consequence of the absorption of working time within the labor process, her working hours spilt over into non-standard working hours. She had difficulty in reconciling high work performance with her caring responsibilities for two children and found that managing her conflicting work/family responsibilities was stressful, as she stated:

> With the IT industry, like, estimations is really hard. So it's quite common people – oh, say 80 percent of people estimate lower because there's so many that have so varied factors in there. So most of the time, you estimate less than that. But for the rest they apply overtime and stress throughout my IT life, is always that. So people put in long hours to make up, to try to meet the deadline. That's very common.

Although the software designer was intentionally using the firm to upskill in the external marketplace, she found it difficult to be assertive in negotiating her wage: 'So one of my weak points is I don't negotiate. I moved here and say, look, I'm going to obtain these skills for a better salary and if I'm not happy, I pick up these skills and I will move on again.' Her fear of failure in the negotiation inhibited her ability to negotiate and she invoked both a gendered and cultural explanation: '. . . it's difficult . . . not my style, I suppose. In general I find negotiating is difficult. Like, my Mum, if she goes to the market she buys anything we need and negotiates a better price. I find that's hard to do . . .'

In summary, this high-growth IT firm offered high remuneration to high-value workers through the peer group expectation of high performance in the labor process of chargeable hours. The firm employed high-skilled knowledge workers performing within tight time margins to maximize the firm's competitive advantage through commercializing breakthrough technologies. The labor process integrated the structure dimensions of a high-skilled IT workforce, the production of global high-end technologies and rapid growth, characteristics which interconnected with the firm's size.

The chargeable hours remuneration practice rewarded accelerated knowledge production and globally marketable skills. Younger male workers in this high-performance based firm could negotiate for higher remuneration due to their advanced skills and potential to commercialize knowledge at the forefront of IT inventions. Their internalized commitment to technical achievement within extreme time constraints of the labor process exemplifies a form of 'masculinity,' which increased the firms' control (see Cooper, 2000; McMullin, forthcoming). The remuneration levels of younger workers generally contrasted with the lower wages of older workers with less valuable, generic skills and women with conflicting family responsibilities.

Canadian Case Study 108

A Canadian case firm of 12 employees which has been operating for around a decade has been selected due to its similarities with the high-end Australian firm of comparable size and duration. This firm was perceived as 'cutting edge' by several respondents and it employed very experienced and highly qualified senior people who were advanced IT practitioners. Both firms recruited for experience using peer group appraisal, with one Canadian firm respondent commenting that recruits were generally no younger than 28 and highly skilled: 'we don't hire anybody with less than five years' experience.' The firm's consultants were generally well-remunerated and experienced workers who could receive a wage range from CAN$100000 to CAN$150000. The CEO had promised profit sharing and equity in the firm, in theory, yet this had not yet materialized.

Assignments were viewed as challenging and the firm had put together groups of IT workers to implement, 'the latest, (the CEO) he's doing this extreme programming thing, which is way out there.' Staying ahead of other firms in the marketplace required disciplined rationalization of labor costs. One respondent's view was that 'I think we're considered a somewhat premium organization . . . We deliver our projects that other people have trouble delivering on, that actually get killed. We come in and finish it, that sort of thing. So we, we get the real difficult kinds of projects.' The male CEO, who was in his 50s, was interested in developing a new software venture and envisaged the firm would expand to 15–20 in the next year, providing a lucrative bridge to his retirement. This aspiration was also shared by the directors of the rapidly growing high-end Australian firm.

Dissimilarities between the Australian and Canadian firms were based in the mix of types of employment contracts. The Canadian firm's complement of IT workers consisted of six contractors and five full-time permanent employees as distinct from the Australian firm's 12 permanent core staff. The firm's fluctuating size and the mixed nature of employment contracts allowed it to adjust its human capital to its fortunes in the marketplace, as the CEO stated: 'we've been through some hard times. We've been through some high times. I think while we're only at in terms of employees now about six now . . . At one time we were 14.'

In this New Economy firm, productivity in the labor process was tightly geared to remuneration measured by performance management systems. To maintain competitiveness, the CEO aimed to restrict working time while maximizing quality in the labor process. As he commented: 'I need to go into an organization and convince them that we can build something better, faster and of higher quality.'

Remuneration systems reflected the business cycle and workers with in-demand specialized skill sets were well-rewarded. From a management perspective, the payment of higher salaries to contractors was seen to be offset by savings on employee benefits and by their contribution to productivity due to their superior levels of technical expertise. Contractors were paid a flat salary and compensation for standard benefits and a contractor respondent recognized that the payments were generally quite 'fair' and that a small firm was not able to provide benefits. Health premiums, extended health, dental, 100 percent drug reimbursement short and long-term disability and life insurance and minimum three weeks' vacation were provided fully-paid to permanent staff. The contractors identified a range of contract status advantages, including higher incomes and tax breaks. The variety of work, the option to be reassigned or renegotiate contracts, and greater flexibility in terms of working time and location were appreciated.

The hybrid employment relationships in the firm incorporated employees and contractors in the way work was organized in the labor process. Contractors and employees were viewed as interchangeable, depending on the applicant pool and nature of the task. A software developer in his 30s who was a contractor, considered that he had the 'best of the both worlds is I can sort of just come in and do the stuff that I enjoy doing with a group of people.' A programmer in his 40s who had worked as a consultant doing most of his work with this firm for over ten years commented: 'Although quite often they bring you in for your specific skill set or your alleged expertise in some area. But when it comes down to it, yeah, you're doing pretty much the same thing as the employee.' As another programmer commented: 'I think he's pretty good and he actually treats his people pretty well and he tried to even treat the independent as part of his team.'

A manager employed as a consultant described the firm's hybrid employment relationships combining the security of full-time internal employment with being 'on call' as a consultant in external sites: 'Now the kind of consulting I'm doing here where I'm a full-time employee at (the President's) beck and call. He basically, he gets a call and we're "call girls." We service the client. It's a common metaphor used in the business ... We're at the high end.' To his mind, the temporary nature of selling his services was disguised by the full-time nature of employment.

The firm was a global supplier of marketing control systems and offered high remuneration levels. The labor process instituted by the CEO in a competitive marketplace exacted high performance from highly skilled IT specialists within a lean competitive contractual environment. Contract workers with advanced marketable skills thrived on the high reward environment. The substitutability between contractual and permanent staff allowed the CEO to flexibly adjust the workforce to the marketplace.

The above arrangements have implications for age and gender relations within the firm. The performance-linked commercial contributions of senior consultants created high margins for remuneration. The firm's consultants were well-remunerated, 'all over $100 000' and new employees were earning above this high wage. Yet the job security of older contractors was limited by the short duration of current IT skills sets in the context of globally driven skills transformations. As a respondent commented: 'Even if you're a consultant, you're faced with all kinds of different environments and you have to be up-to-date with what's going on and what the latest practices are and so on.' Another IT consultant in his 40s commented: 'Oh, to be a consultant you have to be relevant. So to be a consultant at 50, you would have to be quite something.' There was also a coincidence between being older and working with obsolescent legacy technologies in programming jobs. One programmer in his mid-40s was unable to predict that he would be working in IT in five years' time and described IT work as repetitive, detail-oriented and time consuming beyond his current tolerance as there is 'only a certain a palette of colors you use.' A younger IT worker defined older workers as curmudgeons, that is, 'People who have been around since punch cards and usually have the beard and the long hair and haven't progressed probably past the 70s, but they are people that just haven't seen any need to change and progress.' For some, the aversion to the occupation of 'programmer'/developer intensified with age: 'So I kind of just see, if I'm 50 and a developer working with 20-somethings, that's what I don't think I would like.' These views display age-based perceptions of skills obsolescence which restricted the longevity of careers in IT.

The firm recruited younger workers who were employed to implement state-of-the-art technologies. A male programmer in his mid-40s commented on the CEO's expectation that the latest technologies would be adopted: 'I mean, he encourages it, maybe even expects it to some degree. So yeah, definitely, that has to keep the group moving ahead.' Yet while high remuneration was based in advanced and recently commercialized skills, younger contractors were disadvantaged by not having received standard benefits at earlier stages of their life course. As a female business analyst in her 40s maintained: 'Well, and that's always the problem when you're a small company is providing those benefits. And that's why everyone's a contractor so they don't get them. And, yeah it bothers you when people are young, have a young family and they don't have. But often when you're growing a company you're not in a position . . .'

Although there were four female staff members, there were no female analysts at upper management levels. An exception, an experienced business analyst in her late 40s, had owned several firms and was directly recruited by the CEO. He brought her in as a high-level consultant to commercialize the firm's IT, as she recounted: 'I said, "I have no money [CEO's name], I have no money to do this but I have lots of ideas." And he said, "That's fine. I can buy people to do things, but I can't buy visionaries." That's what he said to me.'

In summary, the firm's size and growth depended on the labor process of chargeable hours based on workers' high-skills performance and the global marketability of its IT products. The firm's structure dimensions of high-skills, profitability and growth in the global marketplace were discordant with the age relations in the firm. High performance-based wages demanded advanced skills, but marketplace pressures to self-educate and instantaneously apply advanced technologies continually challenged older workers' capacities to stay abreast of new technologies. Age-based views of older workers' limited capacities also undermined the longevity of their careers. This firm also awarded high remuneration for workers with marketable skills, while for others working with legacy technologies, there was an increased risk of job insecurity.

United States Case Study 507

The United States case study firm, of comparable size to the other case study firms, consisted of 15 employees. It was owned and managed by four partners who were its founders and directors. This firm differs from the Australian and Canadian firms as it provided computer/server/network installation of hardware and technical support, and new customized business software. A tripartite model of administrative, network support and new customized technologies enabled legacy software and hardware applications and future technologies to be produced. As a system analyst in his 40s, commented: 'By being able to bring both products, services, solutions, support all together now that, that's where it's kind of a win–win situation for our customers because most of them can't afford to have a very, very highly skilled set of staff.'

In common with the high-end Australian and the Canadian firms, the company directors held the aspiration that the firm would rapidly increase in size. A systems analyst commented on a recent merger: 'We're more geared to achieve and become even a bigger company now.' The firm was rapidly expanding its directions into vertical specialized global brand software and increasing the financial scale of its operations, shifting its focus, according to one partner, from smaller projects to 'more high-end business consulting and much bigger companies' under the leadership of a new partner. This mainly hardware firm, in the process of transforming its technologies from hardware to software, paid out a lower range of wages compared with the previous two country case study firms, ranging from US$19 000 to US$70 000–US$79 000.

Although 'experience' was ostensibly valued and sought, innovative energy and recent qualifications of younger workers were also highly regarded, in common within the Australian and Canadian case firms. The firm retained workers who were in for 'the long haul,' as many were over 45 and it offered a stable base for employment. Yet the continual necessity to keep learning regardless of age was noted by a male systems analyst in his 40s: 'You cannot stand still. Technology does not stand still. It never will stand still, so if you can't constantly keep l- learning you got a problem. You're never gonna make it.'

Employees were rewarded by maximizing their billable hours through an incentive system of quarterly bonuses. According to a male systems analyst in his 40s, bonuses are based on, 'How well the company does, and how well you did with hours, and how much billing time that you made that quarter.' The firm discussed ideas on bonus systems with workers: 'They consider our input very well. They haven't been long ago had a, a meeting about potential bonuses. And they actually brought back our ideas to the table. So, they do listen to us.' The bonus system was based on remuneration to reward work beyond standard chargeable hours within a 'dual track' performance system. This performance-based system extended hours of employment beyond standardized working hours from nine to five by 'dangling' high-performance incentives:

> So there's certain targets. If you're to bill a hundred hours a week, that's the norm. . . . if you bill a hundred and fifty, you know . . . and, and you maintain that after the quarter, my gosh, you're gonna get a serious bonus check. And they get a piece of the pie, they get a piece of, you know, it's dangling perform-ance. It's performance based so that they'll get their salary. And if you don't, you don't even get your hundred, that's great, everything's cool. You just won't get the bonus, you know.

Certain accommodations beyond financial compensation also occurred in the firm, which were appreciated by workers. Another director chose to preserve base wage rates rather than reduce wages to undercut competitors in the marketplace. This floor on wages protected the low-end of the wage within the 'dual track' remuneration system. The firm also offered its workers direct access to directors which was valued. One respondent had also turned down a salary ($20 000 higher) in a large multi-layered firm as he preferred the direct communication with the director in this smaller firm.

The firm accommodated to family responsibilities by adapting working time and core hours, which could be modified on an individual basis; for example, one technical worker explained that he needed to drop off his child at school and arrived half an hour later than others. Technicians worked autonomously with the customer and were not micro-managed, as a technical worker commented that there is no set policy, 'Do this, this way. There is a "Do the best thing. Use your judgment and, and as long as your, your heart's in the right place, things will be alright."'

The tension between remuneration and high productivity demands was to some extent mitigated by other practices in the working environment. The term 'Work hard, play hard' was used to characterize the working environment in which recreational activities were interspersed amongst project-driven time demands. For example, a director bought lunches for employees, arranged social functions and provided 'toys,' as she described PDAs and cell phones. As has been observed in a study of largely male workplaces in Silicon Valley: 'Beneath the playfulness a serious adult game is being played, in which large amounts of money can be won or lost' (Cooper, 2000: 387–8). The firm's flat hierarchical structure limited promotional paths linked with wage increments, while the CEO rewarded employees through bonus incentives for increasing billable hours.

Compensation benefits were informal rather than formally documented in agreements, offering health insurance, 401Ks, paid vacation, bonuses and limited flexible scheduling. Time flexibilities were offered to cope with family responsibilities and one female employee brought her baby to work. The firm did not have a formal vacation/sick policy and an expectation existed that employees would take time off responsibly; sick leave and vacation time were underutilized. The 'loosey-goosey' practice, as described by a manager, was seen to be limited by the firm's size, which would change with the firm's growth. The camaraderie and the team spirit in the firm mitigated the impact of performance-linked wages to high product outputs.

I now summarize the implications of this case study's working arrangements for age and gender relations. In the US firm, previous technologies of the firm were being replaced by new profitable technologies in the marketplace. The older technical workforce was to some extent not being renewed, as the firm was making a transition to new vertical software applications. The existing age structure of the organization was skewed towards workers over 45 and a manager was concerned that the existing older workforce might not be able to make the transition from a technical orientation to business processes, '. . . a lot of [the technicians] may not be able to make that transition.' A tension existed between the new technology directions and the older technical workforce. As a male IT worker in his 40s expressed it: '. . . knowing where the industry is going is more important and just having, being able to back up your experience, like you can have all these letters after your name . . .' These trends suggest that technological change, a structural dimension of the firm, was discordant with the existing age structure.

There were only two women in the firm: a director and a technical worker. The female director highlighted the age and generational position of this technician, 'the female technician I have, she's over . . . she's one of my oldest workers. She's a grandma.' A male worker also recalled that in the past two female technicians had brought high levels of specialized skills into the firm.

In summary, the US firm's set of remuneration practices was based in an incentive system of bonuses relative to a base wage linked with core hours, which rewarded exceptional contributions to productivity beyond standardized working hours within a 'dual track' labor process. The firm paid base wages for routine skills while leaving the door open for flexibility by rewarding exceptional performance. Structure dimensions of the firm, such as the shift to vertical software technologies, high-skills performance and growth were expected to increase the firm's size. The projected fast-growth trajectory conflicted with the existing skill-base of older workers in the firm, while women were exceptions within the firm's workforce.

Discussion: Chargeable Hours Remuneration Practices

The three case studies that I have examined in order to explore the first set of remuneration practices, exemplify chargeable hours labor processes embedded in highly-skilled, growing firms producing innovative technologies in high-end marketplaces. The interrelated firm structure dimensions of growth, size and profitability enabled the employment of a core group of staff of around 12–15.

The transformation of the industrial economy to the information society is replacing Fordist categories of tasks and defined industrial relations job categories with fluid, multiskilled labor processes measured by outputs. Collective decision-making over value of the 'wage' within the labor/capital relationship has shifted towards employment relations characterized by performance-measured 'remuneration.' Shih (2004: 228) states: 'At its heart, this is an individualist ideology, buttressed by the autonomous nature of work in high-tech, the performance-based evaluations within companies that emphasize individual achievement, and the relinquishing of companies' responsibilities to take care of their workers.'

Labor processes were identified in New Economy firms that were flexible forms of labor adaptation to the rapidly changing global marketplace. This first set of remuneration practices was embedded in the labor processes of chargeable hours, which measured the individualized performance of workers. The market-driven labor processes in firms were connected with the firms' interrelated structure dimensions, of high skills, global marketability and profitability, which consequently enhanced their size and growth prospects. The individualized performance-based remuneration practices were driven by competitive market pressures to reduce labor costs of knowledge-intensive production, which removed intermediaries from the negotiation:

> The worker is not absent from the negotiation but fully implicated. Never was labor more central to value making but never were the workers (regardless of their skills) more vulnerable to the organization, since they had become lean individuals, farmed out in a flexible network whose whereabouts were unknown to the network itself. (Castells, 2000: 302)

Aside from these commonalities, some differences were apparent. The Australian firm workers were audited and constantly monitored by the directors and peers. In this firm, performance expectations rigorously ratcheted to remuneration justified the charge out rate, which effectively limited the ambit for wage negotiation. The process of chargeable hours closely harnessed the work value of the worker to productivity. Intermediaries such as unions were absent and this firm exhibited the most stripped back form of negotiation.

By comparison, the Canadian firm created flexibility in its employment relationships, through its mix of contractors and permanent core staff. The externalization of the labor force through employment of contractors enabled the firm to respond more flexibly to changes in labor requirements. The interchangeability of employees and consultants within the firm's staffing structure enabled the firm to adjust the nexus between its labor supply and production demands and endure the peaks and troughs in productivity.

The United States firm also calibrated bonuses to workers' performance which surpassed workers' average performance within normal billable hours. The 'dual track' remuneration structure provided performance incentives to high performers while maintaining wage constraints on lower tiers of workers. The 'work hard play hard' workplace was considered by several respondents to be a factor 'softening' the extreme demands of project-driven work.

Finally, when we compare and contrast the three country case studies in terms of the implications of work arrangements for age and gender relations, we find that the labor processes presented systematic forms of risk to older workers, which influenced the value of their remuneration. Women's low representation and predominantly non-technical roles suggest that they were initially excluded from equal representations in the IT sector.

Symbolic analysts, generally younger, although with at least five years of experience, formed the higher organizational levels and were remunerated disproportionately for what Castells (2000) calls the 'self-programmable' skills of workers, autonomously creating new knowledge versus the lower rewards for 'generic' skills of workers replicating older technologies. Age segmentation operated as a tendency for older workers to be viewed as holding on to antiquated technologies and not able to master high-end skills leading to commercial value for the firm.

In the Australian firm, the labor process of chargeable hours was embedded in a work intensive environment in which individual remuneration was closely calibrated to commercial profitability. Younger workers with the latest skills sets were highly rewarded for technological inventiveness and breakthroughs. By contrast, an older worker sacrificed wages and mobility to learn the new skills to make himself more marketable.

In the Canadian firm, the mix of permanent workers and younger contractors could assist the firm to accommodate to business cycles. Yet younger contractors with high wages concurrently bore the risks of not accumulating capital early in the life course. Senior contractors could develop market-driven skill sets which connected discrete projects in their career trajectories. Yet their portfolio employment arrangements contained the risks of falling behind current skills sets.

In the United States firm, the high performance billable hours culture was linked to bonuses within a 'dual track' labor process. In this firm, labor force inequities were widening due to the transition from the technical skills base of the older to the new software skills required for vertical integrated software. Shifts from technical to specialist software skills reduced career opportunities for older workers, while catalysing younger workers' career prospects.

Across the case study countries, performance-based wages that were stringently calibrated to enhancing global competitiveness interacted with age relations. Younger workers were able to command high remuneration by proficiency in implementing the most recent groundbreaking new technologies; whereas older workers' skills sets were commonly based in legacy technologies, which attracted lower remuneration and possible job insecurity. The most highly-skilled older workers, nevertheless, were able to prolong their careers by engaging in new sequences of projects. Castells (2000: 302) observed that there are increasing disparities between the top and bottom segments of the labor market in the informational society:

> The dualization of labor markets was manifested by age-segmented reward systems based on rewarding the latest technologies which could compete in the global marketplace. Skills were not enough, since the process of techno-logical change accelerated its pace, constantly superseding the definition of appropriate skills.

Women were under-represented by comparison with the proportion of female IT workers in the labor force in all the firms across the WANE countries. The exceptional women at higher levels, such as a director and business analyst, were able to attract higher salaries. Yet gener-ally, their lower marketability affected their ability to negotiate their wages. Information technology is a masculinized occupation and women's marginal status interacted with gender relations in IT workplaces (see Cockburn, 1985; Duerden Comeau and Kemp, 2007; Game and Pringle, 1984; Wajcman, 2000). Even within these high-end firms, the risks of low remuneration and job security for women was based in their restricted capacity to work beyond standard working hours, in order to absorb the working time costs of chargeable hours. Additionally, a minority status background could compound a female worker's difficulties in being asser-tive in wage bargaining. Schienstock et al. (1999) conclude in a European Union study of social exclusion in the information society that the infor-mation technology sector appears to be dominated by males working in autonomous positions with high status and wages.

2.   LOW-ROAD REMUNERATION PRACTICES

A second type that emerged from the larger comparative case study analy-sis was the set of remuneration practices embedded in the labor processes of low-road market positioning and wages. This set of practices includes firms' structure dimensions of low-level IT skills, low marketability and low-growth, factors which were interconnected with the firms' size.

Australian Case Study 201

The Australian low-end technology web-based technology firm with low profitability had been in existence for five years. Its primary product was secured web-based modular technology projects and it offered a suite of 'boutique' products and consultancy services. Employing five people, the firm was owned by two CEOs, both in their 50s. The future of this slow growth and fragile consultancy was uncertain, and the two CEOs were deriving income streams from alternative employment in new IT ventures.

The fragility of the firm was demonstrated by its small core staff of two and its employment of contingent workers, primarily female migrants with family responsibilities and an international student. In this low profitability firm the hours of casual staff fluctuated, as one CEO commented, '. . . so there are permanents and there are people who do piecemeal work, and that's just, they get paid, and they invoice us.' The terminology of 'piecemeal' work is close to that of knowledge-based 'piece work,' which was undertaken by contingent workers lacking predictable incomes who were at risk of under-employment. In this firm, workers' 'opportunity and advancement are intertwined with temporariness and risk' (Smith, 2001: 7).

The entrepreneurial model in this firm has led to employees bearing risk and job insecurity, as its low market positioning constrained the capacity of the employer to pay higher wages. The employer also saw himself 'as in the same boat myself.' The workers' job security was ultimately risked in this volatile structure of entrepreneurial risk sharing. As one CEO commented: 'so in the end, it's like well, we don't have the money, sorry. . . . You know, well, we'll give you four weeks' pay, but you're going to have to find other work because we just can't afford you. He was an extra employee but there was no extra work.' The low-end positioning and profitability of this firm in the marketplace limited workers' negotiation of the wage, with the ultimate personal cost being borne by the workers who were made redundant.

Age and gender relations were associated with the labor processes of negotiation for 'piecemeal' work. The firm did not employ older workers but recruited from the younger end of the age spectrum. The employment of a young Asian student capitalized on his position as an international student learning IT on-the-job. According to his perspective the training element in the job compensated for the low wage. He perceived that he had an implicit psychological contract with the employer who was 'doing him a favor', so that whatever the employer gave him he should accept:

'I: How did you negotiate your current salary?

R: . . . as I told you I'm just work experience so I . . . whatever they give me I should be happy with, so, they're doing me a favor.'

A female Indian web designer in her 30s who worked from home was offered 'regular working hours' from 9 to 5. Despite the appearance of regularity, her working hours fluctuated in response to the vicissitudes of market demand and she had little control over her actual condition of under-employment. As a mother with gender-based family responsibilities, her commitment to being available for her caring responsibilities compromised her ability to negotiate her wage and working hours. Her ethnic background also created a barrier to her in negotiating with the employees.

> 'I: How do you feel about negotiating your salary?
>
> R: It was very hard for me, for me, it's, I think it's the way of being brought up, . . . it's the culture, . . . talking about money or just, it's just not me, it, it, will be difficult to do.'

Trade-offs between flexibility and the wage were 'chips' to be negotiated within the informal and implicit bargaining process. Working time flexibility was not explicitly valued as a replacement for lower compensation in the negotiation process, but was implicitly traded off. The CEO acknowledged that her requirement for child care flexibility informalized her working hours and he extended the notion flexibility of informalized hours to align with market demand: 'that's normally her hours cause she's got kids and she goes to pick them up, but she takes work home when there's work to do, she gets paid so she'll do it in any hours.' The female worker took into account the low profitability of the firm within her implicit negotiation of the wage and accepted that the low-road firm only had the ability to pay low-end wages:

> I: How did you arrive at the salary and the conditions?
>
> R: Knew he wouldn't be able to pay me the market rate because it is a fairly small company but because I was looking at something like this and my main concern was the flexibility and you know getting home in time for the kids and being there for the kids, that was my number one priority so I had to make a compromise as well, so we sort of yeah, . . . negotiated and . . . I think, we're both happy as of now.

In summary, the low-road trajectory of the firm set the context of the negotiation process which was informalized and implicit, compared with the first set of remuneration practices, which explicitly calibrated performance and productivity. Trade-offs of the wage occurred within the implicit and informal wage negotiation processes. The young international student traded off skills development for a lower wage, while the gendered responsibilities of a female worker implicitly informalized her working hours and remuneration.

Canadian Case Study 109

This Canadian micro-sized firm of four people is a home-based consulting firm specializing in data base management linked with a global software company. The firm operated out of the home of the managing directors, a couple in their 50s. The firm's niche was restricted by the reach of the software company which had secured a small percentage of the global software market. It was aspiring to shift to products beyond this niche, as the firm's profitability was low.

The employees' qualifications were indicative of its market positioning, as only the managing director had tertiary training in a related field, while other employees lacked formal IT-related qualifications. One employee, in his late 50s, noted the absence of a formal training policy while learning occurred on-the-job: 'it's all self taught and learning, and I'm a big proponent of, you know, being paid as you learn so . . . I was lucky enough to be in a position that I got to teach myself while someone was paying me to do a job.'

The firm's employees commonly perceived that centralized control was exercised by the managing directors. It was formed from a coterie of friends and its informal environment had attracted employees who perceived that they were 'unhireable' in more corporate environments. Despite the tertiary qualifications of the managing director, in her own career she had been unable to secure a consistent salary over several years from consulting contracts.

The firm delivered a modular program for a major niche software service provider in contrast with new development and creative programming work. One of the managing directors characterized the firm's work as 'junk work.' The firm's dependence on short-term consultancy contracts positioned it at a low end of the market. One managing director was looking to expand his qualifications into allied areas to create a new niche for the firm's work.

The vulnerability of the firm to collapse is reflected by the personal financial sacrifices of the managing directors. In contrast with the chargeable hours model, the employees' hours were not audited and remuneration occurred through ad hoc distributions of profits from contracts. As one managing director commented: 'No it's shareholder loans we do it by. And, we've all at times put money into the company but years ago we stopped tracking hours cause that, yeah, I'm just trying to figure out how to say it because there's no fixed formula.'

Standardized benefits were not offered in this fragile micro-firm in which employees lacked formal medical or dental benefits or pension plans. The absence of a 'retirement nest egg' was of concern according to one managing director, who expressed how he would like to 'have all the people that are working in our company feel secure.' All of the employees were partners in the firm, and this blurred the entrepreneurial owner/ employee distinction. Yet the partnership had not achieved payoffs at this point. One employee asserted that he preferred the skills and challenge of working in his own firm compared with those working in corporate firms where 'they did a job for 35, 40 years . . . then they retire, but they never, in all of that time, they never learned what else to do.'

The combination of informal friendships and equity partnerships spread the risk of low wages throughout the firm. The friendship-based employment relationship was accompanied by low wages, with some employees earning less than CAN$10000 per annum. The masking of a capital/labor division through profit sharing potentially reduced dissatisfaction with compensation levels.

The implications of the firm's structure dimension of being a low-road and low profitability firm for age and gender relations are now explored. As in the first case, the low trajectory of the firm was paralleled by the low career trajectories of the employees. The firm consisted of workers who were all over 40 and the career trajectories of the workers in the firm indicate that their low wages were accompanied by self-perceptions of their 'unhireability.' The low qualifications, mainly vendor certifications, insecure career trajectories and low remuneration of the employees were mutually reinforcing within this fragile firm.

A technician in his late 50s considered that options for 'taking an incredibly lousy paying job' were greater if you owned your own home. As an older worker with accrued capital, the life course aspect of home ownership enabled him to bear the low wage. As the technician commented: 'Working for nothing here is way better than working for nothing anywhere else, way better, for sure.' A managing director sardonically commented on the hard work yet unmarketable status of the firm's workers:

> if the money runs out it's, I don't know what's going to happen because we're so unemployable . . .We're not day-in-day-out kind of people so I think they'll (employers) probably look at us and say, how long has it been since you've done a 9-to-5 and they don't realize you're working 12 hours a day.

The low remuneration offered in the firm suggests that potential profit sharing possibly masked the insecurity of informal employment. Self-employment is an insecure form of informalization in which the individual bears the risks of sacrificing the wage. The firm offered a group of colleagues an employment relationship which blurred the employer/employee distinction, yet had not at this point achieved profit sharing.

Gender issues were linked with flexibility. For example, an administrative and technical worker with a science qualification worked part-time so she could care for her children. She had forgone benefits as her husband had a 'gold-plated benefits plan.' This flexibility compensated for her low wages and as she commented, she had 'big decisions to make about what was truly important in my life [and] made the choice for family instead of a high powered job.'

In summary, this firm illustrates how the low-road trajectory, low skills and 'unhireability' of workers with low-end positions in the external marketplace, structure dimensions of the firm, restricted wage negotiation by the employees, who were generally older. Compensations of working with colleagues and flexibility existed, while the future profit-sharing promises offered an illusion of independence for its workers as self-employed entrepreneurs.

United States Case Study 509

This micro-firm of four full-time employees and two contractors produced web-based and registration services for equipment hire. The firm acted as an outsourced web-based firm for a larger IT company and received some venture capital funding. This firm, in contrast to the other micro-firms, was a dominant player in the web-based equipment hire field and well-positioned to rationalize the amount of work taken on. The CEO explained that the firm did not market actively: 'They mostly come to us. But, it's a very niche-oriented industry, the equipment hire industry. It's very tight, kind of almost like a family.' The owner had decided that, although he had the opportunity to grow the firm to '10 times the size' he enjoyed the slower pace in a small company and resisted growing it. The scaling back of working pace also was accompanied by low wages, with the majority of staff earning between US$30 000 and US$39 000.

The flexibility of working time and relatively autonomous working situation emerged as a significant reason for the retention of staff, despite the low wages. A web designer in his 30s commented that he was not 'forced to keep a timesheet,' in contrast with the high-end firm employees in type 1. A database administrator compared working for the small firm with a larger firm:

> Here are your tasks and things you're going to do for a particular day. In our case, it is a lot more flexible. We can afford to because we are small, and we have to because we're small. But, it is nice. It is really nice, too, that things are relatively – I guess flexible is the big word.

The flexibility allowed for child care and the stable work environment and friendships were valued over 'toys' such as pool tables, bars and video games, and another employee appreciated the 'defined hours.'

Despite dissatisfaction with the low wages, flexibilities of working time and the relaxed friendship-based culture were seen to compensate for the low wage. The firm's niche market positioning, which guaranteed stable remuneration, was also commented on by one employee:

> It's mostly pay and stability. I think . . . (the CEOs) never missed a pay check in three years . . . and while that sounds like it shouldn't be a big deal, I can tell you about a lot of tech companies in town that don't pay their employees all the time, every week, especially the small ones.

While employees expressed dissatisfaction with the wage, the working environment of the firm was considered low stress. As a web designer in his 30s commented: 'The only reasons I would look for another job would be if I could have compensation that I wanted, (otherwise) I would stay here until I retired.' Another respondent commented: '. . . the salary structure is a lot lower than the average salary for the work, rather significantly lower.'

Wage negotiations were based on implicit assumptions about age and gender relations in the firm. The average age of employees was 35 years and there were no women in the firm. The CEO clearly articulated that he recruited younger people at earlier stages of the life course as he did not have to pay them as much:

> One of the reasons why I like to hire people that are, and I don't want to say younger people, but people newer to the workforce, is that I think there's a lower expectation of salary for the thing, and so . . . I think at 45, which I'm not even there yet, you certainly have a, higher expectation because you typically, married, supporting a family, you have a house.

Older workers were viewed as potentially incapable of learning new technologies as 'mature people who weren't exposed to computer technology and have some fear of it . . . have a certain disadvantage . . . and haven't been as willing to learn it.' The owner has been recruiting people informally from IT acquaintances and has recruited two brothers whom he saw as 'low hanging fruit.'

In summary, the firm's control over working time and the quantity of outputs were factors in the labor process which compensated for the relatively low remuneration. The low-end market position and growth were structure dimensions which were accepted by the employees due to compensations. While the firm did not contain older workers or women, work/life accommodations were offered to younger workers, which compensated for low wages by offering flexibility.

Discussion: Low-road Remuneration Practices

These micro-firms had restricted low-growth markets and were character-ized by low profitability and fragility. The Australian and Canadian micro-firms were at the lower ends of the market and their economic survival was precarious. The US firm which outsourced web-based technologies to a larger IT firm had more stable financial support and the owner voluntarily restricted the firm's production. In all of these firms, employees received low wages and had relatively lower-level skills and qualifications, factors which were interrelated with the firms' low profitability and threatened unviability.

The interrelated structure dimensions of the size of these micro-firms, their low profitability and fragility in the IT marketplace had repercus-sions on individuals' capacities to negotiate for higher wages. The labor process was characterized by informalized wage setting, based largely on employers' unilateral negotiation of wages, which was based on implicit, uncontested notions of workers' value. The lower-skilled workers in these firms were less able to negotiate the wage and bore costs of these fragile businesses. This type contrasts with the first set of remuneration practices that was based in the explicit measurement of chargeable hours.

Recruitment of workers at the low end of the market (expectedly) limited the firms' skills and capacities for innovation and demoted the firms' trajectory in the marketplace. A vicious circle prevailed as the low qualifications and skills reinforced the static low-growth nature of the firm. Firm members were commonly looking outside the firm to other pro-spective employment, largely as a consequence of their relatively poorer career opportunities, lower wages and tenuous job security.

Age and gender relations interacted unfavorably with this type of remu-neration practice positioned in secondary labor markets. Employers were shown to apply implicit assumptions as rationalizations for undercutting wages to labor force segments of younger and older workers, women with competing family commitments and low-skilled international students. Intrinsic and extrinsic factors interacted to constrain their opportunities in negotiating higher wages across the country firms. As Smith (2001: 169) states, compensation is 'socially constructed within a matrix of variables intrinsic and extrinsic to the workplace.' External recruitment at the low end of the market restricted the firms' internal skills for potential inno-vation, their positioning in the external marketplace and future growth prospects.

A perspective expressed in the Canadian firm was that its workers were 'unhireable' outside the firm, indicating that the firm was assumed to occupy a low road in the marketplace compared with firms with more skilled and highly-remunerated employees. Similarly, the precarious Australian firm employed workers at the lower end of the skills market to perform work which fluctuated according to external market demand, which limited the wage. The groups employed in the firm, young immigrant workers and women with family responsibilities had low negotiating power as they were less externally marketable. By contrast, the stable US firm consisted of a group of male colleagues in their 30s. In this firm the pace of the labor process was deliberately reined in by the CEO, flexible working hours were offered and the firm regularly paid its staff salaries, which were perceived as compensations for the low wage.

DISCUSSION: EMPLOYMENT RELATIONS AND THE WAGE

Having described two contrasting types identified in high and low wage small and medium-sized IT firms, I will conclude by relating the sets of remuneration practices to broader characteristics of employment relations in New Economy organizations, harking back to the chapter's introduction. The individualization and deregulation of employment relations in New Economy firms formed the macro-level institutional context for negotiation of the wage. The firms operated within deregulated and individualized industrial relations structures which typified liberal welfare capitalist economies.

The analysis 'inductively' found two major types characterizing the dynamics and sets of employment relations in firms and that these both centered on how the 'the wage' was negotiated. These overlay a mapping of the firms by firm size and were associated with the profitability or fragility of the firm. Labor processes and structure dimensions in firms were identified which explain the outcomes of wage negotiation in New Economy firms. The analyses found two types formed from sets of remuneration practices, which interrelated the firms' structure dimensions and labor processes.

The first type of remuneration practices identified at the high-end of productivity and wages mapped against firms consisting of 12–15 people, exemplified how the market-driven calibration of remuneration to productivity removed individual workers from the negotiation. High-end firms were characterized by structure dimensions of high growth, high skills and market positioning, which interrelated with chargeable hours labor processes which stringently rationed time and money. These workers were generally younger, with state of-the-art skills sets and the ability to commercialize new technologies as global products. They could receive unstandardized wages as their individualized reward systems leapfrogged over regular wage increments.

The second type of remuneration practices identified at the low-end of the IT marketplaces and wages mapped against micro-firms of four to five people, showed how workers with lower marketability were less able to negotiate the wage. Negotiation of the wage contained informalized, implicit labor processes; for instance, employers paid low wages to younger workers and cut the hours and wage of women with family responsibilities. The firms' low level trajectories in the marketplace, less profitable technologies and growth prospects were interrelated structure dimensions which restricted the firm's capacity to pay the 'wage.' In these firms, workers were vulnerable to risk from the firms' fluctuating profitability, despite perceived compensations, such as greater workplace flexibility. As Boltanski and Chiapello (2005: 250) state: 'The individualization of skills, bonuses and sanctions had a further pernicious effect by tending to make individuals exclusively responsible for their own successes and failures.'

Employment relationships in the information society were characterized by individualized relationships between employers and employees. Yet, as the case studies across both types of practices show, individualization of employment relationships meant that those who were least marketable had the lowest negotiating power. The fast-moving information technologies produced within small firms in globally driven marketplaces presented particular risks for workers. Smith's (2001: 7) study of post-industrial firms found these to be characterized by: 'uncertainty and unpredictability, and to varying degrees, personal risk.' The employment relationships in these forms did not allow for 'Collective agreements (which) mention a wage coefficient that corresponds to a minimum wage depending on the wage-earner's position in the scale' (Boltanski and Chiapello, 2005: 299). Thus workers were unprotected by the employment relationship at the labor/capital interface from the risks and uncertainty of entrepreneurial IT businesses.

Across the case study firms in the three countries, remuneration was set through human resources management practices in the firms rather than by industrial relations mechanisms. The case study firms demonstrated a shift from employment agreements to performance management. Remuneration was tightly constrained by the pressure to adjust labor costs to the demands of intense global competition in information technology. In the absence of collective protections, individual workers bore the risks of the marketplace.

The highest negotiating power for employees existed where their skills were congruent with productivity, as in the high-end chargeable time firms.

The stable firms had standardized remuneration structures with some non-standardized incentives. In the low-end firms wages were directly related to profits and workers personally bore the brunt of a declining business. Wages were not linked with award conditions but were rather attached to firms' commercial fortunes as small businesses.

Shih (2004: 227) described the entrepreneurial employment relationship model of IT employment commenting, 'Workers are treated as responsible for their own careers and livelihoods and must continuously develop skills to maintain their own marketability.' Entrepreneurial workers with high-skills in the marketplace were more likely to be able to negotiate their salaries and directly market high-end skills in jobs, while the lack of intermediary advocates, such as unions, could mean that lower-skilled workers in less productive markets were less able to be protected against low wages.

The shift from industrial relations protection to human resources management practices poses difficulties for older and younger workers, women and particular minority groups. Individualization of employment relationships occurred within the space left by deregulation across the countries studied which engendered inequalities in negotiating power.

Age and gender relations interacted with the firm's structure dimensions, which were constantly adapting to the global marketplace. The labor segment which produced high value information labor workers was generally younger, highly skilled inventors of intellectual property that enhanced the firm's global competitiveness. The producers of high volume outputs based on low wages were lower level technically qualified workers, generally younger women, with a few exceptions, who were skewed towards the lower ends of the occupational scale, such as IT support roles. Typically the demand for constant IT upskilling overlapped across family boundaries, lowering their value to employers. The labor segment of redundant producers reduced to devalued labor was exemplified by older workers with earlier IT skills sets, aligned mainly to maintaining legacy technologies.

Exchange theory applied to employment relationships provides a framework for negotiating trade-offs which occurred in age and gender relations (see Emerson, 1976). Bargaining 'chips' were productivity related, and included 'bleeding edge' skills, and ability to bear incursions across work/family boundaries ('zero drag') to enable after-hours learning and work. Carnoy (2000) has described the global age shift towards valuing the productive skills of younger IT workers and downsizing the number of 'obsolete,' higher-priced older employees,

In the high performance organizations analysed in the first type of remuneration practices in firms with 12–15 workers, there was little latitude for negotiation by workers as wages were measures of performance outputs.

Negotiations over the wage operated in favor of younger workers with IT specializations as creators and implementers of new valuable knowledge. The set of remuneration practices posed risks for older workers who risked low wages and job insecurity if they were unable to maintain the high-skills and productivity demands within the chargeable hours labor process. The firms' interrelated structure dimensions of high-end skills, profitability, high market positioning and growth, which in turn influenced their size, enabled this performance-related remuneration.

By contrast, in low-road firms, the set of remuneration practices was characterized by informal and implicit processes of negotiation in the labor processes, which constrained the wages of older workers, younger migrant workers and women who were under-skilled relative to the demands set by the market. The structure dimension of fragile micro-firms with low-road trajectories based on low-skills, profitability and global market positioning influenced the firm's size and growth and individual workers' wages.

In conclusion, despite the wealth generated by the global information society through valuable knowledge creation, divergent rewards for IT workers are emerging within small and medium firms. Individualized employment relations in New Economy IT firms have been shown to lack protection for workers from globally-driven market forces, both at the high and low ends of firms' profitability. For this reason, new mechanisms are necessary to distribute the wage, for instance, new types of unionization at an industry level that can bridge the short-term precariousness of micro-firms. These findings suggest the need for initiatives to support IT workers' negotiation of the wage, which can better align social to the economic opportunities in New Economy IT organizations.

REFERENCES

Australian Bureau of Statistics (2001), *Employment Arrangements and Superannuation, Australia*, ABS Cat. No. 6361.0, Canberra: Australian Bureau of Statistics.
Beck, U. (2006), *Power in the Global Age: A New Political Economy*, Cambridge: Polity Press.
Benner, C. (2002), *Work in the New Economy. Flexible Labor Markets in Silicon Valley*, The Information Age Series, Malden, MA: Blackwell Publishing.
Boltanski, L. and E. Chiapello (2005), *The New Spirit of Capitalism*, London, New York: Verso.
Carnoy, M. (2000), *Sustaining the New Economy: Work, Family and Community in the Information Age*, Cambridge, MA: Russell Sage Foundation Report, Harvard University Press.
Castells, M. (1999), 'Information technology, globalization and social development', United Nations Research Institute for Social Development (UNRISD)

discussion paper 114, Geneva: UNRISD, accessed February 2009 at www. unrisd.org/unrisd/website/document.nsf/(httpPublications)/F270E0C066F3DE 7780256B67005B728C.

Castells, M. (2000), *The Information Age: Economy, Society and Culture. The Rise of the Network Society*, vol. 1 2nd edn, Oxford: Blackwell Publishers.

Cockburn, C. (1985), *Machinery of Dominance: Women, Men and Technical Know-how*, London: Pluto Press.

Cooper, M. (2000), 'Being the "go-to-guy": fatherhood, masculinity, and the organization of work in Silicon Valley', *Qualitative Sociology*, **23** (4), 379–402.

Duerden Comeau, T. (2004), *Cross-national Comparison of Information Technology Employment, (WANE) International Report, No. 5*, London, ON: University of Western Ontario, Workforce Aging in the New Economy.

Duerden Comeau, T. and C.L. Kemp (2007), 'Intersections of age and masculinities in the information technology industry', *Ageing and Society*, **27** (2) 215–32.

Emerson, R.M. (1976), 'Social exchange theory', *Annual Review of Sociology*, **2**, 335–62.

Esping-Andersen, G. (1990), *The Three Worlds of Welfare Capitalism*, Princeton, NJ: Princeton University Press.

Game, A. and R. Pringle (1984), *Gender at Work*, London: Pluto Press.

Glaser, B. and A. Strauss (1967), *The Discovery of Grounded Theory*, Chicago, IL: Aldine.

Godard, J. (1997), 'Managerial strategies, labor and employment relations and the state: the Canadian case and beyond', *British Journal of Industrial Relations*, **35** (3), 399–426.

Human Resources and Skills Development Canada (2008), 'Labour', accessed February 2009 at www.hrsdc.gc.ca/eng/labour/employment_standards/fls/final/page03.shtml.

Marshall, V.W. (1999), 'Reasoning with case studies: issues of an aging work-force', *Journal of Aging Studies*, **13** (4), 377–89.

McMullin, J.A. (forthcoming), *Gender, Age and Work in the New Economy: The Case of Information Technology Firms*, Kelowna, BC: UBC Press.

Schienstock, G., G. Bechmann and G. Frederichs (1999), 'Information society, work and the generation of new forms of social exclusion (SOWING) – the theoretical approach', ITAS, TA-Datenbank-Nachrichten, Nr. 1, 8. Jahrgang – März 1999, S. 3–49, accessed February 2009 at www.itas.fzk.de/deu/TADN/TADN991/scua99a.htm.

Shih, J. (2004), 'Project time in Silicon Valley', *Qualitative Sociology*, **27** (2), 223–44.

Smith V. (2001), *Crossing the Great Divide: Worker Risk and Opportunity in the New Economy*, Ithaca, NY, and London: ILR Press and imprint of Cornell University Press.

Wajcman, J. (2000), 'Feminism facing industrial relations in Britain', *British Journal of Industrial Relations*, **38** (2), 183–201.

Watson, I., J. Buchanan, I. Campbell and C. Briggs (2003), *Fragmented Futures. New Challenges in Working Life*, Annandale, NSW: Federation Press.

Wolfson, W.G. (2003), *Analysis of the Labor Force Survey for the Information Technology Occupations*, analysis report prepared for the Software Human Resource Council, Toronto, ON: WGW Services.

6. Knowledge workers in the New Economy: skill, flexibility and credentials

Tracey L. Adams and Erin I. Demaiter

In the New Economy, information technology (IT) workers have been regarded as quintessential knowledge workers: highly-skilled, educated and knowledgeable people who work with cutting-edge technologies and process information. While this image is not inaccurate, it belies a great deal of complexity. IT workers are found in a wide variety of jobs, some of which demand a great deal of skill, and some of which are more routine. Further, IT workers are not always educated. IT has long been a technical field where the self-trained high-school drop-out might work alongside a PhD in science (Ensmenger, 2003: 154). Even among the educated, people have entered IT work from a wide variety of educational backgrounds and disciplines. Traditionally the significance of education to this kind of knowledge work has not been clear.

Largely because of this ambiguity, and with the desire to demarcate the trained from the untrained, professional and industry organizations have sought to establish education programs, examinations and credentials over the past 50 years (Adams, 2004; Ensmenger, 2001). Creating education programs and curricula for a broad, rapidly changing field has been an ongoing challenge, but organizations in the US, UK, Australia and Canada have nonetheless made great strides. Yet, researchers have raised doubts concerning the importance of these programs. As Benner (2003) argues, there are many ways to acquire IT knowledge and skills. There is little social closure in the field, and it is not the case in IT, as it is in many professions, that one has to gain admittance to and attend an accredited educational institution to acquire the knowledge and skills required for employment.

In this chapter, we explore the significance of education and credentials to IT workers and their skill acquisition activities. In particular, we examine whether education is an important source of skill for these workers, and whether education and the credentials it confers are important for employment in the field. Where do these knowledge workers acquire their knowledge and skills? Do skill acquisition activities vary nationally, or by gender and age? Finding the answers to these questions not only provides insight into the nature of IT employment, but also has broader implications for our understanding of the significance of education and skill acquisition activity in the New Economy more generally.

We pursue these questions with data from the WANE project. Specifically, we rely on the quantitative web-based survey data from Canada, US, England, and Australia. Our sample consists of all study respondents in IT-related and managerial jobs; those in purely administrative roles were excluded. In our analysis, we focus on the variables that look at highest level of education, professional and technical credentials,[1] methods of skill acquisition, pressure to learn new skills, gender, and age. In addition, in several places in our analysis we rely on the qualitative data from the face to face interviews to supplement the quantitative data. In particular, we explore IT employers' ideas around recruitment (how companies hire employees and the skills and traits they look for in recruits).

EDUCATION, CREDENTIALISM AND EMPLOYMENT[2]

A growing body of research indicates that education is the key to success in the New Economy. People with higher levels of education are more likely to be employed and tend to earn more than those with lower levels of education (see Bills, 2004; Wotherspoon, 1998). While education cannot guarantee a good job, obtaining a good job without education is becoming more difficult (McDowell, 2003; Statistics Canada, 2005). Evidence is growing that ongoing economic change provides opportunities for the educated knowledge worker, and further marginalizes the less educated. Castells (2000: 12) argues that workers in the New Economy increasingly fall into two camps. First, there are 'self-programmable workers' who are flexible, adaptable and quick to retrain. Their flexibility brings them success in the New Economy. Second, there are 'generic' workers who, lacking flexibility and skills, are increasingly 'exchangeable and disposable' and forced to compete for work with 'machines and with unskilled labour from around the world' (Castells, 2000: 12).

While there is substantial evidence that being educated and 'trainable' is important in the New Economy, theorists have debated why this is so. Does education provide concrete skills that are required in the labor market, or does it provide credentials, contacts, or other characteristics that enhance workers' ability to obtain employment? In this section we explore the theoretical literature on the link between education and employment, before we turn our attention to education and skill acquisition patterns in IT employment.

There are a number of different theoretical accounts of the significance of education and skill to employment. Perhaps the most influential is human capital theory, which holds that there is a close relationship between education, skill acquisition and labor market success. Education is seen to provide valuable skills and knowledge that help to make workers more productive and, hence, more attractive to employers (Becker, 1975; Hunter and McKenzie Leiper, 1993). Education and training, whether formally or informally acquired, provide workers with capital (knowledge, skills, abilities) that brings benefits to them (in terms of labor market outcomes), as well as workplaces and society more generally (in terms of productivity and social outcomes). While education cannot guarantee a good job, it is clear that those with education are certainly better off than those without (Statistics Canada, 2005).

In contrast, theorists like Collins (1979) and Bourdieu (1996) hold that while education is important for employment, it is less because of the skills it imparts, than the credentials, or symbolic and cultural capital, that it confers. Collins shows that educational credentials can serve as mechanisms of social closure, limiting access to good jobs. As a workforce becomes more educated, existing educational requirements become less effective social closure mechanisms. Credential inflation results: people in positions of influence raise requirements to limit access further. Collins casts the commonly assumed link between education and skill into doubt. So does Bourdieu (1996: 118) who argues that 'the educational institution confers, not just a certificate of technical competence giving one the right to a particular job, but a pass to a job in which the major portion of the necessary technical competence is often acquired on the job.' For Bourdieu, while education provides some skills, it also provides socialization, contacts and credentials that encourage labor market success, and thereby open up opportunities for skill acquisition on the job.

Traditional Marxian approaches to education have also tended to see formal education, less as a source of skill acquisition, than as a means of imparting traits and socialization important to work in a capitalist economy. Bowles and Gintis (1976) argue that the education system instils good work habits, obedience and acceptance of authority and hierarchy among its students. For them, the ultimate purpose of education is to prepare people for their future roles in the industrial, capitalist economy.

Nevertheless, the capitalist economy is changing. According to many "the New Economy no longer requires obedient drones, but rather seeks flexible knowledge workers" (Adams and Demaiter, 2008).[3] Perhaps the role of education (and its relationship to skill and employment) is changing. The recent work of Alan Sears (2006) is relevant here. Sears argues that formal education institutions are still geared towards instilling discipline. He believes that the push for higher education standards seen in Canada and elsewhere in the past decade or two is more about creating disciplined workers who are committed to acquiring marketable skills and skill-upgrading, than it is about providing workers with market-relevant skills. For him, recent educational reform is creating an 'instrumental approach to education' which 'has little to do with skills and a great deal to do with attitudes' (Sears, 2006: 337). Education also provides a mechanism for separating the good, trainable workers, from the 'bad': those who fail or struggle through their schooling are not the disciplined, malleable workers that employers want. Degrees, then, may be indicators of work ethic and attitude, but not of skill.

Signaling theory also sees credentials as distinguishing the trainable from the rest. Like theories of statistical discrimination, signaling theory contends that employers see credentials (and characteristics like gender and age) as indicators of competency and productivity (Rosenbaum et al., 1990). Credentials do not necessarily represent skills learned, but rather potential (Arkes, 1999). Employers may think that 'people with more education are more likely to be smarter and more trainable than those with less education, more motivated and more broadly socialized' (Alic, 2004: 334; Arkes, 1999).

While all of these approaches suggest that education has a direct link to employment, some contend that education is valuable for the skills it brings, while others emphasize the market value of credentials, or the contacts, attitudes, and other capital that education fosters. While insightful, none of these theories seeks to explain the significance of education to knowledge workers, or workers in the New Economy more broadly. How might education and credentials be relevant for IT workers?

SKILLS, EDUCATION AND WORK IN THE INFORMATION TECHNOLOGY FIELD

As noted above, there has been a great deal of professional activity in the IT field which has aimed at identifying and formalizing essential skills and knowledge required for practice in a variety of IT and computing-related jobs (Adams, 2004, 2007; Ensmenger, 2001). University-level programs have been created, and curricula designed and debated. Education in IT has long been a challenge: given rapid changes in technology and techniques, educators have struggled to find a balance between imparting general, theoretical knowledge and teaching concrete skills which may soon become obsolete. Nevertheless, there has been a trend towards formalization and standardization. Expectations for programs have been clearly laid out, and accreditation of educational programs is common. A variety of credentials have been established in the US, UK, Canada, and Australia to help distinguish the skilled and trained, from the lesser-trained.

While these education and credentialing initiatives have fundamentally changed formal education in the IT field over the past 30 to 40 years, their importance for the average IT worker is not clear. For example, a recent study of IT workers in Canada, found that only 50 percent of respondents had a university degree (Gunderson et al., 2005). Moreover, only 44 percent of the latter had a degree in IT fields such as computer science, or computer, software or systems engineering. A further 25 percent held degrees in fields that have traditionally fed into IT employment, like mathematics and electrical or electronic engineering (Gunderson et al., 2005). Many Canadian IT workers have little formal, advanced education in the field. Moreover, only 14 percent of IT respondents held a professional designation – a third of them in engineering. Very few Canadian IT workers have IT-specific professional credentials.

These Canadian statistics raise questions about the significance of education and credentials to IT workers, and suggest that the acquisition of IT skills, for many workers at least, does not happen in university. A growing body of literature on American IT workers supports these findings, and indicates that alternative, more informal methods of skill acquisition are typically more important. Faced with rapidly changing technology, and extensive project and contract-based work, IT workers must continually learn new skills. Kunda et al.'s (2002: 254) study of IT contract workers stressed the importance of self-learning, arguing that it was not simply 'a means of getting a job done or a route of personal satisfaction and growth' but was 'an issue of survival' (see also Chapter 2). Finegold (1999) and Benner (2003) stress the value of networks and organizations in transmitting knowledge. Finegold (1999) argues that IT workers in California tend to value informal over formal learning, and tended to turn to a network of colleagues when they faced a problem that was difficult to solve. On-the-job training and experiential learning are also important (Newell et al., 2002).

An increasing body of literature is raising questions about skill acquisition and education trends within the IT field. While IT workers appear to be generally well-educated, studies increasingly suggest that informal learning is more important to employment and skill acquisition. What is the importance of education, credentials, and informal learning to IT workers? Do IT workers, like the self-programmable workers described by Castells (2000), feel that they must constantly retrain and be flexible? How do they retrain and where do they get their skills? Does the importance of education, and do skill acquisition activities vary cross-nationally? Do they vary by gender and age? How relevant are credentials for employment and skill upgrading? In the following sections, we explore the answers to these questions by drawing on the WANE study data.

EDUCATION AND OTHER CREDENTIALS

Not surprisingly, across all of our study countries, our respondents are typically well-educated. As Table 6.1 indicates, about four-fifths of the respondents to the WANE web surveys have a post-secondary credential of some kind. A baccalaureate degree is not standard for practice in the field: in each country between one-third and half of the respondents claim a bachelor's degree as their highest level of education. Yet, quite a few IT respondents possess graduate degrees, or other kinds of post-secondary credentials. In total, 87.5 percent of respondents in Australia, 85 percent in the US, and 82 percent in England have some kind of post-secondary degree or diploma. The Canadian respondents lag behind the rest: only 78 percent of them hold a college diploma or university degree. If IT has

Table 6.1   Highest level of education

Highest level of education	Canada $n = 108$	US $n = 147$	Australia $n = 89$	England $n = 122$
High school or less	4 (4)[2]	2 (3)	9.5 (8)	5 (6)
'Other' post-secondary education[1]	24 (26)	2 (3)	15.5 (13)	12 (15)
Undergraduate university degree	31 (33)	50 (74)	48 (40)	35 (43)
Graduate/postgraduate university degree	23 (25)	33 (49)	24 (20)	35 (43)
'Other'	18 (20)	12 (18)	4 (3)	12 (15)

Note:
1. The 'Other' post-secondary education category includes: college diplomas, certificate level training (vocational training/trade certificates), and diploma/advanced diplomas. The 'Other' educational category includes: those who report some college/university, overseas qualifications, or unspecified 'other.'
2. The first number in the cells is the percentage of respondents in this category. The second (in parentheses) is the number of respondents in this category.

traditionally been a field where the less educated worked alongside the highly educated, this appears to be less often the case today.

In accordance with Gunderson et al.'s (2005) findings, our data further reveal that respondents in all study countries have training in a variety of subjects, many of which are unrelated to IT. WANE respondents have degrees and diplomas in disciplines like psychology, sociology, anthropology, biology, business, commerce, accounting, art and music, as well as disciplines related to their jobs like mathematics, project management, and human resource management. A number of respondents do have training in IT-related fields, such as computer science, engineering, computer networking, web design, multi-media programming and quality assurance. Some of this training was acquired after workers found employment in the field. Many of our respondents have gone back to school, or are currently upgrading their education to gain additional IT related skills.

Does Education Vary by Gender and Age?

To determine whether educational credentials were more important for some workers than others we considered the role of gender and age. There are several reasons to think that these variables might be important. For instance, there are fewer women than men in computer science courses in universities; perhaps formal education is more important for men entering the field than women. Conversely, studies suggest that young men and boys are more likely than girls to acquire computer skills informally (Looker and Thiessen, 2003), so perhaps formal training and credentials are actually more important for women entering the field. Furthermore, there are reasons to think that the possession of credentials might vary by age: for instance, given credential inflation, newer (and younger) workers may be more likely to need credentials than older workers.

We find that our male respondents are more likely to hold university degrees than are female respondents, especially in Australia, Canada and England (see Table 6.2). The observable gender difference is negligible in the US, where the majority of the respondents of both genders are university-trained. In Canada, Australia and England, women are more likely to hold other kinds of post-secondary credentials than are men. These findings no doubt have significant implications for sex segregation in employment and the gender earnings gap, identified in other studies (see for instance, Demaiter, 2004; Habtu, 2003; Wolfson, 2005).

We also compared the highest level of education obtained by our respondents across major age groupings. These crosstabular results were complex, and there was no observable trend that held across study countries. In Canada and Australia the data suggests that university credentials

Table 6.2 Highest level of education by gender

	Canada		US		Australia		England	
	Male n = 71	Female n = 19	Male n = 86	Female n = 33	Male n = 45	Female n = 22	Male n=89	Female n = 24
High school or less	6 (4)[1]	0 (0)	1 (1)	3 (1)	7 (3)	14 (3)	6 (5)	4 (1)
'Other' post-secondary education	22 (16)	26 (5)	2 (2)	0 (0)	7 (3)	36 (8)	10 (9)	21 (5)
Undergraduate/grad/ postgraduate university degree	58 (41)	47 (9)	85 (73)	85 (28)	84 (38)	50 (11)	73 (65)	62.5 (15)
'Other'	14 (10)	26 (5)	12 (10)	12 (4)	2 (1)	0 (0)	11 (10)	12.5 (3)

Note: 1. The first number in the cells is the percentage of respondents in this category. The second (in parentheses) is the number of respondents in this category.

are more common among younger IT respondents. This finding may reflect credential inflation in the field across these countries: university education may be more important for entry into the field today, than it was in the past. Regardless, the trend is not generalizable to other countries. As noted previously, the vast majority of IT respondents in the US are university trained, and there is no indication that older workers are significantly less educated than younger respondents. There is some indication that educational attainment varies by age in England, but no clear pattern is evident.

To summarize, while IT workers in our study countries are typically well-educated, it is clear that people enter IT work from a variety of disciplinary and educational backgrounds, and (with the general exception of the US) with training at various levels. Men typically have higher levels of educational attainment than do women in most study countries, and in Australia and Canada, educational attainment is higher among younger workers in general.

DO IT WORKERS POSSESS OTHER KINDS OF CREDENTIALS?

Because practitioners have entered the IT field from a wide variety of training backgrounds, IT professional groups have attempted to establish professional credentials to distinguish the experts from the amateurs. Have IT workers embraced these credentials as adjuncts or alternatives to educational credentials? If our respondents are representative, they have not. The vast majority of workers in our study do not possess credentials established by professional associations. In Canada, only 12 of 104 respondents claim any such credential. In the US, 23 of 136 respondents claim a professional credential, and in Australia only 21 of 76 respondents possess credentials established by professional associations.[4] Moreover, there is little overlap among respondents with respect to the type of credential possessed.

Other types of credentials in the IT field have been established by large software companies (like Microsoft) to signify expertise in specific software systems and applications. Nevertheless, only a minority of our respondents possessed any kind of technical certification. For example, 36 out of 104 (35 percent) Canadian respondents, 24 out of 138 (17 percent) American respondents, 22 out of 122 (18 percent) British respondents, and 21 out of 77 (27 percent) Australian respondents report the possession of a technical certification. The most common technical certifications cited by our respondents were the Microsoft Certified Professional designation, the Microsoft Certified Systems Engineer, and the Oracle Database Certification.

These technical credentials do not seem to be particularly valuable to respondents. Although they were rarely mentioned in the qualitative interviews, some workers indicated that they sometimes looked good on a résumé, even though experience tended to be more highly valued. The difficulty is that these certificates are often considered valid for a short period of time before they become obsolete, given rapidly changing technology. To keep them up-to-date requires frequent retraining. It is little wonder that workers do not pursue these credentials in large numbers.

Overall, few respondents possess either technical or professional credentials. These credentials seem to do little to demonstrate skill or expertise. Educational credentials appear to be much more important for practitioners in the field. Is education also a primary means of skill acquisition, or do IT workers acquire skills in other ways? Where do they learn how to do their jobs?

WHERE DO IT WORKERS GET THEIR SKILLS?

When asked where they acquired the skills they needed to do their jobs, our IT respondents emphasized the importance of informal methods of skill acquisition: most notably, self-learning, previous work experience and on-the-job training (see Table 6.3). Most consistently emphasized was self-learning valued by 90 percent or more of Canadian, American

Table 6.3　Where do IT workers acquire skills[1]

	Canada *n* = 105	US *n* = 141	England *n* = 122	Australia *n* = 78
Self learning	93	92	90	88.5
Previous work experience	87	82	77	77
On the job training	84	96	87	91
Seminars/conferences	45	33	33	32
Vendor/proprietary training	34	25	20	35
Private/business school	16	11	6	N/A
Community college/university	64	47.5	55	42
Other	6	8	7	97

Note: Each cell provides the number of respondents in each nation reporting they have acquired skills from these sources. Respondents were free to choose as many sources of skill as they felt were relevant.

and England respondents, and 88.5 percent of respondents in Australia. On-the-job training was also highly emphasized, especially by respondents in the US (96 percent of whom rated this as a source of skill) and in Australia (91 percent).

Formal methods of skill acquisition, such as community colleges and universities were less often emphasized, but were consistently the fourth most common source of skills for respondents across all study countries. Thus formal education, is an important source of skill, but it was not deemed as important for our respondents as self-learning, on-the-job learning, or previous work experience. Seminars, conferences, and vendor/ proprietary training were mentioned by only one-third of the respondents on average; these types of 'network' activities are important sources of skill for some.

Gender, Age and Skill Acquisition

We also explored whether workers differ in their means of skill acquisition by gender and age. Although we ran into difficulties with small survey sample sizes, we found some indication of noteworthy differences.

With respect to gender, we find that (with few exceptions) women respondents are more likely than men to learn skills on the job, while men emphasize self-learning and formal education more (see Table 6.4).[5] This latter finding is not too surprising given women's tendency to have lower levels of academic attainment in three of our study countries. The other differences deserve more research. Women may lack opportunities to acquire skills more informally on their own (given their family responsibilities), and through informal networks and acquaintances, as some have speculated (Adams and Demaiter, 2008; McGuire, 2002). These findings may also in part reflect sex segregation in the field, where women predominate in low-skilled jobs in which it may be easier to acquire skills on the job, while men predominate in high-skill areas requiring advanced training and innovation (Demaiter, 2004; Habtu, 2003; Wolfson, 2005).

It is also notable that cross-cultural variations exist. For example, while women tend to emphasize self-learning less than men, this is not the case in the US. And women in England appear more likely than their male counterparts to see college and university as an important source of skills (see Table 6.4). These cross-national differences are also deserving of more study.

With respect to age, few key findings emerged from the data analysis, although younger IT respondents were typically more likely to list college and university training as being important than were older workers. For example, in Canada 81 percent of IT respondents in their 20s and 61.5

Table 6.4 Skill acquisition by gender

	Canada		US		England		Australia	
	Male $n = 71$	Female $n = 19$	Male $n = 86$	Female $n = 33$	Male $n = 89$	Female $n = 24$	Male $n=45$	Female $n = 22$
Self learning	97 (69)[1]	84 (16)	89.5 (77)	100 (33)	95.5 (85)	71 (17)	93 (42)	86 (19)
Previous work experience	87 (62)	84 (16)	87 (75)	70 (23)	79 (70)	75 (18)	82 (37)	64 (14)
On the job training	79 (56)	100 (19)	95 (82)	97 (32)	86.5 (77)	83 (20)	89 (4)	95.5 (21)
Seminars/conferences	51 (36)	32 (6)	33 (28)	30 (10)	35 (31)	25 (6)	40 (18)	23 (5)
Vendor/proprietary training	41 (29)	21 (4)	28 (24)	21 (7)	21 (19)	8 (2)	42 (19)	27 (6)
Private/business school	17 (12)	16 (3)	10.5 (9)	12 (4)	4.5 (4)	8 (2)	N/A	N/A
Community college/university	70 (50)	58 (11)	46.5 (40)	45.5 (15)	49 (44)	62.5 (15)	51 (23)	27 (6)
Other	7 (5)	0 (0)	3.5 (3)	15 (5)	8 (7)	4 (1)	100 (45)	91 (20)

Note: The first number in the cells is the percentage of respondents in this category. The second (in parentheses) is the number of respondents in this category.

percent of IT respondents in their 30s listed college and university training compared to a much lower 55 percent of workers in their 40s. This pattern held true for England but was less evident in Australia and the US. It should be noted that there are so few respondents in each age category, we cannot be confident that this finding is generalizable, even though it is logical that workers recently out of school would find these skills more up-to-date and job relevant than would older workers.

Notably, IT respondents in all the case study countries, regardless of their age, tend to emphasize self-learning as important. Over 75 percent of all respondents report self-learning as a key method of skill acquisition. Moreover, workers age 30 and over emphasize previous work experience.

Education and Skill Acquisition

We also examined the extent to which educational attainment shaped skill acquisition patterns. Do workers with more education acquire skills differently than workers with less education? Are they more likely to see education as an important source of skill?

Although the value of n in most cells are too low for good analysis, the clearest findings were found for the Canadian data presented here in Table 6.5. Canadian respondents with a university degree generally listed more skill acquisition activities than those with other post-secondary education and other types of education (disregarding those with a high school

Table 6.5   Skill acquisition by education in Canada

	High school or less $n = 4$	Other post secondary education $n = 26$	Undergrad/ grad university degree $n = 55$	Other $n = 18$
Self learning	100 (4)	92 (24)	94.5 (52)	100 (18)
Previous work experience	100 (4)	81 (21)	93 (51)	83 (15)
On the job training	100 (4)	81 (21)	87 (48)	83 (15)
Seminars and conferences	25 (1)	35 (9)	58 (32)	28 (5)
Vendor/proprietary training	75 (3)	31 (8)	36 (20)	28 (5)
Community college and university	0 (0)	61.5 (16)	78 (43)	44 (8)
Private and business school	25 (1)	23 (6)	9 (5)	28 (5)

education or less, given the extremely small *n*). University degree holders are among the most likely to list self-learning, previous work experience and on-the-job training as means through which they acquire skills. They are also more likely to draw on seminars and conferences, and college and university courses. While they are not very likely to draw on private and business schools for training, they are more likely than most others to pursue vendor and proprietary training (see Table 6.5).

The findings for the Australian data (not presented here) are similar, although not quite as marked. Here too, in general, the university-educated tend to engage in more skill acquisition activities than do others. The England data provide some evidence that people with different levels of education engage in different skill acquisition activities, but with small N's in many cells, it is difficult to be confident in this result. In the US, the poor distribution of respondents across the education variable renders analysis impossible.

Overall, respondents across nations appear to acquire skills from a variety of sources. While formal education is an important source of skill, more informal means are ranked more important. There are some differences across nation, and across gender, in terms of which informal means are rated most highly. Moreover, in Canada, there is some indication that the more educated engage in more skill acquisition activities, but this trend is not as strong in other nations (except for, perhaps the US, in which the vast majority of respondents are both educated and highly likely to engage in informal learning activities).[6]

It is clear that our respondents engage in many activities to keep their work skills up-to-date. In this sense, they appear to be 'self-programmable' workers, in Castells' (2000) sense. Is skill upgrading essential to employment? Do IT workers feel pressure to upgrade their skills continually?

DO IT WORKERS FEEL PRESSURE TO UPGRADE THEIR SKILLS?

As discussed, the literature suggests that workers in the New Economy must retrain and upgrade their skills frequently to maintain employability. This depiction appears to fit many of our respondents: the majority of whom agree with the statement 'I feel pressure to continually learn new skills.' The results are remarkably consistent across nations, with Americans being slightly more likely than those in Canada, Australia and England to state they experience pressure (see Table 6.6). While these percentages are high, it is notable that a sizeable minority of the respondents said they felt no such pressure.

Table 6.6   Pressure to continually learn new skills

	Canada $n = 105$	US $n = 140$	England $n = 122$	Australia $n = 78$
Yes, I feel pressure to continually learn new skills	60 (63)	67 (94)	61 (74)	64 (50)

Variations across Gender, Age and Education

To determine whether some IT workers feel more pressure to learn new skills compared to others, we also considered the role of gender, age, and education. With respect to gender, we find the largest gender gap between men and women in Australia. For instance 76 percent of men compared to a much smaller 45.5 percent of women report feeling pressure to upgrade their skills. Similarly, although the gender gap is small, Canadian men are also more likely to report feeling pressure to upgrade their skills than are Canadian women. In contrast, in the US women (70 percent) are more likely to report feeling pressure to upgrade their skills than are men (64 percent). In England, men and women are quite similar with 62.5 percent of women and 61 percent of men reporting pressure (see Table 6.7).

With respect to age, we find two distinct trends. In Canada and England, there was an overall tendency for younger IT respondents to report feeling more pressure to learn new skills. For instance, in Canada, 69 percent of respondents in their 20s, and 56–59 percent of respondents in their 30s and 40s reported pressure to learn new skills, compared with only 50 percent of IT respondents in their 50s. The opposite trend appears to characterize the US and Australia. For instance, 64 percent of US respondents in their 20s and 76.5 percent of respondents in their 50s agreed they felt pressure to acquire new skills continually. Similarly, 69 percent of Australian respondents in their 20s compared to 78 percent of respondents in their 50s agreed they felt pressure to acquire new skills continually. Older Australians (in their 50s) were more likely than all other age groups across all nations to state they felt pressure to learn new skills. It must be noted, however, that the values of *n* in each age category were quite low, and there was a great deal of variation by country. It is unclear why there would be regional differences in the way in which age is associated with pressure to learn new skills.[7]

We also explored the link between education and pressure to learn new skills. There is no trend that holds across the study countries, but there are some country-specific trends. For instance, in Canada, the data seem to suggest that more educated workers generally report pressure to continually learn new skills (see Table 6.8). Australian IT respondents with

Table 6.7 *Pressure to continually learn new skills by gender*

	Canada		US		England		Australia	
	Male n = 71	Female n = 19	Male n = 86	Female n = 33	Male n = 89	Female n = 24	Male n = 45	Female n = 22
Yes, I feel pressure to continually learn new skills	62 (44)	58 (11)	64 (55)	70 (23)	61 (54)	62.5 (15)	76 (34)	45.5 (10)

Table 6.8 *Pressure to learn new skills by education*

	High school or less	Other post-sec.	Undergrad/ grad/ postgrad	Other
Canada				
	n = 4	n = 26	n = 55	n = 18
Yes, I feel pressure	50 (2)[1]	61.5 (16)	58 (32)	72 (13)
Australia				
	n = 6	n = 13	n = 50	n = 2
Yes, I feel pressure	17 (1)	54 (7)	82 (41)	50 (1)
US				
	n = 3	n = 2	n = 119	n = 16
Yes, I feel pressure	67 (2)	100 (2)	65.5 (78)	75 (12)
England				
	n = 6	n = 15	n = 86	n = 15
Yes, I feel pressure	83 (5)	47 (7)	559 (51)	73 (11)

Note: The first number in the cells is the percentage of respondents in this category. The second (in parentheses), is the number of respondents in this category.

some form of post-secondary education (be it certificate level, diploma, advanced diploma, or some form of university degree) also tend to report greater pressure to learn new skills. The US and England data hint that it is those without a post-secondary credential that feel the most pressure to upgrade. Additional research with larger sample sizes is necessary to assess whether any trends hinted at here are significant and generalizable.

The above analyses illustrate that both education and a variety of skill acquisition activities are important for IT workers in our four study countries. IT workers are typically well-educated, even though many do not have formal education in IT fields. Many IT workers feel pressure to continually upgrade their skills. Skill acquisition does occur through education, but informal means of skill acquisition, especially self-learning and on-the-job training are particularly important. In some countries, like Canada, it is educated workers who engage in more skill acquisition activities, and it is clear that educated workers in all the countries feel pressure to upgrade their skills. If skill acquisition comes primarily outside education, and many educated workers have degrees in other fields, how or why is education important?

EDUCATION, SKILL AND IT EMPLOYMENT

Education clearly provides some human capital, but it does not appear to be the primary source of job-related skill. Our analysis further suggests that IT-related credentials are not terribly important for employment in the field – with the possible exception of the US in which a university degree appears to be standard in the firms we studied. We suggest instead that perhaps education functions here in accordance with signaling theory. Educational credentials may signal trainability and adaptability to employers. This may be particularly true in Canada and Australia where educated workers report feeling more pressure to upgrade their skills than do others, and where workers with credentials engage in more skill acquisition activities than others.

To assess the role of education in skill acquisition among IT workers, we examined the qualitative WANE data, with a focus on Canada, to determine whether employers viewed education as an indicator of adaptability and trainability, as signaling theory predicts. We found general support for this idea.

When asked about hiring practices, and what they are looking for in an 'ideal' IT employee, employers tended to emphasize skills and attitudes over educational credentials. Particularly emphasized were soft skills, positive attitudes, and the ability to learn:

You know attitude and ambition can overcome a lot of education. Education is sometimes overvalued because you get somebody, they can be smart as a whip and have all kinds of degrees, if they don't have the right attitude they're not an asset to a company.

(IT firm 112)

Attitude and ability seems to be more highly valued by many, than education per se. Some employer respondents did discuss the value of educational credentials. For instance, some stated that they preferred to hire people with degrees or college diplomas, believing them to have a good skill sets and abilities. Again, while education was valuable it was not necessarily essential. In the words of one respondent, 'my preference is towards people who've been through a university program but ah, that only describes maybe half of our people here.' (IT firm 101) Many other respondents emphasized the value of work experience,[8] trainability, technical and communication skills, the ability to adapt to a changing environment, a willingness to learn quickly, and 'cultural-fit.' The following quotes are indicative:

the first thing that I primarily look for are soft skills rather than hard technology skills. Obviously I'm interested in people who've got relevant experience and skills with what we do . . . but more than that, I'm more attuned to looking for people who are bright, have an aptitude and a passion for what we do first and foremost because you can learn other skills but having a passion for what you do you've got it or you don't . . . Being innovative and having a flair for creativity and the confidence to express that are kind of natural soft qualities that some people express better than others. I first and foremost look for those because I know that the other things can be learned, so . . . if I know that they're bright and they can learn quickly the fact that they might not know the Java language doesn't bother me at all . . . [but] experience is a factor.

(IT firm 101)

[A good employee is] . . . someone who's willing to learn new things and who has a good base knowledge of language and what works. Whatever the job is that they would be hired for they would obviously need to know the minimum amount, but someone who's creative, I think is an easy person to work with. I think [that] is probably the most important thing.

(IT firm 103)

You definitely want people people right. So people who can get along well, listen, you know classic listener skills, acknowledging, reacting, positive attitude type stuff. It's not a – you're not going away in a trench, building something and then just passing it over to someone you never see. There's a lot of people interaction. You've got to have those skills.

(IT firm 115)

I look for how quickly they think on their feet, how effectively did they think out of the box, how well will they function in a team environment.

(IT firm 117)

In addition to these characteristics, employers also emphasized having a good work ethic, a positive attitude, problem-solving skills, time-management skills, an ability to work autonomously, and an ability to meet deadlines:

> Ah, well they have to be motivated, they have to like to code . . . that's perhaps the most important parts of IT and then [there] are things that are general to employees. You know their ability to a to get things done on a good time schedule . . . manage their own time and keep adequate notes and documentation and work within whatever systems that we require for and the specifications we require for a particular project.
>
> (IT firm 110)

How do employers decipher who is going to be the hard-working, trainable, flexible employee who satisfies the above-mentioned 'ideal' worker characteristics? Signaling theory suggests that employers use education as an indicator. There is some evidence, that employers in our study use education in this manner. For instance, one employer explains 'in terms of academics I use that as an indicator of how bright they are . . . or hope they are.' (IT firm 101) Another appears to consider education as an indicator of one's ability to learn. Thus, field of study is not terribly important:

> I wouldn't be too concerned about educational background because I come from a totally different background than programming, so I don't see the education so much as just the ability, the ability to teach yourself I guess. The ability to learn for yourself . . . You can take somebody who's come from a different discipline and as long as that person knows how to learn for themselves I think they can do just about anything. (IT firm 103)

While many other employers did not explicitly state that they use education as an indicator of other valued traits and skills, it is at least plausible that they do so. Previous research has argued that employers see post-secondary training as teaching students valuable employment skills such as time-management, the ability to work to deadlines, the ability to learn, and communication skills (Evers et al., 1998). IT employers in our study emphasize these same traits.

To sum, there are many reasons why IT employers might seek out educated workers. While some note that college and university graduates possess valuable skills, it is also clear that employers stress experience, skill and attitude, no matter where acquired. Moreover, they expect workers to learn while on the job, and want to hire those who are able to do so. Educated workers are believed to have the ability to learn. Educational credentials, then, appear to be tools employers can utilize to identify adaptable, trainable workers.

CONCLUSION

In exploring the significance of education and credentials to IT workers and their skill activities, in Canada, the US, England, and Australia, some general conclusions can be made. Most important, the data presented in this chapter demonstrate that most IT workers are educated, and that they consider education to be a source of skill. Nevertheless, they are more likely to emphasize informal sources of skill. Most workers feel pressure to learn new skills, and they appear to acquire skills predominantly through learning on the job, and learning on their own. The literature suggests that many rely on network and colleague contacts as well. IT workers appear to be self-programmable in Castells' sense – frequently adapting and learning new things to maintain employability. For employers, skills appear to be more important than educational (or other kinds of) credentials; education may serve more as an indicator of good work habits and trainability, than a source of important job-related, cutting-edge skills.

Our international analysis demonstrates some differences by country, gender, educational attainment, and to some extent, age. Given small sample sizes and the study focus on predominantly small-size firms, we cannot be sure whether the international differences noted here are generalizable. What is most striking, though, is that many international differences are differences of degree. The value of education and methods of skill acquisition are remarkably similar from one international context to the next, even when the varying educational systems are taken into account. Whether real differences in the importance attached to post-secondary degrees, and in the relationship between education and skill acquisition exist (and why), are important issues for future research to consider. In a similar vein, future research should explore how the skill acquisition activities of older and younger workers may differ, and whether true international differences exist here as well.

There is a growing body of literature identifying gender differences in IT (Crump et al., 2007; McMullin, forthcoming; Wright, 1996). This current study adds to this literature by suggesting that men and women in IT typically have differing kinds of education, and that they tend to acquire skills in different ways. Further research is needed to understand the implications of these findings for women's participation in the field and patterns of sex segregation. If, for instance, women have less access to knowledge through network groups and colleagues, and are less able to engage in self-learning activity because of family care responsibilities, they would appear to be at a disadvantage in keeping their skills up-to-date and hence may be less attractive to employers than men. Our study suggests that women are typically most likely to say they acquire skills on-the-job, but given occupational segregation and their clustering into a limited number of lower-end IT jobs, they may have access to a narrower range of skills, and hence have fewer employment opportunities. The implications of men's and women's skill acquisition activities for employment is deserving of greater attention.

Ultimately, education appears to be important in the New Economy, both as a source of skill (as human capital theory indicates), and as an indicator of attitudes and adaptability valued by employers (as Sears, Bourdieu and others argue). Education may signal employability in a wide range of jobs. At the same time, workers in the IT sector appear to engage in a wide variety of skill acquisition activities. While these self-programmable workers are the fortunate ones in the New Economy, according to Castells, the requirement of constant skill-upgrading can be problematic. The demands of self-learning may bring too much extra work to employees who may already be over-burdened (Hyman et al., 2005). Moreover, it may serve as an additional form of managerial control (Barrett, 2005; Rasmussen and Johansen, 2005). The constant need for upgrading may place women at a disadvantage, especially those with children who already undertake a double day. Given stereotypes about the limited learning skills of older workers (Chan et al., 2001), they too may find it hard to maintain a job in which 'learning new things' is a constant requirement.

In the end, it remains to be seen whether IT workers in the small firms studied here are harbingers of trends affecting others in the economy, or whether their industry and employment situation makes them relatively unique. Are workers in other fields required to be self-programmable, and is there increased pressure to acquire skills through a variety of means to maintain employability? Further research is required to find out. Nevertheless, the evidence is growing that education and skill acquisition are becoming more important for today's workers and that there is a new emphasis on characteristics such as flexibility, adaptability and self-learning. The impact of these trends on workers is a topic deserving further investigation.

NOTES

1. In England, respondents were not asked about possessing credentials established by professional associations.
2. Some material in this section is taken from the following article: Tracey L. Adams and Erin I. Demaiter (2008), 'Skill, education, and credentials in the new economy: the case of information technology workers', *Work, Employment and Society* **22** (2): 351–362.
3. It should be noted that Bowles and Gintis (1976) highlighted the significance of streaming. Traits like obedience were stressed more with working-class children to prepare them

for industrial jobs, while middle-class children were encouraged to be more independent, to prepare them for management and professional roles.

4. In England, respondents were not asked about possessing credentials established by professional associations.

5. Respondents were asked the following: 'Through which of the following methods did you acquire the IT skills that are needed for your current job (self-learning, previous working experience, formal training, on-the-job/informal training, private business school/training institute/community college/CEGEP/University, vendor/proprietary training, seminars/conferences, and other.' In the US, 100 percent of women value self-learning, while in England, men are slightly more likely to report on-the-job training as important.

6. We also explored whether workers with professional or technical credentials were more likely to engage in certain types of skill acquisition activities, but no significant or notable patterns were evident.

7. In an additional Canadian-based analysis, we examined responses to the question on pressure to learn new skills by occupation; most likely to report pressure are engineers (80 percent), technicians (67 percent), CEO's (64 percent) and programmers (60 percent).

8. It should be noted that a number of IT respondents talk about how work experience is important when hiring an 'ideal' IT employee; however, because of the small size of the firms and the financial insecurity that comes along with that, some employers discuss how it is not always feasible to hire employees with a great deal of on-the-job experience.

REFERENCES

Adams, T. (2004), *Professionalization in Computing-related Occupations: Canada, the US and Britain, WANE Working Paper, February 2004*, London, ON: University of Western Ontario, Workforce Aging in the New Economy (WANE).

Adams, T. (2007), 'Interprofessional relations and the emergence of a new profession: software engineering in the United States, United Kingdom and Canada', *Sociological Quarterly*, **48**, 507–32.

Adams, T. and E. Demaiter (2008), 'Skill, education and credentials in the new economy: the case of information technology workers', *Work, Employment, and Society*, **22** (2), 351–62.

Alic, J.A. (2004), 'Technology and labor in the new US economy', *Technology in Society*, **26** (2–3), 327–41.

Arkes, J. (1999), 'What do educational credentials signal and why do employers value credentials?', *Economics Education Review*, **18**, 133–41.

Barrett, R. (2005), 'Managing the software development labour process', in R. Barrett (ed.), *Management, Labour Process and Software Development*, New York: Routledge, pp. 76–99.

Becker, G. (1975), *Human Capital: A Theoretical and Empirical Analysis, with Special Reference to Education*, 2nd edn, New York: Columbia University Press.

Benner, C. (2003), '"Computers in the wild": guilds and next-generation unionism in the Information Revolution', *International Review of Social History*, **48**, 181–204.

Bills, D.B. (2004), *The Sociology of Education and Work*, Malden, MA: Blackwell Publishing.

Bourdieu, P. (1996), *The State Nobility*, Stanford, CA: Stanford University Press.

Bowles, S., and H. Gintis (1976), *Schooling in Capitalist America: Educational Reform and the Contradictions of Economic Life*, New York: Basic Books.

Castells, M. (2000), 'Materials for an exploratory theory of the network society', *British Journal of Sociology*, **51** (1), 5–24.

Chan, D.J., J. Marshall and V. Marshall (2001), 'Linking technology, work and the life course: findings from the NOVA case study', in V.W. Marshall, W.P. Heinz, H. Krüger and A. Verma (eds), *Restructuring Work and the Life Course*, Toronto, ON: University of Toronto Press, pp. 270–87.

Collins, R. (1979), *The Credential Society: A Historical Sociology of Education and Stratification*, New York: Academic Press.

Crump, B.J, K.A. Logan and A. McIlroy (2007), 'Does gender still matter? A study of the views of women in the ICT industry in New Zealand', *Gender, Work and Organization*, **14** (4), 349–70.

Demaiter, E. (2004), 'Understanding women's experiences in male-dominated professions: a case study of women in the information technology (IT) sector', unpublished MA thesis, University of Western Ontario.

Ensmenger, N. (2001), 'The "question of professionalism" in the computer fields', *IEEE Annals of the History of Computing*, **23**, 56–74.

Ensmenger, N. (2003), 'Letting the "computer boys" take over: technology and the politics of organizational transformation', *International Review of Social History*, **48**, 153–80.

Evers, F.T., J.C. Rush and I. Berdrow (1998), *The Bases of Competence: Skills of Lifelong Learning and Employability*, San Francisco, CA: Jossey-Bass.

Finegold, D. (1999), 'Creating self-sustaining high-skill ecosystems', *Oxford Review of Economic Policy*, **15** (1), 60–81.

Gunderson, M., L. Jacobs and F. Vaillancourt (2005), 'The information technology (IT) labour market in Canada: results from the national survey of IT occupations', report prepared for the Software Human Resource Council.

Habtu, R. (2003), 'Information technology workers', in *Perspectives*, cat. no. 75-001-XIE, Ottawa: Statistics Canada.

Hunter, A., and J. McKenzie Leiper (1993), 'On formal education, skills and earnings: the role of educational certificates in earnings determination', *Canadian Journal of Sociology*, **18** (1), 21–42.

Hyman, J., D. Scholarios and C. Baldry (2005), 'Getting on or getting by? Employee flexibility and coping strategies for home and work', *Work, Employment and Society*, **19** (4), 705–25.

Kunda, G., S. Barley and J. Evans (2002), 'Why do contractors contract? The experience of highly skilled technical professionals in a contingent labor market', *Industrial and Labor Relations Review*, **55** (2), 234–61.

Looker, D. and V. Thiessen (2003), *The Digital Divide in Canadian Schools: Factors Affecting Student Access to and use of Information Technology*, cat. no. 81-597-XE, Ottawa: Statistics Canada.

McDowell, L. (2003), *Redundant Masculinities? Employment Change and White Working Class Youth*, Malden, MA: Blackwell.

McGuire, G.M. (2002), 'Gender, race, and the shadow of structure: a study of informal networks and inequality in a work organization', *Gender & Society*, **16** (3), 303–22.

McMullin, J.A. (forthcoming), *Gender, Age and Work in the New Economy: The Case of Information Technology Firms*, Kelowna, BC: University of British Columbia Press.

Newell, S., M. Robertson, H. Scarborough and J. Swan (2002), *Managing Knowledge Work*, Basingstoke: Palgrave.

Rasmussen B. and B. Johansen (2005), 'Trick or treat: autonomy as control in knowledge work', in R. Barrett (ed.), *Management, Labour Process and Software Development*, New York: Routledge, pp. 100–122.

Rosenbaum, J., T. Kariya, R. Settersten and T. Maier (1990), 'Market and network theories of the transition from high school to work', *Annual Review of Sociology*, **16**, 263–99.

Sears, A. (2006), 'Education for an information age?', in V. Shalla, (ed.), *Working in a Global Era: Canadian Perspectives*, Toronto, ON: Canadian Scholars Press, pp. 320–44.

Statistics Canada (2005), *Labour Force Historical Review, 2004*, 71F0004XCB, Ottawa: Statistics Canada.

Wolfson, William G. (2005), *Analysis of Labour Force Survey Data for the Information Technology Occupations 2000–2004*, Ottawa: Software Human Resource Council.

Wotherspoon, T. (1998), *The Sociology of Education in Canada: Critical Perspectives*, Toronto, ON: Oxford University Press.

Wright, R. (1996), 'The occupational masculinity of computing', in C. Cheng (ed.), *Masculinities in Organizations*, London: Sage Publications, pp.77–96.

7. Formal training, older workers, and the IT industry

Neil Charness and Mark C. Fox

INTRODUCTION

In 1990, a paper in the *Monthly Labor Review* noted (Anonymous, 1990) that there was little agreement on the definition of training in the workplace, though it is recognized that training decreases with age. In this chapter we examine some aspects of training, particularly, the relationship between formal training and age, as well as other demographic variables such as gender and work status. The goal is to understand some of the correlates of training for older workers, particularly for workers in the information technology (IT) industry.

Why examine age and training? Some economists are concerned that an aging workforce is likely to be a less productive workforce (for example Jorgenson et al., 2004; Tang and MacLeod, 2006). The methodology employed in those macro-economic analyses relies on proxy variables for indices of worker productivity such as the level of university education in an aggregate unit such as a province or state (Tang and MacLeod, 2006). Psychologists, using micro-level analyses, examine the relation between age and individual productivity and typically find a near zero (McEvoy and Cascio, 1989; Waldman and Avolio, 1986) or slight positive (Sturman, 2004) relationship. Such analyses focus on individuals using both direct productivity measures, such as work items completed, and indirect ones, such as supervisor and peer ratings. A major difference between the two approaches to measuring productivity is that psychological studies of productivity typically ignore input costs (for example salary) whereas economic models usually incorporate such measures.

The discrepancy between conclusions from different disciplines may also relate to which worker is considered. Psychological studies of elite performers (see Ericsson et al., 2006, for a review of expertise) typically show an inverted J-shaped function between age (more specifically, career age) and productivity (for example Simonton, 1988, 1997). Although there are discipline-specific curves (mathematicians peaking well before historians), the general finding is that productivity for experts climbs from the teen years to the 30s, peaks in that decade (or that of the 40s: Roring and Charness, 2007), and declines thereafter.

But, most disciplines would agree that a well-trained worker is likely to be more productive than a poorly trained one (for example the human-capital model in economics: Frazis and Spletzer, 2005). Meta-analyses cast doubt on whether older adults benefit from training to the same extent as their younger counterparts (Kubeck et al., 1996); however, too little is known yet about effective training techniques in older populations to be able to draw too many conclusions about age and training based on the efficacy of usual training (Charness and Czaja, 2006). Moreover, there is a long-standing finding that older workers are less likely to be offered or accept job-related training than younger ones (for example Belbin and Belbin, 1972).

There are many possible reasons for the age gap in training and career development. These explanations can be classified according to two recip-rocally operating factors: the willingness of the company to offer training and the willingness of the worker to accept training. Firms are likely to weigh the costs of training and lost time at work while an employee is being trained against potential future gains in productivity following successful training. Rather than offer training to existing workers, a firm may find it less expensive to add (or substitute) new staff already possessing the req-uisite skills. Managers sometimes express the concern that they have less confidence in recovering training costs from older workers than younger ones, as well as the concern that training will be less successful with older workers (Finkelstein et al., 1995). Nonetheless, analyses suggest that older workers, given their lower turnover rates, are likely to be a cost-effective trainee population (Brooke, 2003).

However, business cycle considerations probably weigh heavily into the decision process about training. In times of labor surplus (for example the IT industry after the 1990–1991 IT-bubble collapse), management may choose to assign the risk of training to the worker, whereas in tighter labor markets (1989–1990), the risk of training may be assumed by management.

Workers generally (and older workers in particular) may be concerned that training is of low value to them given their perceptions of limited promotion opportunities following training as well as some fear that they will be unable to learn new skills successfully (Noe and Wilk, 1993). Reciprocal relations can develop between these sets of factors when the beliefs of managers are transmitted and accepted by workers and vice versa. There is evidence that there are negative societal stereotypes about aging that affect perceptions about older workers (for example Finkelstein et al., 1995; Gordon and Arvey, 2004; Kite et al., 2005). The estimated age bias effect size can be small (d=.11) and Gordon and Arvey (2004) note that it depends on a variety of contextual influences (for example, some decline in bias across study publication date and greater bias toward job applicants than toward job incumbents). Such beliefs can influence managers (Cleveland and Shore, 1992) and affect worker beliefs about aging. When such stereotypes are activated in a learning context they can have negative consequences for performance (Hess and Hinson, 2006).

AGE-RELATED PARTICIPATION IN DEVELOPMENTAL ACTIVITIES

A number of questionnaire-based studies have examined the relation between age and participation in work/career developmental activities, such as training courses. In general, they find a small ($r < .20$) but consistent negative age effect. Birdi et al. (1997) found a significant bivariate relation with age of $r = -.10$ in voluntary job learning activity, though a non-significant $r = -.04$ in work-based developmental activities in a large sample (n=1798) of vehicle manufacturing workers in the UK. Maurer et al. (2003) found a significant negative relation, $r = -.13$, between age and participation in employee development activities (frequency indicated on a 1–7 rating scale) in a random (phone dialing) sample of 800 US workers.

The IT industry has some useful features for testing out theories about age and training. This industry is an important source of growth for the economy as a whole in North America (Harchaoui et al., 2002) and in OECD countries generally (OECD, 2003). Knowledge obsolescence within this sector of the economy can be extremely rapid (for example Sparrow and Davies, 1988) and probably has increased given the accelerating pace of technology development and dissemination (Charness, 2008). Thus, the pressure to update knowledge is likely to be stronger here than in more staid industries and so we might expect to find less of an age-related decline in participation in training activities.

Knowledge updating can be seen as the firm's responsibility to its workforce or the workforce's responsibility to the firm, or a shared responsibility of both, as seen in IBM's recent introduction of training and education savings accounts for workers (Lohr, 2007). It is fairly clear that the perception of the firm as lifetime employer has diminished in the US and that a career is no longer perceived as a joint responsibility of firm and employee (Ekerdt, 2008; Marshall, 1998).

However, it is unclear whether the perception matches reality (Cappelli, 2003; Jacoby, 2003). Jacoby (2003) has argued that since the 1980s through 2000 indices such as job tenure (for example, employment with the same firm for 10-plus years) have shown modest change that depends on industry and gender, with decreases for some middle-aged male managers and increases for middle-aged women. Cappelli (2003) differs on the dimension of job security, particularly the perception of job stability. Perceived job insecurity seems to be a major factor in workers' pursuit of job training opportunities in the form of additional formal education (Elman and O'Rand, 2002). The potential unraveling of the career social contract may be even more evident in the very fast-paced IT industry environment given the rapid turnover of firms through both merger and failure. Thus, the IT industry may serve as a 'canary in the coal mine' case for tracking trends that may foretell the future of career development more generally. However, the IT industry has its own demographic peculiarities, as seen in reports by IT associations. For instance, in North America, this industry sector is unrepresentative of the general population in terms of having more males and more young workers (see Jovic et al., forthcoming).

We analyse data from the Workforce Aging in the New Economy (WANE) project, an international collaboration that included a web-based questionnaire filled out by manager and non-manager employees. A description of the study can be found in Chapter 1. WANE focused on sampling information technology companies in the small to medium-sized (<250 employees) category with an emphasis on small firms (4–20 employees). The sample was opportunistic, relying on a mix of cold calls and existing contacts for access. Thus, the generalizability of the data to the IT industry as a whole is uncertain. Despite potential problems with representativeness, it is feasible to test some hypotheses about age and training within this sample.

Hypotheses

Training and age
Given prior results in the literature that argue for a negative relationship between age and participation in training, we would expect a slight negative relationship between worker age and participation in training. That is, because of the premium on being cutting edge in the IT industry, the expected age–training relationship should be weakened. Based on a lifespan capital investment perspective (for example Diamond, 1986), we would also expect older workers (as they near retirement) to perceive less benefit from training and hence to avail themselves of less training even when it is offered, hence also predict a negative relationship between training intensity and age for those who do report training.

Training and job status

Training needs are likely to reflect life-cycle changes in career progression. Training in production level skills is most important early in a career as people acquire needed skills that were not met through prior educational venues such as high school, college, and university. As people move into management positions later in their careers, they are likely to need management training. Hence we expect to see a decline then a rise in training with age as people move from line to management positions.

Training and gender

Given that formal training sometimes requires travel or evening and weekend attendance, we would expect that women, who have more family responsibilities, hence more difficulty with work–family balance, might perceive more difficulty in accessing training and perhaps experience less training.

METHOD

Materials

A comprehensive questionnaire was constructed by WANE researchers, featuring 1327 items pertaining to demographics, health, family life, work satisfaction, and other issues related to work. The need to complete certain items was contingent on previous responses, and thus participants did not need to answer each item to complete the survey. For present purposes, the survey featured several sets of items pertaining to the extent and nature of employee training as well as satisfaction with the availability and outcomes of various forms of training.

Procedure

The questionnaire was completed by IT workers employed by companies of varying size in the United States, Canada, Australia, and England during the period November 2004 to April 2006. Criteria for selection of firms are discussed in Chapter 1. Employees were directed to a website to fill out the surveys. Response rates varied from country to country. A total of 461 participants completed at least part of the survey. Detailed information about response rates from specific firms in each region is presented in Chapter 1.

Respondents

Of 384 respondents indicating gender (83 percent of the total), 73 percent identified themselves as male and among 378 employees providing age (82 percent of total), 52 percent identified themselves as age 40 or less. Seventy percent of respondents identified themselves as younger than 50. Mean age was 37 years with a standard deviation of 10.5. A histogram depicting the distribution of age within the sample is shown in Figure 7.1.

For our purpose of assessing some of the age relations to training, we also divided the respondents into those above and below age 40 (slightly above the sample mean of 38). In the US, for instance, the Age Discrimination in Employment Act originally was formulated to protect older workers, defined as those of age 40 and above. Information on respondent race and ethnic group suffers from low response rates to these items (21 percent).

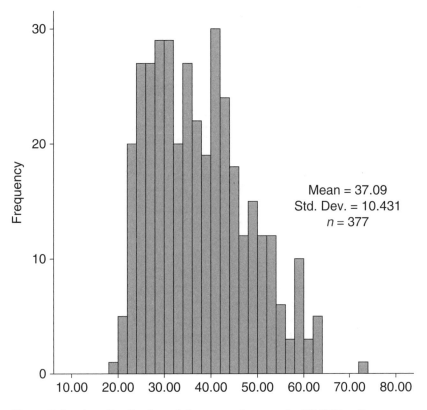

Figure 7.1   Age distribution of the respondents to the WANE online questionnaire

However, 84 percent of those respondents identified themselves as white. Among 91 percent who responded to a question indicative of managerial status (Q6, 'Do you supervise (manage) other people in your current job?'), 39 percent reported supervisory duties. Of 418 respondents identifying themselves as either IT workers or non-IT workers (response rate of 79 percent; question 3, sub-item 27, 'other, Non-IT'), 71 percent reported having IT-related responsibilities.

RESULTS

Because the survey did not solicit current age and every respondent did not complete the survey at the same time it was necessary to calculate age at the time of survey completion. A variable representing the difference between the date of completion and reported date of birth was created in SPSS 14 and is used in all age-related analyses. For bivariate analyses, scatter plots were examined for possible non-linear relationships.

Analysis

A total of 30 items from the web survey (most requiring a yes/no response) addressing the issue of workforce training, specifically, formal training, were chosen for the present analysis. In an effort to reduce the data, a principal components factor analysis was performed. However, due to the low rate of fully completed surveys – each individual did not answer every item of interest – it was not possible to pool these items into a single analysis. For this reason, clusters of consecutive items addressing the same construct were pooled together and individual analyses were performed for each of these groups of items. The criterion for deciding on the factor structure for a group of items (number of factors) was an eigenvalue greater than one, and varimax rotations were performed to minimize correlations between component scores. This data reduction technique yielded three component scores accounting for 56.3 percent of the variance, two accounting for 59.6 percent of the variance, and four accounting for 45.8 percent of the variance. Tables 7.1–3 show the rotated component scores and the factor loadings for each of the items. Survey items were recoded from '1' for yes and '2' for 'no', to '0' for 'no' so that names and directionality of factors would correspond.

Several questions addressed the types of training workers had experienced in the last 12 months. The two scores yielded by the analysis of these items reflect a network and hardware specialization training component, a management training component and a product and sales training

Table 7.1   Factor scores for training type from questions 58a–h

Did you receive formal training in the last 12 months in:	Component		
	1	2	3
a. Management	–.043	.799	–.148
b. Systems software	.545	.002	.332
c. Applications software	.003	–.078	.779
d. Telecommunications or computer networking	.805	.089	–.119
e. Computer language and/or programming	.352	–.371	.012
f. Computer hardware	.765	–.046	.149
g. Communication or interpersonal skills	.138	.806	.065
h. Company's products	.143	.001	.768

Note: Factor 1 is termed 'network and hardware specialization training'; Factor 2 is termed 'management training,' and Factor 3 is termed 'product and sales training.'

Table 7.2   Factor scores for perception of type of support from questions 60a–e

Did your employer support this training by:	Component	
	1	2
a. Paying for course materials	.132	.782
b. Providing paid time off for training or educational leave	.040	.754
c. Providing premises or supplies	.719	.307
d. Providing transportation or accommodation	.622	.095
e. Organizing and/or giving the training	.874	–.089

Note: Factor 1 is being termed 'other support'; Factor 2 is being termed 'paid support.'

component. The network and hardware specialization component is associated with items assessing training in areas such as systems software, telecommunications or computer networking, and computer hardware. The management training component was captured by items assessing training in management, and communication or interpersonal skills. Products and sales training was reflected in items that queried about training in company's products and applications software.

Table 7.3   Factor scores for reasons for not training from questions 62a–m

Reasons you did not take training or development course(s) in the past year:	Component			
	1	2	3	4
a. I have the skills I need	.617	–.089	.023	–.168
b. Training program suitable to my needs is not available	–.005	–.206	–.206	–.382
c. Too late for me at my age	.077	–.095	.131	.534
d. Not interested	.600	–.035	–.031	.402
e. Not needed to keep up with my job	.776	.017	.040	.014
f. Not needed to progress in my career	.764	–.057	–.028	–.010
g. I work too many extra hours	.193	.175	.631	.066
h. Too embarrassed	–.120	–.104	.495	–.058
i. Health reasons	–.137	–.381	.106	–.268
j. Family responsibilities don't leave enough time	–.001	–.101	.724	.113
k. Not permitted/selected by manager to take courses	–.159	.767	.063	–.003
l. Courses too difficult	–.183	–.038	–.160	.625
m. Employer did not offer	–.096	.791	–.077	–.158

Note: Factor 1 is 'training unnecessary,' Factor 2 is 'training unavailable,' Factor 3 is 'no time for training,' and Factor 4 is 'low self-efficacy.'

Other questions focused on the means by which employers helped respondents acquire formal training and yielded two components, as seen in Table 7.2, that could be described as assistance in the form of 'paid compensation' and 'other training resources.' Items loading high on the paid compensation factor were employer 'paid for course materials,' and 'provided paid time off for educational leave.' Items loading high on the 'other training resources' were 'providing premises or supplies' and 'organizing and/or giving training.'

Several questions dealt with reasons for not having taken training courses in the past year and yielded four factors that could be described as 'training unnecessary,' 'training unavailable,' and 'no time for training,' and 'low self-efficacy,' as seen in Table 7.1. Items loading high on 'training unnecessary' were 'not interested,' 'I have the skills I need,' and 'Not needed to progress in my career.' Items with high loadings for 'training unavailable' were 'not permitted/selected by manager to take courses,' and 'employer did not offer.' The items 'I work too many extra hours' and 'family responsibilities don't leave enough time' loaded high on 'no time for training.' The factor we term 'low self-efficacy' represented items 'too late for me at my age,' and 'courses too difficult.'

The resulting factors were compared to the case of generating scales by summing only items with high loadings (greater than .5). Both methods yielded very similar results, and the original factors are used in the following analyses. Because a multivariate analysis of variance revealed no regional/country differences among these factors, regions were pooled together.

Who Receives Formal Training?

First we assess whether having any formal training was related to age, gender, and other variables. Then we discuss, for those reporting some training, whether the amount of training related to such variables.

Contrary to expectations from prior studies in non-IT settings, age was not related to reporting training in the prior year, defined by a response to the question: 'In the last 12 months, did you receive any formal training related to your job while being employed.' Of those responding yes or no (96 percent), 26 percent received training and 74 percent did not. The participation rate in formal training is comparable to the 30 percent figure reported by Bird et al. (1997) for their sample of manufacturing workers using a similarly worded question (how often they had attended a training course in the previous 12 months).

Gender was not related to having received training in the last 12 months (or to the number of days of training over the year prior to the survey). Job type was also unrelated to having received training in the past year and how many days of training were accrued in the last 12 months as workers identifying themselves as having IT-related jobs did not differ from non-IT workers on these variables. Managerial status, as defined by responses to the question: 'Do you supervise (manage) other people in your current job?' (coded 1 for management, 0 for non-management) was also uncorrelated with whether or not training had been received in the past year.

ANOVA revealed no interactions for any of these variables in predicting number of days of training using age split at 40. Thus, contrary to results observed in other studies, formal training in the prior year seems relatively uniformly distributed within the firms as a function of age, gender, type of work, and managerial status with the majority of workers receiving no formal training.

Amount of Training and Age

However, among workers who reported receiving formal training in the last 12 months, age correlated negatively with the number of days of training reported, but this relationship was marginal using a two-tailed test of significance, r (95) = $-.20$, p = .054. Regression revealed significant linear, quadratic, and a marginal cubic relation to age. The quadratic relationship between age and days of training is shown in Figure 7.2. Days of training decrease with age from the twenties and remain relatively flat until a slight increase is seen in the late 50s. It should be noted that report of days of training was quite skewed. The mean was 14.4 days, with a standard deviation of 37.6.

Type of Training

An analysis of the types of training reported by older and younger workers revealed some differences. Age was moderately correlated with the products and sales factor score, r (88) = $-.28$, p < .01, and was not related to seeking out network specialist or management training. In this sample

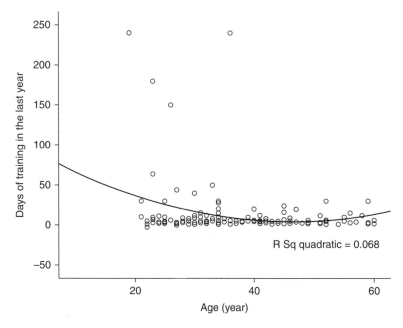

Figure 7.2   Relationships between age and amount of formal training in the prior year

younger workers received more 'product and sales-related' training but not other forms of training. Gender (coded as '1' for male, '2' for female) in this sample was unrelated to the types of training being pursued. The type of job held by workers was not correlated with type of training reported in the past year. However, workers who identified themselves as performing jobs that are IT-related (in question 31, coded '1' for IT and '0' for non-IT) reported more product and sales-related training than non-IT workers, $r(83) = .23$, $p < .05$, but did not differ from non-IT workers on other forms of training. Management status (coded 1 for management and 0 for non-management based on item 6) was related to having had product and sales-related training, $r(97) = -.30$, $p < .01$ and network-specialist training, $r(83) = -.23$, $p < .05$, in the past year. Those who reported supervising other workers had less product and sales-related training and network specialist training, but the groups did not significantly differ in the amount of management training. However, those who supervised more workers did have more management training, $r(52) = .36$, $p < .01$. A 2 (age: 40 and younger/above 40) × 2 (gender: male/female) × 2 (management status: management/non-management) × 2 (work type: IT/non-IT) MANOVA revealed no interactions between the variables in predicting any of the three training factors.

In accordance with our initial hypotheses about career progression and training, management status was negatively associated with having received IT training reflected by the network specialization and product and sales factor scores. However, contrary to our hypotheses, those in management did not have significantly more management training.

Reasons For Not Training

For the majority of workers who reported no formal training in the past year, analyses revealed that age correlated with low self-efficacy, $r(268) = .15$, $p < .01$, but none of the other three factor scores representing reasons for why workers did not seek out training in the last year. Older adults were more likely to decline (or not be offered) training because of lack of confidence. Age was not related to forgoing training because it was perceived as unnecessary, unavailable, or precluded by time constraints. Apparently older and younger adults in this sample do not avail themselves of training or are not offered training for similar reasons.

Gender, on the other hand, did predict reasons for declining training as it correlated weakly with the training unnecessary factor, $r(271) = -.15$, $p < .05$. Males tended to decline training opportunities in part because they considered them unnecessary. IT workers differed from non-IT workers in that they were more likely to decline training because they considered it unavailable, $r(259) = .19$, $p < .01$. Managerial status correlated weakly

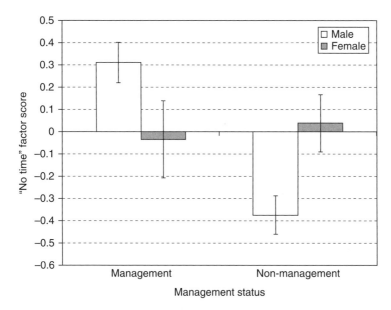

Figure 7.3   *Management by gender interaction for training factor of 'no time for training'*

with component scores representing unnecessary, r (294) = .12, p < .05, unavailable, r (294) = −.17, p < .01, and no time for training, r (294) = .21, p < .01. Non-management employees were more likely to consider training unavailable, while those in management positions were more likely to decline training because they considered it unnecessary or lacked time.

To examine the joint relationships among status variables, we also performed ANOVAs. A 2 (management status: manager/non-manager) × 2 (work type: IT/non-IT) × 2 (age group: 40 and younger/above 40) × 2 (gender: male/female) MANOVA revealed a four-way interaction in predicting factor scores on unavailable, $F(1, 233)$ = 4.13, MSE = .875, p < .05, and low self-efficacy, $F(233)$ = 4.94 , p < .05. However, a low number of IT workers in some cells (often fewer than five) led us to exclude work type as a factor. The resulting 2 (management status: manager/non-manager) × 2 (age group: 40 and younger/above 40) × 2 (gender: male/female) MANOVA revealed an interaction between management status and gender in predicting the 'no time for training' factor score, F (1, 262) = 9.11, MSE = .716, p < .01. As can be seen in Figure 7.3, while management status did not affect how much women reported not having time for training, men in management reported having no time for training and men in non-management positions did not report having no time.

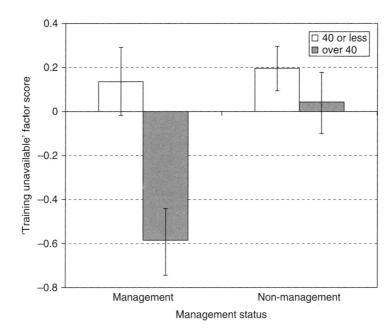

Figure 7.4   Management by age interaction for factor 'training unavailable'

Management status also interacted with age in predicting to what extent workers perceived training as unavailable, $F(1, 262) = 4.05$, $MSE = .904$, $p < .05$. As seen in Figure 7.4, workers under the age of 40 reported similar levels of perceiving training as unavailable, regardless of whether or not they were in management, while workers over 40 in management positions did not consider training unavailable relative to the other groups. The three-way MANOVA did not reveal any three-way interaction between management, age group, and gender, as the previous four-way may have portended. This is likely because an additional 29 participants were included in the three-way analysis for having answered every necessary item except for work-type.

Employer Support for those Reporting Training

In this sample, age was not related to the degree to which employees perceived employers as providing opportunities for training. Employers did not provide more direct (paid) or indirect (other) support for older versus younger adults. Nor did gender influence the degree to which employees believed they were receiving employer support. However, IT workers

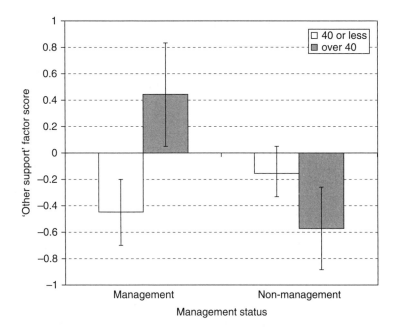

Figure 7.5   Management by age interaction for factor 'other resources'

reported more paid support, r (88) =.21, p <.05, than non-IT workers, and those in management positions reported more paid support than non-management workers, r (103) = .30, p < .01. A 2 (management status: manager/non-manager) × 2 (work type: IT/non-IT) × 2 (age group: 40 and younger/above 40) × 2 (gender: male/female) MANOVA revealed an interaction between age group and management status in predicting scores on the other resources support factor score, $F(1, 69) = 4.82$, $MSE = .964$, $p < .05$.

As seen in Figure 7.5, whereas non-management workers tended not to differ in how much non-paid support for training was reported, management employees over age 40 tended to report more compensation than those under 40 in the form of non-paid support. Thus managers over the age of 40 perceive more support for training (training available, other support available) than managers under age 40.

Perceived Benefits of Training

The WANE data also queried respondents about the extent to which they were making use of the training they had acquired over the past year. Responses to this item did not correlate with age, gender, or work type.

However, those in management were slightly more likely to report using the skills they had attained in formal training, r (105) = .21, p < .05. A 2 (age: 40 and under/above 40) × 2 (gender: male/female) × 2 (work type: IT/non-IT) × 2 (management status: manager/non-manager) ANOVA revealed no interactions between these variables.

CONCLUSIONS

In this sample of IT firms, age was not a significant predictor of experiencing formal training in the past year. The failure to find an age effect on whether such training was received in the past year may be due to differences between the IT industry and other industries, or to a lack of power to find a small (r < .20) effect with this moderate-sized sample. However, for those reporting training, on the dimension of intensity of training – number of days reported – age was a significant, though weak, negative predictor (r = −.21) at a value somewhat higher that that reported in prior studies of participation in work-related developmental activities.

There are a number of plausible reasons for this discrepancy between training at all (no age effect) versus training amount (negative age effect). First, very young IT workers may in some cases be fresh out of university and report estimates of days of training that include their last formal classes. Note that a few young adults report very high amounts of training (see Figure 7.1) and they may be the outliers responsible for showing a training intensity relation to age. Consistent with this interpretation is the finding of a significant quadratic trend with age. The bivariate correlation becomes non-significant, r = −.04, when selecting only workers above age 30, suggesting that very young adults drive the intensity–age relationship. Second, it may be the case that although training, both formal and informal, is seen as necessary by firms and by workers in the IT industry, there remains a bias against providing intensive training to older employees or a bias among older workers against accepting training that is offered to them.

The examination of factor scores allowed a more in-depth explication of these findings. When training is factor analysed into categories such as network and hardware, product and sales, and management-related, age was moderately negatively related (r = −.28) to products and sales training, implying that older workers were less likely to experience that type of training than younger ones.

Further the role that a worker plays is also a significant predictor of type of training. Workers who identified themselves as performing IT-related jobs reported more product and sales training than those not directly involved in IT. Those reporting supervision of more workers also had

more management training. Such findings are consistent with a career progression explanation that training is offered (and accepted) to suit current
needs and that workers progress in an age-normative fashion from line to
managerial work.

One benefit of the WANE question set is that it sought some of the
reasons for not participating in formal training. Recall that 74 percent of
the sample did not report any formal training in the prior year. Here age
was a modest predictor. For those reporting no training, age was modestly
($r = .15$) related to the low self-efficacy factor score, indicating that lack
of confidence may play a role in whether training is sought or accepted by
older workers. This finding implies that effective training programs need
to attend to building confidence about the efficacy of training particularly
for older employees.

We also observed a gender effect for the factor of 'training unnecessary' with men slightly more likely to give that reason for not taking part
in formal training. IT workers, compared to non-IT ones, were more
likely to cite the reason for not training as being training was unavailable.
However, both of these tendencies showed interactions with other factors.
Women, perhaps surprisingly given that they are more likely to suffer from
time constraints, showed little variation in perceiving 'no time' as a reason
for not engaging in training. Men in management, conversely, were more
likely to endorse that reason for why they did not train. The age and management status interaction further revealed that older managers were the
least likely to perceive training to be unavailable.

We also were able to delve into the perceptions of types of support for
training, the factors we termed paid and other (indirect) support. The
age by management interaction we observed revealed that older managers reported more other support than both managers and non-managers
under 40.

Finally, managers were slightly more likely to report that they used the
skills from formal training. In short, management has its benefits when it
comes to access to and support for formal training, and this may be particularly true for older managers. The perception that there is inadequate
time for training may simply reflect our sampling of small firms. Recall
that managers in many cases were the owners of the firms and had to
juggle training opportunities with their management responsibilities in a
highly competitive and stressful industry.

Caveats

Because of the nature of sampling, emphasizing very small and small
firms, it is possible that our results would not generalize to large IT firms.

For instance, formal training appears to be offered more by larger than smaller firms (Black et al., 1999; Chaykowski and Slotsve, 2003). Further, the relatively high non-response rates in some regions preclude drawing strong conclusions about differences among regions for formal training and perceptions about training. Finally, the questionnaire items that we analysed emphasized formal training rather than informal training, so we do not have a complete view of skill development activities.

Given the increasingly prevalent view of workers as entrepreneurs within a firm, it seems likely that much of the training and education that workers engage in is informally organized or self-organized. This may be due to several factors. IT firms may be in such highly competitive situations that they are forced to emphasize current performance over future development and this tendency to be focused on immediate performance may be exacerbated in firms with smaller resource bases. Those in cutting edge businesses may also be the ones developing the tools and procedures that will eventually be codified into formal instructional programs, so formal training opportunities are simply unavailable.

REFERENCES

Anonymous (1990), 'What we do and don't know about training in the workplace', *Monthly Labor Review*, **113**, 36–8.

Belbin, E. and R.M. Belbin (1972), *Problems in Adult Retraining*, London: Heinemann.

Birdi, K., C. Allan and P. Warr (1997), 'Correlates and perceived outcomes of 4 types of employee development activity', *Journal of Applied Psychology*, **82**, 845–57.

Black, D.A., B.J. Nowel and Z. Wang (1999), 'On-the-job training, establishment size, and firm size: evidence for economies of scale in the production of human capital', *Southern Economic Journal*, **66**, 82–100.

Brooke, L. (2003), 'Human resource costs and benefits of maintaining a mature-age workforce', *International Journal of Manpower*, **24**, 260–83.

Cappelli, P. (2003), 'Career jobs are dead', in O.S. Mitchell, D.S. Blitzstein, M. Gordon and J.F. Mazo (eds), *Benefits for the Workplace of the Future*, Philadelphia, PA: University of Pennsylvania Press, pp. 203–225.

Charness, N. (2008), 'Technology as multiplier effect for an aging work force', in K.W. Schaie and R. Abeles (eds), *Social Structures and Aging Individuals: Continuing Challenges*, New York: Springer, pp. 167–92.

Charness, N. and S.J. Czaja (2006), *Older Worker Training: What we Know and Don't Know*, American Association of Retired Persons (AARP) Public Policy Institute, Pub ID: 2006-22, Washington, DC: AARP, accessed 20 February at www.aarp.org/research/work/issues/2006_22_worker.html.

Chaykowski, R. and G. Slotsve (2003), 'Employer-sponsored training by firm size', Skills Research Initiative, Human Resources and Skills Development Canada working paper B02, Social Sciences and Humanities Research Council of Canada, Ottawa.

Cleveland, J.N. and L.M. Shore (1992), 'Self- and supervisory perspectives on age and work attitudes and performance', *Psychology and Aging*, **77**, 469–84.

Diamond, A.M., Jr. (1986), 'The life-cycle research productivity of mathematicians and scientists', *Journal of Gerontology*, **41**, 520–25.

Ekerdt, D.J. (2008), 'No career for you. Is that a good or bad thing?', in K.W. Schaie and R. Abeles (eds), *Social Structures and Aging Individuals: Continuing Challenges*, New York: Springer, pp. 193–211.

Elman, C. and A.M. O'Rand (2002), 'Perceived job insecurity and entry into work-related education and training among adult workers', *Social Science Research*, **31**, 49–76.

Ericsson, K.A., N. Charness, P. Feltovich and R. Hoffman (eds) (2006), *Cambridge Handbook of Expertise and Expert Performance*, Cambridge: Cambridge University Press.

Finkelstein, L.M., M.J. Burke and N.S. Raju (1995), 'Age discrimination in simulated employment contexts: an integrative analysis', *Journal of Applied Psychology*, **80**, 652–63.

Frazis, H.J. and J.R. Spletzer (2005), 'Worker training: what we've learned from the NLSY79', *Monthly Labor Review*, **128**, 48–58.

Gordon, R.A. and R.D. Arvey (2004), 'Age bias in laboratory and field settings: a meta-analytic investigation', *Journal of Applied Psychology*, **34**, 468–92.

Harchaoui, T.M., F. Tarkhani, C. Jackson and P. Armstrong (2002), 'Information technology and economic growth in Canada and the US', *Monthly Labor Review*, **125**, 3–12.

Hess, T.M. and J.T. Hinson (2006), 'Age-related variation in the influences of aging stereotypes on memory in adulthood', *Psychology and Aging*, **21**, 621–25.

Jacoby, S.M. (2003), 'Are career jobs headed for extinction?', in O.S. Mitchell, D.S. Blitzstein, M. Gordon, and J.F. Mazo (eds), *Benefits for the Workplace of the Future*, Philadelphia, PA: University of Pennsylvania Press, pp. 178–202.

Jorgenson, D.W., M.S. Ho and K.J. Stiroh (2004), 'Will the US productivity resurgence continue?', *Current Issues in Economics and Finance*, **10**, 1–7, accessed 15 July, 2007 at www.ny.frb.org/research/current_issues/ci10-13.pdf.

Jovic, E., J.A. McMullin and T. Duerden Comeau (forthcoming) 'Appendix A methods', in J.A. McMullin (ed.), *Working in Information Technology Firms: Intersections of Gender and Age*, Kelowna, BC: University of British Columbia Press.

Kite, M.E., G.D. Stockdale, B.E. Whitley, Jr. and B.T. Johnson (2005), 'Attitudes toward younger and older adults: an updated meta-analytic review', *Journal of Social Issues*, **61**, 241–66.

Kubeck, J.E., N.D. Delp, T.K. Haslett and M.A. McDaniel (1996), 'Does job-related training performance decline with age?', *Psychology and Aging*, **11**, 92–107.

Lohr, S. (2007), 'IBM plan ties training and accounts', *New York Times*, 25 July, accessed at http://news.com.com/IBM+plan+ties+training+and+accounts/2100-1022_3-6198716.html.

Marshall, V.W. (1998), 'Commentary: the older worker and organizational restructuring: beyond systems theory', in K.W. Schaie and C. Schooler (eds), *Impact of Work on Older Adults*, New York: Springer, pp. 195–206.

Maurer, T., M. Weiss and F. Barbeite (2003), 'A model of involvement in work-related learning and development activity: the effects of individual, situational, motivational and age variables', *Journal of Applied Psychology*, **88**, 707–24.

McEvoy, G.M. and W.F. Cascio (1989), 'Cumulative evidence of the relationship between employee age and job performance', *Journal of Applied Psychology*, **74**, 11–17.

Noe, R.A. and S.L. Wilk (1993), 'Investigation of the factors that influence employees' participation in developmental activities', *Journal of Applied Psychology*, **78**, 291–302.

Organisation for Economic Co-operation and Development (OECD) (2003), *ICT and Economic Growth: Evidence from OECD Countries, Industries and Firms*, Paris: OECD.

Roring, R.W. and N. Charness (2007), 'A multilevel model analysis of expertise in chess across the lifespan', *Psychology and Aging*, **22**, 291–99.

Simonton, D.K. (1988), 'Age and outstanding achievement: what do we know after a century of research?', *Psychological Bulletin*, **104**, 251–67.

Simonton, D.K. (1997), 'Creative productivity: a predictive and explanatory model of career trajectories and landmarks', *Psychological Review*, **104**, 66–89.

Sparrow, P.R. and D.R. Davies (1988), 'Effects of age, tenure, training, and job complexity on technical performance', *Psychology and Aging*, **3**, 307–14.

Sturman, M.C. (2004), 'Searching for the inverted u-shaped relationship between time and performance: meta-analyses of the experience/performance, tenure/performance, and age/performance relationships', *Journal of Management*, **29**, 609–40.

Tang, J. and C. MacLeod (2006), 'Labour force ageing and productivity performance in Canada', *Canadian Journal of Economics*, **39**, 582–603.

Waldman, D.A. and B.J. Avolio (1986), 'A meta-analysis of age differences in job performance', *Journal of Applied Psychology*, **71**, 33–8.

8. The structure of IT work and its effect on worker health: job stress and burnout across the life course

Kim M. Shuey and Heather Spiegel

The Information technology (IT) industry is a key player in what Manuel Castells (2000) describes as an emerging 'network society' within today's New Economy – an economy characterized by a number of trends, including rapid growth in the service and technology sectors and an 'accelerated pace of technological and scientific advance as well as equally rapid obsolescence' (Powell and Snellman, 2004: 201). Compared to businesses in previous decades, today's firms face more intense worldwide competition, leading to greater pressure to increase productivity and reduce costs through means such as labor market flexibility. Firms in high-wage economies, such as information technology, face additional pressures to adapt in ways that allow them to more easily absorb their high wage costs, accomplished through strategies such as the development of niche markets and work intensification to increase productivity (Taplin and Winterton, 2002). The demand for flexibility is in part responsible for the disappearance of the 'life-long career' and the era of long-term employment contracts and mutual commitments between employer and worker. Accompanying a focus on increased flexibility, ideas of permanency have given way to a rise in non-standard work arrangements and a labor market in which employees are faced with greater uncertainty and insecurity, along with a decreased ability to control their own working lives and plan for the future (Brown, 1997; Carnoy, 2000; Korczyk, 2001). As a result of these broader economic changes, risks that were once borne by employers are increasingly shifted to workers (Beck, 2002). In today's economy, individual workers and their families are being saddled with greater responsibility for managing growing labor market risks brought about by changes such as the downward pressure on wages and occupational pension systems, the rise of job insecurity, and an accelerated pace of technological advance (Carnoy, 2000; Phillipson, 2006; Powell and Snellman, 2004; Shuey and O'Rand, 2004).

As earlier chapters in this volume have demonstrated, understanding the complexities associated with working in the new economy requires that our investigations consider not only broader labor market change, but also how these macro-level processes and their associated practices affect the situation of individuals within their work environments. One particularly salient aspect of work for individual lives is its effect on health and well-being. Despite a large body of literature on the relationship between paid work and health, relatively little is known about how macro-level pressures that are transforming the nature of work in today's economy affect job-related stress. For individual workers, industry and occupational requirements translate into larger workloads, uncertainty regarding job security and continuity, and increased work–home interference – all of which are associated with higher amounts of job-related stress. Research suggests that as a result of these workplace practices, an increasing number of workers are experiencing job-related stress and stress-related health problems (Mansell et al., 2006).

Overall, more research is required in order to understand the ways in which industry and workplace practices affect worker well-being. This chapter will address this issue by examining the ways in which economic changes, and subsequent organizational practices associated with the new economy, have social implications that affect individuals' lives through the creation of workplace stress. Our analysis draws on data from qualitative semi-structured interviews with 343 IT respondents from 40 small and mid-sized firms in four countries. This is supplemented with quantitative data collected from employees of these firms via web-based surveys ($n = 403$). Findings from our study are presented below, situated within the context of existing research.

The life course perspective provides a conceptual framework within which we can analyse the complex relationships between individual lives and the new economic realities reflected in today's workplace practices. Several themes reflecting basic life course concepts and principles have emerged over the course of this analysis. Our findings speak to the ways in which life course transitions, linked lives, and age-associated roles and status positions (Elder, 1995) influence the effect that the structure of work in the New Economy has on individual experiences of job stress. In addition, results also demonstrate the relevance of the life course concept of human agency, which acknowledges the individual choice-making processes that take place within structurally imposed constraints and opportunities (Elder and Johnson, 2003). To begin our analysis we first present a number of emerging themes related to the creation of job stress in a new-economy industry. We discuss the normalcy of stress and burnout among IT workers, aspects of IT work that lead to job stress and burnout, and the pressures that company and industry environments place on individual workers to conform to job demands. We then situate our findings within a life course framework to better understand age-graded variation in the stress associated with the structure of employment in IT.

STRESS AND BURNOUT AS A NORMAL PART OF THE JOB

It's stressful, yeah . . . and it's not just me. I feel it's everyone. Yes, I do.
(5508030, woman, age unknown, IT sales/marketing, US)

Over half (52 percent) of web survey respondents across the study countries said that their current job affected their stress levels. As Table 8.1 shows, this pattern is consistent across the study countries, ranging from 54 percent in the US to 48 percent in England. In addition to high levels of stress, many interviewees discussed burnout, either in relation to themselves or to their colleagues. Burnout was acknowledged by many of the workers as a normal part of the job. Some referred to burnout as the result of working too hard – long work hours coupled with persistent pressure to meet expectations. Burnout was described as 'hitting the wall' – as a 'brutal wake-up call when you just literally don't want to get out of bed in the morning' (1102003, man, late 20s, CEO, Canada). This Canadian CEO referred to this condition as 'classic burn-out' that almost everyone at his

Table 8.1   Measures of stress and health by region (n = 403)

	All countries	Canada (n = 94)	Australia (n = 69)	England (n = 117)	US (n = 124)
Current job affects level of stress?	52.1*	53.2	53.6	47.9	54.4
Current job affects level of anxiety?	22.8	20.2	11.6	29.1	25.2
Current job affects fatigue?	37.0	38.7	41.2	37.6	33.3
Current job affects sleep?	18.6	16.1	20.6	17.9	20.3
Work situation has a negative impact on health?	38.0	27.7	26.0	40.2	50.4

Note: * Percent of respondents who agree with the indicated questions regarding their current job.

company has gone through at one point or another. Another IT executive noted that 'so many people have mentioned burnout that you know it seems to be present' (1112016, man, early 60s, CEO, Canada). Meanwhile, others pointed out that many IT workers are acutely aware of the possibility, and the dangers of burnout – noting that it was important to pace yourself in your work, or risk burnout at an early age, clarifying that an 'early age' meant 30 to 35. As one Canadian respondent described:

> You have people in this field who are incredibly intelligent and resourceful and they're being burnt out going nowhere . . . It's a black hole, taking your energy and your intelligence . . . I've talked to a lot of people in the field and they're all tired.
>
> (CANLFW08K, woman, mid 40s, CEO, Canada)

Workers across the study countries discussed a number of physical and mental health-related concerns stemming from the stress and demands of their work. On average, over one-third (38 percent) of web survey respondents across the study countries said that their work had a negative impact on their health. This negative relationship between work and health varied significantly across the countries, with a higher proportion of US and England respondents (50 percent and 40 percent respectively) reporting the negative effects of work, compared to 28 percent of Canadian and 26 percent of Australian workers (see Table 8.1).

In face-to-face interviews, some workers described physical health concerns that they attributed to their work, such as weight gain resulting from poor eating habits and lack of exercise, headaches, pain and disability. Many talked about the lack of sleep and exhaustion they faced, even dreaming about work. Table 8.1 shows that of web survey respondents across the countries, 37 percent indicated that their current job led to fatigue (ranging from 41 percent in Australia to 33 percent in the US), and 19 percent indicated that it led to sleep problems (ranging from 21 percent in Australia to 16 percent in Canada). One England respondent said, 'It's [work] constantly on my mind, day and night, night and day' (4404253, woman, late 20s, analyst, England). Another discussed the relationship between work and ability to sleep, stating that 'when I go to bed, if the pressure is on, sometimes you've got so many things going through your mind that you can't switch off, you can't go to sleep, even though I've been at home for a couple of hours and not thought about it at all, it's when you get into bed' (4402094, woman, early 40s, programmer, England). A few people also mentioned waking up in the middle of the night because work was on their minds – and proceeding to get up and send e-mails or do some other work-related task. Some talked about 'crashing' after working particularly hard, or sleeping for 12 hours at a time on weekends.

Meanwhile, workers also described the effects of work on their mental health, which included work-related symptoms of sadness and depression. Nearly one-quarter (23 percent) of respondents across the countries stated that their current job led to anxiety – a number that ranged from a high of 29 percent in England to a low of 12 percent in Australia (see Table 8.1). In face-to-face interviews, one worker described how he had a breakdown, was off work for weeks and was currently on anti-depressants and receiving counseling as a result of pressures at work. Another referred to previous employment for an IT company as leaving her clinically depressed, referring to her job as 'designed to destroy your self esteem completely' (4405062, woman, late 20s, technical writer, England). A third respondent, employed as a customer services manager, described the environment at a previous employer as follows, noting, however, that this was 'an unusually horrible environment to work in':

> we found the stress levels at the organization were so high that we had an actual suicide, an attempted suicide, and one person removed from the office with a straightjacket on, and another person who suffered a heart attack.
>
> (4407006, woman, late 30s, manager, England)

Overall, the data presented above suggest that work-related stress and burnout are a normal part of the employment experience in IT with implications for the mental and physical health of workers.

THE STRUCTURE OF IT WORK AND THE CREATION OF STRESS AND BURNOUT

Understanding the complexities of work in the New Economy requires that we examine how individual lives are affected by broader labor market forces and organizational practices. Thus, in this section we turn to a consideration of the structural factors that have emerged from our data as contributing to high levels of stress and burnout among IT workers. We begin with results related to the heavy work demands in IT, and individual-, company-, and industry-level pressures to conform to these demands. In the section to follow we situate our findings within a life course framework, which facilitates our understanding of the effect of work conditions on stress as workers' age. Next we present results that demonstrate the effect that the pressure to keep skills current in a rapidly changing industry has on worker stress and burnout. We end the section with a discussion of findings that illustrate the influence of life course context on skill-related stress.

The Pace of Work and Work Overload

> It was great the first year . . . I could go a hundred miles an hour. Second year I think I slowed down a little bit. The third year is when it . . . affected me physically and I think I had burnout . . . as soon as I left that job I got pneumonia . . . I got physically sick . . . and then I went into a depression when I left. It was like . . . I'd worked so hard and for so long that I didn't realize what it did to me.
>
> (5508186, woman, mid 40s, manager, US)

One organizational consequence of macro-level labor market trends is changing expectations regarding employee workload and pace of work. Research suggests that today's workers are spending more hours at the office and are more likely to take additional work home than in the past. Pressures on employees to work longer and harder are in part the result of an increase in quantitative workload, or in other words, an increase in the amount of work required and a reduction in the time frame in which it must be completed (Blyton and Dastmalchian, 2006). Having to work under time pressure to meet deadlines is a major source of quantitative overload for workers (Cooper et al., 2001). Research shows a growing proportion of North American and European workers reporting that they 'mostly' or 'always' work 'under a great deal of pressure,' and that their job involves 'working at high speed' or 'working to meet tight deadlines' (Blyton and Dastmalchian, 2006).

On the whole, excessive workplace demands resulting from work intensification have negative mental and physical health consequences (Barnett and Brennan, 1995; Janssen et al., 1999; Wichert, 2002). In terms of physical health, individuals who work excessive hours show more symptoms of ill health than their co-workers who work fewer hours (Cooper et al., 2001). Work overload is related to high levels of anxiety and depression (Cooper et al., 2001), as well as difficulties initiating sleep, maintaining sleep and achieving restorative sleep (Knudsen et al., 2007). Additionally, high job demands and high levels of pressure are associated with psychological strain and job dissatisfaction, as well as an increased incidence of cardiovascular disease (Mansell et al., 2006). In sum, existing research suggests that today's workers face pressure to work longer and harder than in the past, and that the strains associated with being overworked have consistently negative behavioral, psychological, and physiological outcomes (Harvey et al., 2003).

Consistent with previous research, the IT workers in our study acknowledged that long hours were a routine part of the job. Workers, particularly programmers, pointed out that it was normal to work very long days, and even pull 'all-nighters.' Some even reported keeping futons and air mattresses in their offices for periods when they were working day and night on important projects. They noted that in IT, the work day never really ended:

> I used to do lots of twenty-four-hour and twenty-hour-plus days . . . You figure you just stay up, you can get it done . . . I used to get so tired of getting over-night parking tickets.
>
> (1108029, man, early 50s, technician, Canada)

The workday continued into the night, with workers awaking from sleep to attend to work-related tasks:

> I was working from maybe about nine in the morning straight through 'til about one or two in the morning. And I would wake up in the middle of the night at around three or four, like I would be reminded of things in the middle of my sleep. And I would get up and e-mail whoever to give them instructions, things I had forgotten.
>
> (1112055, man, late teens, programmer, Canada)

Beyond putting in long hours at the office, workers reported the negative effects of feeling like they were always on call. Many provided examples of the frequency with which they are consulted throughout the course of the day and night, with one worker indicating that his cell phone rings between 30 and 50 times a day. He also described the feeling this created for him as a sense that '. . . you've got to be on your game all the time, you don't have any time to *not* be. And it's just . . . everyone has access to you 24 hours a day, seven days a week' (1110016, man, age unknown, manager, Canada). Another talked about feeling like she was always on call because she needed to be right there for the company if anything ever went wrong. As described by one Canadian administrator, this 24 hour access is stressful and makes it difficult for IT workers to make any plans or to relax:

> It's difficult making plans to do something. You know, to go on vacation or do those sorts of things because you don't know what's coming . . . and that's more the stress that I don't like, always having to be available . . . I don't want to have to be available all the time, and that's the biggest problem I guess. That's the stressful part.
>
> (1109042, woman, early 40s, administrator, Canada)

Although it appears that many IT workers who remain in the industry strive to meet the demands of their job, our data suggest that a sizeable proportion are not happy with their workload and the pace of their work. Of the workers who responded to the web survey, 42 percent said they would like to reduce the number of hours they worked. Of those, over one-third wanted to reduce their hours because of work-related stress. Nearly half of workers (46 percent) agreed or strongly agreed with the statement that there was not enough time to get their required work done. Over half (52 percent) reported that they most or all of the time worked to tight deadlines, and to meet those deadlines, 40 percent reported that they worked very quickly most or all of the time. In sum, our findings confirm that for many IT workers, there is no way to escape the demands of work. Long hours in the office and 24-hour access means the blurring of boundaries between work and home life, and an inability to relax or make plans for the future. Many feel pressured to work very quickly and to meet tight deadlines. Overall, these work conditions are a routine part of work in IT and create a great deal of stress for workers.

Structural factors promoting work overload

Previous research suggests that a combination of individual and organizational pressures explain why many workers conform to the long hours and fast pace of work in IT. For some workers, it may reflect a particular attachment to work or a desire to show commitment and to prove themselves, thereby improving job security or chances for advancement (Blyton and Dastmalchian, 2006). For others, it may reflect a pressure to conform to an organizational culture where long hours and overloaded schedules are viewed as a badge of honor that symbolizes economic and social success (Roxburgh, 2004). This is particularly evident in the software industry, where workers often compete over the number of hours spent working in the office (Fraser, 2001). Below we discuss relevant findings from our research related to individual-, company-, and industry-wide pressures on the length and pace of work and the subsequent job stress and burnout experienced by IT workers.

Individual Pressures

The workers interviewed in our study confirmed the perception that career advancement and success in IT is related to a willingness to work long hours. Our data show that adherence to these industry-wide norms for success are enforced both by internal and external pressures. One US informant mentioned that workers who did not conform to the 24-hour schedule of the industry were not successful. He suggested that peer pressure is one way in which the intensive work ethic in IT is enforced, stating:

> It's not an 8-to-5 industry . . . everything involved here, especially here, is 24 hours, all the time . . . We've seen that most people that have kind of gravitated to wanting to be 8-to-5 type workers haven't been successful. Because either

through the pressures of their peers or through feeling like they're [not] doing their job fully.

(KI11, man, early 30s, CEO, US)

In addition, several of the respondents suggested that self-imposed pressures associated with a desire to finish a particular task contribute to the long hours that people in the industry are willing to work. One Human Resources Manager in England observed that some of his co-workers felt the need to work as long as it takes in order to get the job done, referring to them as 'gladiators' who simply work longer and harder if faced with a problem (4404422, man, late 50s, HR/office manager, England).

Others explained that people in the industry put in long hours because they feel stressed by the amount of work and pressure to complete the work 'no matter what.' One IT Manager in England described working extra hours at home in the evenings in order to 'get myself back on track so I don't have to feel that stress, or feel any of that tension' (4407020, man, late 20s, manager, England). This strategy to relieve job stress by working harder can, however, backfire and have a negative effect on health and personal life. According to a British Office Manager, a co-worker's decision to work longer in order to stay on track at work contributed to her downward health spiral:

> All of a sudden her work started going down. 'Well, that's easy, I know how to cope with this, I'll work longer.' Indeed she did. Her social life started going downhill. . . . work started to go down even more, work harder, it was a vicious circle. She developed ulcers big time, such she had to go into hospital and nearly died.
>
> (4404422, man, late 50s, HR/office manager, England)

Overall, our findings suggest that individual workers internalize cultural ideals within the industry that reinforce the importance of an intensive work ethic for achieving success. Pressure to keep up with heavy workloads generates a 'get it done no matter what' attitude among workers, who work long hours in order to stay on track and avoid the additional stress created by falling behind.

The Role of Companies
Respondents also discussed the role that companies play in establishing the pace and demands of work. Some referred to the importance of the office environment and workplace culture in generating a precedent for long hours. A 'long hours' workplace culture was not viewed positively by some of the respondents. For example, one worker in England reported

that he did not like the atmosphere in the office, stating that 'there was a lot of tension, there was a lot of pressure to do a lot of hard work all the time. The sort of feeling was you'd be asked to do far more than you possibly could . . .' (4404682, man, late 20s, engineer, England). And, as another worker in England pointed out, the long hours required by the company in turn have a negative affect on workplace morale because all the workers are continually exhausted.

In addition, many of the companies included in the study were described as 'product driven companies,' where success is determined by ability to bring products quickly to market. Thus, workers within these companies felt pressure to get things done as quickly as possible in order to get a product out the door and bring in revenue. One manager in the US described the work as follows:

> Oh, it's high pressure. It's pressurized. It's pressurized because things need to get done . . . the pressure is applied externally. Somebody needs to have something done right now. The phone rings and somebody's having a problem, and they need it fixed now.
>
> (5503073, man, mid-40s, manager, US)

Some workers pointed out that the number of hours and the speed at which they work was determined by the promises that their company made to clients. For example, one explained that the company was responsible for the long hours that were required, 'pushing people harder' in order to meet the unreasonable deadlines and commitments they had made to their clients (5504008, man, early 30s, manager, US). Workers described how their company accepted contracts without knowing whether the workers could actually meet the deadlines. Some felt that management was insensitive to the challenges of meeting deadlines, and the difficulties that might be encountered over the course of the project that may make a deadline impossible to meet. They described this lack of understanding from management as stressful:

> Another problem I find is a lot of times, management just doesn't understand that when you get into something it will take longer . . . You get roadblocks as you go, it's like that with anything. But sometimes they don't understand, so when you give them an actual date they expect it to be done by that date regardless, which can be very stressful.
>
> (1104185, woman, mid-20s, programmer, Canada)

In sum, a long-hours organizational culture and the lack of congruence in goals and expectations between employees and managers made the demands of the IT industry even more stressful for workers.

Macro-level Industry Changes

In addition to factors related to company and management structures, workers also identified broader, macro-level industry changes as a source of growing demands on workers in IT. First, historical changes in the industry related to the technology boom and subsequent bust in the early 2000s shifted the relative power of employers and employees. Following the industry collapse, jobs became more scarce, and as a result, employers gained more power over workers. The result for workers was an increase in work demands, and subsequently, greater stress and pressure than existed during the technology boom. One worker in Australia discussed the changes in the power of workers as follows, drawing a parallel between the demands on IT workers following the industry collapse and factory work:

> In the dot com boom days . . . you had a lot of very mediocre people being paid a lot of money and thinking they were very self-important but not actually getting much real work done . . . After it all imploded and there had been all this great publicity about how the IT job market has collapsed, a lot of employers . . . used that to put the pressure back on to employees and treat them very much as, you know, factory worker-style things. You know, just be grateful you've got a job. Work long hours, no overtime, just be grateful.
>
> (2202029, man, early 30s, engineer, Australia)

Meanwhile, a software engineer in the US pointed out that these broader industry changes are positive for employers, but have created more job stress for workers:

> [recent industry changes] have become better for business from a business perspective . . . that is, if I had a business I would be happy because people are working hard. But maybe from an individual perspective, who are not quite used to the stress that goes with it, it's a little tough.
>
> (5502099, male, age unknown, engineer, US)

Additionally, our respondents elaborated on how the pace of work in IT today is related to expectations within the broader industry regarding the immediate need for action – that everything needs to happen very quickly. They noted that the speed up of work within IT is increasing over time. Some referred to the pressures imposed by the industry as being in a pressure cooker, or being on a treadmill:

> you're just never out of the pressure cooker. You know, I get phone calls Saturday night from customers, Sunday mornings from customers . . . constantly. In the old days, well, they'd contact you Monday and that was acceptable. Now for them to be successful everybody's on this treadmill and we've

just kept turning the speed up and up and up and up. I want to just step off to one side.

(1110016, man, age unknown, manager, Canada)

This worker's perception was that the incidence of burnout resulting from these industry pressures will only increase in the future. Similarly, a CEO working in the US observed the following about industry changes and their effect on job-related stress:

> You have a contract due, they didn't fax it anymore. They don't mail it anymore. When they mailed it, you had three or four days and nobody cared. Three, four days you could wait, and it was all right. But today, I e-mailed it an hour ago, I need it in my in-basket right now, and there's something wrong. I've got a virus in my e-mail. Stress is so high. I mean the timeframe for us to resolve a problem has gone from *weeks* to hours.
>
> (K2 ID1, man, age unknown, CEO, US)

He concluded that the biggest issue in IT today is the negative effect that the increase in the pace of work and changing expectations regarding response times has on levels of job stress. He suggested that these broader changes make it more difficult and stressful for workers because 'they just feel so ultimately responsible. I mean . . . it's like they've got monkeys hanging on their back and they feel so responsible. You know, they *have* to fix this' (K2 ID1, man, age unknown, CEO, US).

In sum, our data suggest several forces that encourage conformity to a culture of long hours and fast pace in IT. Workers reported feeling both self-imposed and external pressure from co-workers to put in long hours at the office and to work quickly. Company-level factors, such as a work-intensive culture and management's desire to please customers irrespective of the pressures placed on workers, contribute to the fast pace of work and subsequent job stress for the workers in our study. In addition, changing expectations within the broader IT industry regarding the need for immediate action and problem solving, combined with a reduction in worker power following the industry bust, exert pressure on workers to keep up with the pace of work as well. Although many IT workers (who remain in the industry) conform to these pressures, our data suggest that a result of work overload is a high level of job-related stress for workers resulting from management's establishment of unrealistic deadlines, industry expectations regarding rapid response times, and from the encroachment of work into personal life.

Work Demands and Stress in Life Course Context
Our data demonstrate that the job-related stress generated by the structural demands of work in the IT industry, described above, is not uniform

across workers. The life course perspective provides a number of organizing principles that facilitate a better understanding of this heterogeneity. In this section we discuss emerging themes from our study that highlight the influence of life course transitions on job-related stress. In addition, we present findings highlighting the utility of the life course principle of 'linked lives' for understanding the incompatibility between the demands of IT work and connections and responsibilities to others.

Life Course Transitions and Job Stress
A life course transition represents a discrete change in status and roles that is embedded within a broader trajectory of individual experience over time (Elder, 1995). Transitions have personal and social consequences, and a transition in one life sphere, such as family, has the potential to generate a shift in other life spheres, such as work. Much previous research acknowledges the multiple consequences of a life transition, such as the transition to parenthood, on work life. However, little attention has been given to the effects that such transitions, and the new pressures that they create for workers in a high-demand work environment, have on individual well-being.

In general, the workers in our study acknowledged the influence of age-associated roles and responsibilities on the stress generated by heavy job demands in IT. Many pointed out the relationship between life course transitions related to family and a change in desire and ability to work long hours. Workers discussed how a transition such as the birth of a child forced them to change their priorities and their willingness to conform to the excessive time demands in IT. One worker in the US stated that he 'basically made a commitment when our child was born that I wasn't going to put in the same hours that I did prior to that' (5508117, man, mid-40s, administrative, US). Another software developer described the change in work habits following the transition to parenting as follows:

> I now have two young children and I don't work exactly like I used to. I worked, I literally slept at the office . . . one day a week I never went home. So for four years . . . I would just work through the night. And my wife hated that, but especially now that my daughter, my oldest daughter is five, she knows when dad's not there. And you know, she doesn't like it, and I don't like it so, so I know even for me my tendency is to want to do less of that [working long hours]. I think that's just common, you know, as you start getting families and stuff.
>
> (5504008, man, early 30s, manager, US)

Even temporary transitions into a position of greater responsibility for the care of a family member forces a renegotiation of work, with one worker describing how driving a sister to work forced her to stick to her hours rather than working longer, 50 hour weeks (4402120, woman, late 20s, programmer, England). In the end, our data suggest that the inability to reconcile the changing priorities accompanying the transition to parenthood with the demands of the industry is one reason IT workers decide to leave the industry. For example, according to one US programmer:

> It requires long hours . . . so, a lot of people tend to work in IT until they have families. I would think a lot of bachelors would be in IT because it requires long hours . . . Your priorities do change over time. You get a family and stuff like that. Your focus might change.
>
> (5502060, man, mid-20s, programmer, US)

Most workers who discussed the difficulties of balancing the responsibilities of work and family life agreed that the transition to parenthood compounds work-related stresses. A female IT manager in the US described the resulting worry that she experiences as follows:

> When I started having children it changes your priorities, because work is not number one any longer and you don't have the time to be at work, especially when they're younger and so . . . the stress level, I think, goes up. Because you're always worried about everything that goes on with the kids and then you have to worry about work and being there and having your meetings and being able to produce what you need to do in the time frame.
>
> (5508186, woman, mid 40s, manager, US)

A few workers described the conflict they experienced between work-related responsibilities and family obligations. For example, some pointed to higher levels of stress created by work-related travel for parents of young children compared to those without children. The observations of others suggest that higher levels of stress among older workers is due in part to pressure to keep up with and perform work in the same manner as younger co-workers who face fewer non-work responsibilities. These difficulties are described by an Australian programmer:

> People feel like if you've got a deadline hopefully you try to meet that . . . and the deadline is always too ambitious. Young, single people, they're quite happy to put in the hours, and I feel pressured to put in the hours as well. So, it's quite common.
>
> (2202094, female, early 40s, programmer, Australia)

In sum, our data suggest that life course transitions involving greater responsibilities outside the sphere of work increase the level of job stress for IT workers. The workers in our study indicated that the transition to parenthood highlights the inherent incompatibility between family responsibilities and a job that requires long hours and creates few boundaries between work and home. The transition forced our workers to make choices and redefine their priorities – something that younger workers without family responsibilities did not face. Many of the workers who talked about this tension between work and family noted a decline in their willingness to put in long hours following the transition to parenthood. Both men and women discussed the difficulties and stress that they felt from trying to balance work and family demands. Although their priorities and work patterns changed, the pressures imposed by the structure of work in IT did not, resulting in worry about the ability to continue to meet the requirements of the job.

Linked Lives: Stress and the Incompatibility of IT Work and Relations with Others

The concept of linked lives highlights the interdependence of lives, and the effect that labor market experience can have on an individual's connections to others (Elder, 1995). This concept provides a useful framework for understanding the way in which work demands generate stress. Our data confirm that the demands and pressures of work have a negative affect on the ability to establish and maintain connections to others. Nearly one-quarter of web-survey respondents across the study countries agreed or strongly agreed that their working hours interfered with family responsibilities. A similar proportion of our sample agreed or strongly agreed that their work interfered with their ability to develop or maintain personal relations. In face-to-face interviews, respondents elaborated on the negative effect that work has on relationships with others. For example, one worker explained how work caused him to miss family events, while another described how he returned home from work in a 'stressed state,' and that it often took time to 'wind down' after work – both of which, he acknowledged, had an impact on his relationship with members of his family and family life (4405000A, man, late 30s, product manager, England). Some noted that they try to put family relations first, 'but the pressure doesn't allow us to do so' (4401055, man, early 40s, programmer, England). A few proceeded to give examples of the ways in which the pressures and demands of work place a strain on their relationships with their family members. For example, one Australian programmer described how her husband, also in IT, worked straight through a visit from his parents, who lived outside of the country. Another Australian quality assurance manager explained that his work prevented him from seeing his child for days at a time and had a negative impact on his young son:

> I've been away for up to four weeks on end, coming home at weekends, but you get home late on Friday night, and you either take off on Sunday night or early

on Monday morning. Well that certainly had an impact a couple of years ago when my son was younger. He really missed having me around . . . I would be leaving home at six and getting home at eight so I wouldn't see him for three or four days at a stretch. Apparently his teachers certainly knew that something had changed, and so you don't like to see that sort of impact on your kids.

(2207240, man, late 40s, manager, Australia)

In addition, some explained that the pressures of work completely prevented them from having other hobbies and relationships, even making it difficult to have a pet. One woman in England discussed her situation as something that she would not be able to sustain:

I can't continue like this for a long time . . . I don't have time for any other hobbies . . . just to get my dog out for a walk . . . just to get home in time to get him out. It's very, very intensive. It's not only the amount of work, it's the pressure.

(4404240, woman, mid-30s, sales/marketing, England)

Although only 8 percent of web survey respondents agreed or strongly agreed with the statement that their personal relationships interfere with their ability to get their work done, respondents suggested during face-to-face interviews that additional demands of family and personal life increase stress levels because they sometimes create the need to work ever harder than others in order to meet work obligations. One female graphic designer explained that she found it extremely difficult to catch up on work and meet deadlines after she returned from time off with a sick child. Another talked about working straight through the day without breaks or lunch breaks in order to spend more time with her child; a practice that she acknowledges is not good for her health. A third speculated about how stressful it will be at work when the health of an ill family member, for whom he is partially responsible, declines even further, requiring more of his time and emotional energy (4404682, man, late 20s, engineer, England). One US owner described the interconnectedness of work and obligations to others, and the stress that it generates, as follows:

So, if they bring in even the slightest [problem from home] . . . 'The kid was up until 2 o'clock this morning not sleeping' . . . 'My mother is sick in bed' . . . 'My father just died' . . . if they bring in any of those kinds of things in addition to what they're dealing with [at work], it stresses them. It's a big issue in IT. I mean it's a really big issue in IT. It is at every level, too.

(K2 ID1, man, age unknown, CEO, US)

In sum, findings related to the life course concept of linked lives suggest that the demands of work in IT make if difficult and stressful for workers to develop and maintain relations with others. An inherent incompatibility between heavy work demands in the industry and connections with others outside work generates an increased level of exhaustion, stress, and worry among IT workers. In addition, these negative effects extend beyond workers, affecting the lives of the people with whom they are connected. In general, our results in the previous two sections have demonstrated that examining work within a life course framework helps increase our understanding of age-graded variation in the stress associated with the structure of employment in IT. We turn next to a discussion of a second structural feature of work associated with high levels of stress for IT workers.

The Pressure to Remain Competitive in a Rapidly Changing Industry

In addition to workload changes, job skill requirements have been shifting across all sectors as a result of new technologies. The introduction of new technologies entails automation and consequently a simplification of jobs and general deskilling of the labor force; machines with microprocessors can now be programmed to do many of the routine activities that less-skilled workers used to perform. Concurrently, the increased use of computer systems generates greater demand for highly skilled labor in the form of technical staff who operate and repair equipment, develop and install software, and build and monitor networks – as well as greater demand for the analytical, problem-solving, and communication skills of workers, managers, and other professionals. These employees, known as 'knowledge workers,' require non-routine cognitive skills such as abstract reasoning, problem solving, communication and collaboration (Karoly and Panis, 2004).

Technological advancements also require a continuous process of skill acquisition for all individuals, making 'education and training . . . a continuous process throughout the life course involving training and retraining that continues well past initial entry into the labor market (Karoly and Panis, 2004: xiv). In addition, technological change and globalization are associated with less stable employment relationships, which necessitate life-long learning if employees want to remain employed or transition into more competitive sectors (Karoly and Panis, 2004). For individuals, the introduction of new technologies into the workplace can be extremely stressful. Unless adequate training and preparation are provided for workers, research suggests that individuals experience substantial distress and often feel unable to cope with the innovations (Cooper et al., 2001). In short, the literature suggests that broader economic changes generate industry-wide skill requirements that have ramifications for work-related stress. We next discuss relevant findings from our research.

The pressure generated by the need for constant skill acquisition and updating was a salient part of work for our respondents. Fully 62 percent of web survey respondents said that they felt pressure to continually learn new skills, and nearly a third reported that they worried quite a bit or a great deal about failing to keep their IT knowledge and skills current. Although our workers acknowledged that workers in any profession that is highly affected by technology would feel pressure to stay current and acquire new skills, they felt there was a difference between the continual training that is required in IT and the training requirements of other occupations. In particular, respondents indicated that skills (and by extension, workers) do not retain their market value in IT the way they do in other industries. The lack of a stable knowledge base means that workers face a high degree of uncertainty regarding their future value and qualifications in the industry. For example, as one Canadian analyst remarked:

> In the medical field what a herb does doesn't change overnight. You know, you learn what a herb does and that herb does that for as long as you live. You might find new things that it does in addition to that, but it [is] still with the original thing it does, it still works. So your knowledge is stable and you build on that knowledge, and build on that knowledge and you feel useful and valued as a person. But if you're in IT, you're going to feel everything that you knew doesn't even MATTER anymore.
>
> (1118018, man, early 30s, analyst, Canada)

Another pointed out the differences between working in IT and working as an architect:

> I think that when you study hard to become an architect, and you go out and hang your proverbial shingle, you're an architect for 40 years. Sure materials come and go, you know styles come and go, but the baseline things you believe in are solid. In IT almost none of that is true.
>
> (1115042, woman, mid-30s, other IT, Canada)

Many of the workers acknowledged that one of the unique aspects of IT is that training and upgrading of skills is a never-ending process. One Canadian worker reported that this never-ending cycle of learning makes workers feel like they never get a chance to relax and 'take a breather' (1115042, woman, mid-30s, other IT, Canada). This need to constantly adapt to 'what is currently hot' creates stress and pressure to 'always be on your toes and keep in touch with what's going on around you' (5502099, man, age unknown, engineer, US). According to one Canadian respondent, this pressure to maintain one's value is tiring for workers:

> I'm tired of doing the catch-up. I mean if you do another field your skills just add to your experience level and your value. In this field you have no value. Your value's obsolete very quickly.
>
> (1118018, man, early 30s, analyst, Canada)

In sum, rapid technological change in the IT industry creates pressure on workers to continually update their job skills. IT workers view their situation as unique because their skills, and the knowledge-base in which they are rooted, do not retain their value the way they do in other industries. Insecurity surrounding the value of their skills, and thus their ability to find other employment, creates a great deal of uncertainty for IT workers. The constant need to upgrade and adapt to the latest technology, and the inability to establish and build upon a skill-set that retains its value across the course of one's career is perceived as a salient source of stress.

Skill Acquisition and Stress in Life Course Context
One emerging theme in our data is the relationship between age and skill-associated stress. Some respondents provided an individual-based explanation for this relationship, citing an age-associated decline in individual desire to learn new things:

> I think there's a relationship between age and people's, well, desire maybe. I do know people who don't want to have to keep learning forever. And so I think there is often a relationship between age and wish to sort of lower the pressure and not do new things. Stick to the ideas you already know.
>
> (2202055, man, late 30s, programmer, Australia)

Other workers, however, attribute this relationship to the structure of IT work rather than individual preferences. They suggest that the requirement for continued skill acquisition throughout one's entire career, not just in the early years, is perceived as a drain and a contributor to worker burnout. As one Canadian owner describes:

> To stay in your career track you have to go through the hard part of skills acquisition that the rest of the world does before they're 25, for the most part. And, the people [in IT] have to go through it, you know, in every decade of their life to remain an IT specialist . . . that's a contributor to burnout.
>
> (1105016, man, early 40s, CEO, Canada)

In addition, this quote suggests that the process of skill acquisition may have a cumulative negative effect on levels of stress, with workers growing increasingly tired of the never-ending process of skill upgrading over time. Such a process is more consistent with the life course concept of duration rather than reflecting an age-graded desire for learning, as indicated in the first quote. This life course concept suggests that the length of time spent in a particular role is an important predictor of individual experience. One possible result of this cumulative process is that the stress associated with the need to keep skills current throughout one's career in IT drives older workers out of the industry, and is one potential explanation for why this disproportionately young industry is structured the way it is in terms of age.

Other statements provided by our respondents suggest a recognition that age-graded associations between skill requirements and stress result not from a biological process of aging or age-based preferences, but from additional, and often conflicting, responsibilities associated with life stage. For example, one worker talked about younger workers as 'having all of the time in the world' to learn new things, suggesting that they have no other commitments while 'living at home with mum and dad' (2207383, man, early 30s, manager/programmer, Australia). Another explained that age is related to ability to handle work-related stress, with younger workers more resistant to stress than older workers because they have fewer responsibilities outside of work, such as family obligations:

> Who is the least resistant to stress? I mean, young kids can take stress. You start talking about my technicians . . . when the majority of them are over 45 years old, they have families that they are dealing with. Granted a lot of them have a lot more patience than a 19-year-old . . . but, I mean, they can't take too much stress.
>
> (K2 ID1, man, age unknown, CEO, US)

In sum, the skill-related stress associated with IT work affects workers differently depending on life course position. What appears to some as a relationship between age and a desire to keep skills current instead may be more of a reflection of the duration of time that an individual has spent in a career characterized by a never-ending process of learning and retraining. The cumulative stress created by this aspect of IT work may lead some to leave the industry entirely or to seek positions within IT with fewer training requirements. Overall, as the previous sections discussing work overload and skill acquisition demonstrate, structural features of the IT industry not only contribute to job-related stress and burnout among workers, but also affect individual workers differently based on life course position.

HUMAN AGENCY: STRATEGIES USED TO DEAL WITH STRESS AND THE THREAT OF BURNOUT

The life course perspective recognizes that individuals are not passively acted upon by structural constraints, but instead make choices and act within the constraints of their social circumstances (Elder et al., 2003). Themes emerging from our analysis demonstrating this life course principle of human agency suggest a number of potential strategies used to create workplace structures and experiences in response to the stress created by conditions of work in the New Economy. Results suggest purposeful attempts by employers to organize the workplace in response to the normative, institutionalized demands of the IT industry. They also suggest strategies on the part of employees to control and adapt their work lives in an attempt to reduce levels of stress. Below we discuss results related to the active management of work-related stress by both employers and employees.

Company Strategies – Altering the Work Environment

Across the study firms there was variation in the level of acknowledgment by company owners and managers of the stresses faced by workers. Some owners and managers seemed unconcerned about workplace stress and demands on workers. They attributed stress to individual choice to work too hard without drawing a connection between the structure of the work-place and the experience of individual workers – and as a result they did little to actively manage the demands of work. Meanwhile, the actions of owners and managers in other companies indicated an awareness of limits regarding what could be asked of workers, and a sense that the structure of work needed to be altered in order to prevent worker burnout. Across all of the study countries, data from face-to-face interviews showed that many of the employers who recognized the stress and pressure felt by their workers resulting from the demands of the IT industry were actively involved in managing and altering the work environment.

Owners and managers employed a number of different strategies to alter the work environment in order to reduce worker stress and burnout. Some of these were codified into written company policies designed to enforce limits and accommodate workers' needs, while others were reinforced through their incorporation into the culture of the workplace. One strat-egy that emerged was the placement of limits on workers' hours. Some employers recognized that the high workloads and normatively long hours associated with the IT industry are not sustainable for employees. One Canadian CEO stated that he was against 'people having to work 60 hours, 70 hours a week for months at a time because they're an IT worker . . . I don't buy into that' (1105016, man, early 40s, CEO, Canada). His strategy was to avoid worker burnout by establishing a workplace culture in which his employees were encouraged to work intensively for shorter periods of time – a 'good' eight hours every day, rather than extremely long days. A manager in the US referred to this same strategy as working hard to create an environment in which everybody can 'finish the marathon, not finish the hundred yard dash' (KI#20, man, mid-50s, CEO, US). In England, one manager described how he discouraged his employees from working extra hours because he felt they could not keep up working long, intense days for very long without negative consequence (4405244, man, early 50s, manager, England).

In addition, many managers talked about the importance of allowing workers flexibility in the scheduling of their work day in order to accommodate other life events and responsibilities. One manager discussed the workplace culture in his firm as oriented toward helping workers balance work and family lives, stating, 'if people have got sick children or sick partners or elderly parents or whatever, that's number one and we work around that to help them . . . we try and make it as easy as possible' (2202133, man, mid-40s, owner, Australia). Giving workers control over their hours was discussed by some managers as a conscious strategy that was designed to help reduce workplace stress and burnout. As one manager put it:

> We felt quite strongly that you're not just the person you are while you're in the office, you have a whole life, and that we wished to be more accommodating of people. So what that means is we all choose our own working hours. I told each of them when they joined that as long as they did roughly a certain number of hours a day they could work whenever they wanted. They choose their hours, and that was partially to allow people not to travel in the rush hour and contribute to congestion, to accommodate family arrangements if they have those, and just generally lead a stress-free working life. I think giving people control is what helps reduce the stress that they feel.
> (4407006, woman, late 30s, manager, England)

Another strategy involved attempts to force workers to take time off and to take breaks throughout the course of the workday. In order to avoid a situation where 'you get to the end of the year and people had only taken a quarter of their holiday entitlement . . . [and are] so stressed that they're falling down from exhaustion' (4407006, woman, late 30s, manager, England), some company managers reported actively trying to force workers to take their leave. One company owner gave workers an extra day off each month, while another included in the company handbook the requirement that everyone take 15 minute breaks every few hours.

A final strategy utilized by employers to address workplace stress was to cultivate a fun workplace culture that provided relaxing distractions for workers. In some companies this took the form of organized activities for workers to participate in – for example, one company in England reported having football and badminton clubs and pub crawls. For other employers it meant setting up activities in the workplace for workers to participate in over the course of the day, such as billiards, ping-pong, and fußball tables, pinball machines and video games. Some encouraged their employees to wear casual attire to the office. One manager reported that her company brought in a massage therapist as a preventative measure to proactively enhance workers well-being and to reduce the effects of stress.

Overall, the sense from many of the employers was that the structure and demands of IT work required company-level interventions in order to preserve the mental health of the workers and reduce the incidence of burnout. Owners and managers developed a number of strategies to counteract the stresses associated with work, ranging from giving workers control over their schedule, to creating a workplace culture that encouraged workers to take breaks and to engage in collaborative and social activities. The data demonstrate the role of human agency in the management of workplace stress and the attempts by employers to exert change within the particular limitations imposed by the IT industry.

Individual Strategies – Escaping and Creating Boundaries

In addition to decisions at the managerial level to adapt the workplace to reduce levels of stress, our findings suggests a number of strategies that workers actively engage in to exercise control over the stress levels in their work environment. The first is an attempt to escape the stresses of the current job by constructing a narrative in which the grass is greener elsewhere – in other jobs or positions either within, or outside of the IT industry. Some strive toward achieving the alternate reality that they describe, while others appear to use it as a distraction from the stresses of their current job. First, face-to-face interviews suggested that some workers constructed a narrative that romanticized other positions within IT. Programmers in particular reported that work life and stress levels would be different, and will be different, once they have paid their dues and moved up into a managerial or ownership position. As one worker stated, 'In the end, no one wants to be sitting there and going, yeah, in twenty years I still want to be a programmer. Like I think everyone thinks of it as a lot of people get into it as a stepping stone to get into management' (1114045, man, early 30s, programmer, Canada). This Canadian programmer talked about coming out of university and being assigned 'grunt work,' working hard to climb the company hierarchy – taking on increasingly difficult projects, and experiencing higher levels of stress and pressure – all with the hopes of one day making the transition to management. The implication was that this job shift into a management position is the payoff for many years of hard work and stress. A second programmer confirmed this strategy of discounting current stress and work demands in hopes of achieving a better position in the future. He stated:

I don't see myself as a developer for the rest of my time here. [Interviewer: Where would you like to go?] Some sort of senior-level, management . . . A lot of times I go home just exhausted . . . And that's something that, that's why I don't see myself as a programmer, because I don't want that feeling a lot of the time.

(1116071, man, age unknown, technician, Canada)

The data suggest a disconnect between the programmers' optimism regarding the stress levels in management and the actual reports from managers and owners about the nature of their job. In contrast to the programmers' hope for lower levels of stress and fatigue after transitioning into management, reports from managers refuted the notion that their jobs were any less demanding or stressful. Both company owners and managers reported getting little sleep, and that their job was very stressful on their families, who they acknowledged have made sacrifices in order to keep the business going. One company owner in Australia drew a contrast between owning the company and working for the company:

I've got a lot of grey hair, and I'm 28 and I can say an awful lot of that comes from the pressures of knowing what can go wrong because things aren't as good as they should be, so it added a lot of strain to me. Now in a normal situation where it wasn't my business . . . that probably would not have affected me nearly as much.

(2203068, man, late 20s, network administrator, Australia)

Owners and managers reported that their jobs involve a 'different kind' of stress. Some reported that they have known people in management who have relinquished their managerial roles and gone back to a lower level job because the stress levels were even higher for them as a manager. Consistent with the romanticized perceptions held by programmers discussed above, one company owner suggested that he used to think that coding was the most stressful part of IT. Now that he owns a company, however, his perceptions have changed – in addition to the normal job stress he also worries about the welfare of his employees and the future of the company.

Another strategy used by employees to deal with the stress and demands of their job involves escapism by romanticizing the benefits of working in jobs outside IT and dreaming about leaving the industry. Across the study countries, many workers reported that they contemplated leaving the industry for jobs that they perceived as having fewer demands – jobs that had lower levels of stress or were more enjoyable. For example, one Canadian worker reported a desire to be a FedEx driver. Others romanticized working in other 'low stress' jobs, like driving a Zamboni or the machine that clears snow from sidewalks, or serving coffee and doughnuts at Tim Hortons or Starbucks. Some said they thought about going back to school for training in a new career such as veterinary technician, or holistic health practitioner. As a strategy to 'focus on my family and reduce the stress,' one worker in the US fantasized about doing the following:

> take a little bit of the money we have, go buy a house in full that's, you know, rather modest. Get an easy job and, you know, relax . . . we both [referring to his wife] daydream about doing something like that.
>
> (5501045, man, late 40s, analyst, US)

Some workers referred to this process of fantasizing about leaving the industry as something they would engage in during times when they are experiencing high levels of stress at their current job. One worker in England talked about wanting to leave his job when he gets stressed at work. Another Australian worker described thinking that 'it must be easy just being a gardener, a council gardener attending the parks' (2208032, man, mid-40s, manager, Australia). He described this fantasy as something he engages in as a last resort, at times when he is stressed and having a bad day.

Rather than just daydreaming about better jobs either inside or outside the IT industry, another strategy workers employ is to exit the industry completely. This was presented as something that many workers, particularly older workers who have been in the industry for a long time, want to do. However, as one Canadian worker pointed out, many people cannot get out: 'Everybody I know that's in this field that's older wants to get out. But they can't get out, because they're kind of stuck . . . I want out of this, it's like a demon, you know' (1118018, man, early 30s, analyst, Canada). Across the study countries there were tales of individuals who chose to leave the industry for a job in another field, sometimes as a result of witnessing the negative experiences of a friend or colleague in the industry. For example, as one worker explained:

> I'll just briefly tell you an anecdote that a colleague of mine, who runs another business, told me the other day. One of his programmers, senior programmer very important to his business, was found in one of those bizarre things that you only see on TV. Sitting in his car parked by the side of the road in the middle of nowhere, unable to say who he was or what he was doing there, or what he did for a living or, you know, why he'd had a complete loss of memory incident. I guess you'd call it a breakdown. His colleague on the programming team was so destabilized by the experience of having his counterpart suffer this episode that he decided he could no longer worker in the IT industry and he up and left.
>
> (4405272, man, early 40s, CEO, England)

Respondents spoke almost longingly about knowing individuals who did make the transition out of IT. According to one Canadian worker:

> It's brutal, it's tough. People get out, you know. I know a lot of people, that guy was a web developer, or was a developer, or was a designer, or was a coder. And now they make pizzas . . . farmers and all sorts of things. People just get out. Some people just walk away from it.
>
> (1115060, man, late 20s, analyst, Canada)

Some reported knowing people who left IT for other types of jobs because they offered less stress. Others had colleagues who left with hopes of more job security, or a more fun work environment. Still others knew people who were threatening to leave the industry as a way to deal with the frustration of not feeling that their skills were adequate. For example:

> I've got a good friend who's . . . very disturbed that he suddenly feels like he has no skills at all anymore, absolutely hates the industry, just a culture that he's in, just swears that all they do is deskill people . . . This guy is seriously considering just finding something outside of IT altogether.
>
> (2211032, man, early 30s, programmer, Australia)

Others expressed that they themselves were on the verge of a transition out of IT. Some expressed feeling that they could not tolerate working in IT anymore – that they had been pushed into action. As one respondent told the interviewer:

> You're getting me at a bad time because I'm at a point where I'm done. I don't want to deal with this industry anymore, I've been in it for 20 years, I don't want to deal with it anymore . . . I'm done with computers actually.
>
> (1107081, man, early 40s, programmer, Canada)

Another way that workers dealt with the stresses and demands of the job was by devising strategies that involved resistance to the normative, institutional constraints of the IT industry. These strategies were mainly aimed at preventing work from encroaching into personal life by setting boundaries related to when, and where, they worked. One example from our data comes from an Australian programmer who reported making 'conscious decisions' about the type of company he pursued employment with because he did not like 'working ridiculous hour weeks . . . and the mentality of the company comes first and your life comes second' (2202029, man, early 30s, programmer, Australia). Some workers talked about setting limits on the length of the workday – only working a 9 to 5 schedule, setting an hour beyond which they would not work, or making a point of not working from home. As one worker put it:

> From my point of view I would rather come to work than work at home. I do like that separate life, I like the fact that I work here and I don't work at home.

I very rarely do take work home. I very rarely work at home at the weekend. If I need to work at a weekend, I'll come into the office. Whereas if I had to work from home . . . then you can't switch off. If your computer's there, I don't like the idea that it's always there, and if I'm thinking about stuff from work at home, I might then end up working every evening, and I don't think that's healthy.

(4404370, man, early 30s, manager, England)

And finally, resistance among our workers also took the form of turning off cell phones and computers. One worker in England described making a conscious decision to:

switch my telephone, my mobile phone off, and I shut my laptop down or disconnect from the work network so I can't get an e-mail from work. I think you've got to try pretty hard not to work at the weekends, or to only work on a Sunday evening for an hour or something like that and try and have the weekend as free as you can. And try not to go bonkers, basically.

(4405000A, man, late 30s, manager, England)

In sum, despite the structural demands and constraints of the IT industry, our data suggest that workers engage in a number of strategies that provide some control over the way they perform, or view, their job. Strategies range from mentally escaping the stresses of work by daydreaming about other jobs and planning for a future in another industry, to resisting the normative pressures in IT by creating boundaries that limit the encroachment of work into personal life. Similar to employers, the sense from many of the employees was that the demands of IT work could not be sustained across the life course and required individuals to strategize about how they could preserve their mental and physical health.

SUMMARY AND CONCLUSIONS

Despite a large body of research on the relationship between paid work and health, relatively little is known about how the transformation of employment relations and the changing nature of work in today's labor market affect individual well-being. In this chapter we investigated the creation of job-related stress in a New Economy industry, and examined the demands and stresses of work within a life course context. Findings confirm that structural features of employment in the New Economy related to work intensification and lifelong skill acquisition undermine the health and well-being of workers through the creation of stress and burnout. Our data suggest that stress is perceived as a normative part of working in IT, and that the amount of stress experienced by workers differs based on life course position.

Workers in our study firms confirmed the long hours and high job demands required in the industry. These demands contributed to an inability to escape work and blurred boundaries between work and personal life that left workers feeling unable to relax or plan for the future. A large proportion of our sample of workers were not happy with their workload and the fast pace of their work. Nearly half wanted to reduce the number of hours they worked – many because of the work-related stress they experienced. However, despite workload dissatisfaction, many of the IT workers who remain in the industry strive hard to meet the demands of their jobs. Our findings suggest that individual-, company-, and industry-level factors create pressure for workers to conform to the normative long hours and fast pace of work. Workers felt external pressure from co-workers, as well as self-imposed pressure to meet work demands. Some felt they needed to work hard in order to achieve career advancement. Others felt that they needed to keep up with the pace of their co-workers. And still others worked long and hard because they experienced high levels of stress from the amount of work they had and hoped to get themselves back on track. Company-level factors such as a work-intensive culture and the desire of management to meet the needs of customers created pressure, and stress, for the workers in our study. Expectations within the broader IT industry regarding the need for immediate action and problem solving also created pressure and stress for workers. These expectations, combined with the reduction in worker power following the industry bust, decreased workers' ability to resist work demands for fear of job loss.

A second structural factor of work in IT associated with job-stress is the pressure to keep skills current that is created by rapid technological change within the industry. Two main aspects of this process generate stress for workers. First, training is perceived as a never-ending process. Workers experience the lifelong training and learning required by their job as tiring and stressful. Second, the process creates uncertainty and questions about value and employability within the industry. Workers described IT as different from other occupations, which allow workers to acquire a stable base of skills early on in their career upon which they can build. In contrast to other industries, the skills necessary for work in IT do not provide a foundation of knowledge and do not retain their value. This insecurity surrounding the value of IT workers' skills creates a great deal of uncertainty for workers. Many reported that they worried about failing to keep their knowledge current. In sum, the constant need to upgrade skills, and the inability to establish and build upon a skill-set that retains its value across the course of one's career, is perceived as a source of uncertainty and stress.

A second goal of our analysis was to examine the way in which life course position intersects with the structural features of work that generate stress for workers in a New Economy industry. This is important to consider in light of labor force aging and the desire to retain and retrain older workers. Not surprisingly, one main finding suggests that life course transitions involving greater responsibilities outside work, particularly caregiving responsibilities, increase levels of job-stress. For workers, transitioning to parenthood highlights the incompatibility between the demands of work in IT and family responsibilities. Long hours and lack of boundaries between work and home are viewed as increasingly problematic when combined with parenting. Workers indicated that the transition forced them to make choices and redefine their priorities – something that younger workers without family responsibilities did not face. Some expressed a change in the way in which they viewed, and performed, their job. A primary source of stress for workers faced with such a life course transition was the disconnect between their changing priorities and newly established work patterns, and the unchanging pressures imposed by the structure of work in IT. As a result, workers experienced stress and worry surrounding their continued ability to meet job requirements.

Second, as the life course perspective illustrates, workers' lives are interconnected with the lives and experiences of others. Our findings confirm that the demands of work in IT make it difficult and stressful for workers to build and maintain relations with others outside work. Heavy work demands interfere with personal relationships, reducing the amount of time available to spend with family and friends. The stress generated by work also follows workers home, spilling over into personal relationships and negatively affecting the people to whom workers are connected – partners, children, parents, and friends. The ability to meet work-related demands while also maintaining relationships and responsibilities is a source of stress and worry among the workers that we interviewed.

Third, the pressure to keep skills current affects workers differently depending on life course context. Some of our respondents attributed age-associated burnout and industry exit to the stress involved in keeping skills current. Many recognized that variation in responsibilities outside work affect the level of skill-related stress that workers experience. In addition, our data indicate that the process of skill acquisition has a cumulative negative impact on levels of stress, with workers growing increasingly tired of the never-ending process of learning and retraining over time. Within this context, age serves as a proxy for the duration of time that a worker has been exposed to these industry pressures. Thus, length of time in the industry rather than age may be a stronger predictor of skill-associated burnout and industry exit.

Finally, our results speak to the role of human agency in organizing work environments and work lives in response to the stress created by the normative demands of the IT industry. Both employers and workers attempted to exert change within the particular limitations imposed by the industry. Many employers recognized the negative effect of work demands in IT and the inability of workers to withstand these demands across the life course – and as a result some devised strategies to alter the workplace in order to preserve the mental health of their workers. Purposeful interventions ranged from providing flexible work schedules to creating a workplace culture that encouraged employees to take breaks and to engage in collaborative and social activities. In addition to employers, employees also developed strategies that allowed them to exert control over the encroachment of their job into their personal life. These strategies ranged from resistance through boundary setting, to escapism through romanticizing about jobs in other industries. Setting clear boundaries regarding hours and location of work can be viewed as resistance in light of work obligations in the New Economy – specifically, technological advancements that have extended the ability to continue working while away from the workplace, and norms that reward long hours at the office rather than performance. Both create a situation where a growing number of workers feel forced to work outside normal business hours or take work home with them in an attempt to keep on top of an increasingly heavy workload (Duxbury et al., 2006).

Of interest is the relative lack of findings identifying job insecurity as a source of stress. Previous research suggests that job insecurity is a normative feature of work in the New Economy that leads to decreased levels of psychological well-being (Burchel et al., 2002; Kuhnert et al., 1989; Wichert, 2002). Job insecurity has been referred to as 'one of the single most salient sources of strain for employees' (Cooper et al., 2001: 45). A few of our workers did discuss the lack of stability in IT and concerns about being laid off, while others mentioned that the financial uncertainty of working in IT was a source of stress. In the quantitative portion of our analysis, nearly half of web survey respondents indicated that job security was very important, although less than 10 percent strongly agreed that their job security was good. However, on balance, our workers gave little mention of job insecurity as a source of stress in face-to-face interviews. This, perhaps, reflects the nature of the IT industry, which is unique in that it is structured around a workforce required to embrace industry norms of flexibility and risk, rapid industry change and job turnover. This is an industry that, from its inception, has faced different competitive markets and risks than those historically borne by employers and employees in other sectors, such as manufacturing. Absent in IT is a history of institutions of welfare capitalism, such as unions and human resource departments aimed at sustaining labor stability and worker loyalty. The IT industry is disproportionately staffed by cohorts of workers who began their working lives at a particular point in history, in an industry that from its inception lacked the long-term employment contracts and mutual commitments between employer and worker of previous decades. In sum, in an era and an industry characterized by technological advances that accelerate the speed of production, high rates of turnover, and pressures to remain competitive in global markets, it would not be surprising to find that the demands resulting from work intensification create more stress than job insecurity for cohorts of workers who began their working lives, and choose to stay, in IT.

REFERENCES

Barnett, R.C. and R.T. Brennan (1995), 'The relationship between job experiences and psychological distress: a structural equation approach', *Journal of Organizational Behavior*, **16**, 259–76.

Beck, U. (2002), '*Risk Society: Towards a New Modernity*, London: Sage.

Blyton, P. and A. Dastmalchian (2006), 'Work-life integration and the changing context of work', in P. Blyton, B. Blunson, K. Reed and A. Dastmalchian (eds), *Work-life Integration: International Perspectives on the Balancing of Multiple Roles*, New York: Palgrave Macmillan, pp. 17–27.

Brown, R.K. (ed.) (1997), *The Changing Shape of Work*, New York: Macmillan Press.

Burchell, B., D. Ladipo and F. Wilkinson (eds) (2002), *Job Insecurity and Work Intensification*, London: Routledge.

Carnoy, M. (2000), *Sustaining the New Economy: Work, Family, and Community in the Information Age*, New York: Russell Sage Foundation.

Castells, M. (2000), *The Rise of the Network Society*, 2nd edn, Malden, MA: Blackwell Publishing.

Cooper, C.L., P.J. Drew and M.P. O'Driscoll (2001), *Organizational Stress: A Review and Critique of Theory, Research, and Applications*, Thousand Oaks, CA: Sage Publications.

Duxbury, L., I. Towers, C. Higgins and A. Thomas (2006), 'From 9 to 5 to 24 and 7: how technology redefined the work day', in W.K. Law (ed.), *Information Resources Management: Global Challenges*, Hershey, PA: Idea Group Publishing, pp. 305–32.

Elder, G.H., Jr. (1995), 'The life course paradigm: social change and individual development', in P. Moen, G. Elder, Jr. and K. Luscher (eds), *Examining Lives in Context: Perspectives on the Ecology of Human Development*, Washington, DC: American Psychological Association, pp. 101–39.

Elder, G.H., Jr. and M.K. Johnson (2003), 'The life course and aging: challenges, lessons, and new directions', in R.A. Settersten, Jr. (ed.), *Invitation to the Life Course: Toward New Understandings of Later Life*, Amityville, NY: Baywood, pp. 49–84.

Elder, G.H., Jr., M.K. Johnson and R. Crosnoe (2003), 'The emergence and development of life course theory', in J.T. Mortimer and M.J. Shanahan (eds), *Handbook of the Life Course*, New York: Kluwer Academic/Plenum Publishers, pp. 3–19.

Fraser, J.A. (2001), *White-collar Sweatshop: The Deterioration of Work and its Rewards in Corporate America*, New York: W.W. Norton.

Harvey, S., L. Duncan-Leiper and E.K. Kelloway (2003), 'Trust in management as a buffer of the relationship between overload and strain', *Journal of Occupational Health Psychology*, **8** (4), 306–15.

Janssen, P.P.M., W.B. Schaufeli and I. Houkes (1999), 'Work-related and individual determinants of the three burnout dimensions', *Work and Stress*, **13** (1), 74–86.

Karoly, L.A. and C.W.A. Panis (2004), *'The 21st Century at Work: Forces Shaping the Future Workforce and Workplace in the United States*, Santa Monica, CA: Rand Corporation.

Knudsen, H.K., L.J. Ducharme and P.M. Roman (2007), 'Job stress and poor sleep quality: data from an American sample of full-time workers', *Social Science and Medicine*, **64**, 1997–2007.

Korczyk, S. (2001), 'Risk in employment arrangements', in J.A. Turner (ed.), *Pay at Risk: Compensation and Employment Risk in the United States and Canada*, Kalamazoo, MI: W.E. Upjohn Institute for Employment Research, pp. 53–81.

Kuhnert, K.W., R.R. Sims and M.A. Lahey (1989), 'The relationship between job security and employee health', *Group and Organizational Studies*, **14**, 399–410.

Mansell, A., P. Brough and K. Cole (2006), 'Stable predictors of job satisfaction, psychological strain, and employee retention: an evaluation of organizational change within the New Zealand customs service', *International Journal of Stress Management*, **1** (1), 84–107.

Phillipson, C. (2006), 'Aging and globalization: issues for critical gerontology and political economy', in J. Baars, D. Dannefer, C. Philipson and A. Walker (eds), *Aging, Globalization, and Inequality*, Amityville, NY: Baywood Publishing, pp. 43–58.

Powell, W.W. and K. Snellman (2004), 'The knowledge economy', *Annual Review of Sociology*, **30**, 199–220.

Roxburgh, S. (2004), '"There just aren't enough hours in the day": the mental health consequences of time pressure', *Journal of Health and Social Behavior*, **45** (2), 115–31.

Shuey, K. and A. O'Rand (2004), 'New risks for workers: pensions, labor markets, and gender', *Annual Review of Sociology*, **30**, 453–77.

Taplin, I.M. and J. Winterton (2002), 'Responses to globalized production: restructuring and work re-organization in the clothing industry of high wage countries', in Y. Debrah and I.G. Smith (eds), *Globalization, Employment and the Workplace: Diverse Impacts*, London: Routledge, pp. 259–82.

Wichert, I. (2002), 'Job insecurity and work intensification: the effects on health and well-being', in B. Burchell, D. Ladipo and F. Wilkinson (eds), *Job Insecurity and Work Intensification*, London: Routledge, pp. 92–111.

9. Flexibility/security policies and the labor market trajectories of IT workers

Martin Cooke and Kerry Platman

INTRODUCTION

In recent years public policy thought in Europe, and to a lesser extent in North America, has struggled to cope with two interrelated phenomena. Economic changes including the increase in international flows of goods, capital, and labor have presented problems for promoting the competitiveness of national firms and industry in global markets. The other trend, the demographic aging of the populations in these countries, has caused concern about the potential implications of a smaller and older labor force.

Since the late 1980s, countries have attempted to mobilize labor and increase productivity by changing the structure of social provision. Income replacement programs that absorbed surplus labor in the 1980s have been restructured to reduce their rolls and to encourage work. The precise changes have been very political and country-specific, but in general there has been a focus on 'active' labor market policies and measures to improve labor force flexibility by increasing firms' ability to set the conditions of work. Recently there have been attempts to create a policy framework that balances this flexibility with workers' rights to security and protection. The research program on 'flexicurity' (Wilthagen, 2002; Tros, 2004) and the 'transitional labor markets' (TLM) approach of Günter Schmid (Schmid, 2001, 2006) represent the most well-known of these efforts, which are much better developed in Europe than in the North American welfare states.

Although the flexicurity and TLM projects were not developed primarily to address the aging of populations and labor forces, they may hold some promise in that regard. Linked to the idea of the life course, it has been suggested that increasing the flexibility of transitions into and out of work across working ages might lengthen working life and help to counter slower labor force growth (Policy Research Initiative, 2005). Adult retraining has been long advocated by the Organisation for Economic Co-operation and Development (OECD), which supports 'active aging' and 'life-long learning.' As part of his TLM program, Schmid argues that allowing flexible transitions when people need them, as in the case of working parents with young children, would reduce stress and help to reverse the decades-old trend to early retirement. By encouraging an average of only 30 work hours per week, while extending average working life an extra five years, Schmid claims that lifetime stress and burnout could be reduced and that work could be better balanced with other activities (Schmid, 2001; Schmid and Gazier, 2002). In Canada, the Policy Research Initiative (PRI) has explicitly proposed encouraging flexibility, not only in retirement options but also over the entire life course, to deal with the challenges of a smaller and older workforce (Policy Research Initiative, 2005). In the European Union (EU), a common set of flexicurity principles were agreed upon in December 2007, covering four areas: flexible and reliable contractual relations; comprehensive lifelong learning strategies; effective labor market policies; and modern, adequate and sustainable social protection systems (European Commission, 2007). A central aim of the principles is to help frame national policy options in a way which supports employment transitions:

> The inactive, the unemployed, those in undeclared work, in unstable employment, or at the margins of the labor market need to be provided with better opportunities, economic incentives and supportive measures for easier access to work or stepping-stones to assist progress into stable and legally secure employment. Support should be available to all those in employment to remain employable, progress and manage transitions both in work and between jobs. (Council of the European Union, 2007)

Despite the current popularity of these approaches in policy discussions, there are few examples of how they would work in practice. How, exactly, policies would be formulated to allow flexibility for employers and employees as well as providing sufficient security largely remains to be seen. This is even more the case in the United Kingdom (UK) and North America, where labor markets have historically been less regulated, and employment and income protections less comprehensive than in Europe (Esping-Andersen, 1999). An understanding of current employment careers is critical to identifying the types of programs that might work in this regard and which could lengthen labor force attachment. In particular, we need to understand how employees currently navigate insecure employment, and how policies might be formulated to better provide security. To that end, this chapter uses data from the Workforce Aging in the New Economy (WANE) project to improve our understanding of working careers of employees in one industry that has had considerable instability in recent years, the information technology (IT) industry. We use interview and survey data with IT employees and managers in the UK and Canada, two countries with somewhat similar sets of social and employment policies, to explore the strategies and resources that helped IT workers make key transitions in employment and to maintain their employability in a turbulent industry.

BACKGROUND: FLEXIBILITY/SECURITY AND POPULATION AGING

It has been widely observed that the nature of work in wealthy countries has changed considerably in recent decades. Rapid changes in technology have meant changing skill requirements of employees. Economic globalization and the mobility of capital, goods, and labor have put pressure on firms to be able to compete internationally, and to be able to respond quickly to changes in demand. In this context, countries have sought to reduce the tax burden of social provisions while mobilizing their labor forces and increasing productivity. In countries in which social protection has been historically minimal, it has been fairly easy for governments to further reduce the relative generosity and availability of various types of income replacement. In the Canadian case this has been done by decreasing the length of employment insurance protection after job loss and by removing the universality of social welfare programs, a change which has allowed provinces to impose work tests as a condition of receiving benefits (Evans, 2002). Similarly, the prime focus of initiatives in the UK over the last decade has been to use the social security system to encourage people back into work, moving away from universal benefits and towards means-testing. The UK ranks as one of the least generous spenders on labor market initiatives in the European Union, with expenditure at 0.8 percent of gross domestic product in 2004, compared to about 2.1 percent for the EU-15[1] (European Commission Employment and Social Affairs 2006).

These countries have also undertaken specific measures to address the possible economic effects of demographic aging, thought to include higher public pensions and health care costs and lower tax revenues. The OECD has been particularly active in encouraging member countries to prepare for demographic change by ensuring the solvency of pension plans, but also by creating policies to improve labor force participation in older ages (Organisation for Economic Co-operation and Development, 2000). These have ranged from 'active' policies that assist older workers to find employment, to the restriction of pensions and other routes to retirement and the banning of age discrimination (Cooke, 2006). Not surprisingly, changes to social welfare, pensions, and employment protection have been criticized when they increase the risk for workers and former workers, while increasing the relative power of employers (Maxwell, 1995). However, as Pierson (1994) points out, the policy responses to globalization have been largely dependent on the existing systems of social provision, and few countries have been able to undertake fundamental restructuring (Pierson, 1994). In the northern European countries, which have traditionally had stronger welfare states and employment protection, it has been more difficult to remove these protections and reduce levels of taxation. It is therefore not surprising that it is in these countries that researchers have proposed alternative policy frameworks that would balance employer flexibility with employee security. These are the 'flexicurity' framework proposed by researchers at Tilburg University, and the 'Transitional labor market' (TLM) framework of Günter Schmid.

Flexicurity

The flexicurity framework has been promoted as a pragmatic response to the pressures of globalization and demographic change facing advanced economies. Its starting point is the need for regulatory and legislative mechanisms that foster both a competitive economic environment and social, income and employment protection. Wilthagen (2002) argues that these two goals are not necessarily at odds but trade-offs are usually made between them, which are possibly more detrimental to citizens in times of economic downturns. The flexicurity approach is concerned with four dimensions of security for individuals: job tenure; employment security in the labor market; income protection during spells of unemployment or under-employment; and 'combination' security, the ability or inability to combine paid work with domestic or caring responsibilities. Most recently, the framework has been developed at a series of expert meetings funded by the European Commission to incorporate a set of common principles relevant to the contrasting welfare and labor market systems of the 27 Member States. Principles include a number of flexicurity pathways to which the Social Partners should aspire, and emphasize the importance of lifelong learning and vocational training systems both within and outside organizations. One pathway seeks to embark on 'a higher road towards a knowledge-oriented economy by deepening investment in skills' through improving institutional structures, workplace agreements and government intervention (European Expert Group on Flexicurity 2007: 29).

Transitional Labor Markets (TLMs)

The other widely cited approach to balancing flexibility and security is the TLM framework of Günter Schmid (Schmid and Gazier, 2002; Schmid, 2006) Schmid's approach was originally suggested as a means of promoting full employment and higher labor force participation, especially among women. The main idea behind the TLM approach is that barriers between work and other socially meaningful activities should be more fluid. The problem with traditional unemployment and social insurance plans is that they lead to social exclusion, which TLMs would prevent by promoting flexible transitions between various forms of paid work and care giving, education, disability, full retirement, and between employment and unemployment. These policies would make not only work pay but also self-guided and supported transitions (Schmid and Gazier, 2002).

'Making transitions pay' requires a new set of institutions that would 'flexibly coordinate' these activities. These institutions would be transitional labor markets which, Schmid argues, already exist in a variety of forms in all countries. For example, among media workers and in other artistic fields, social networks help freelance and temporary workers to manage short-term risks (Schmid and Gazier, 2002; Platman, 2004). Another form might be retraining pools in which redundant workers would be paid to retrain while looking for other work. These institutions would help workers deal with the risks of unemployment and promote social inclusion and 'positive' transitions while not reducing the competitiveness of local employers. However, encouraging TLMs throughout the labor market requires that monetary, wage, and financial policies must be better coordinated to stimulate economic productivity, and the thorough reform of social and labor market policy to favor flexibility and transitions (Schmid, 2002). Similarly, Tros (2004) has argued from a flexicurity perspective that, although recent management responses towards older workers have tended to favor early retirement and premature exit, other strategies such as part-time work and flexible retirement could facilitate transitions within and across organizations, and between education, home and the workplace. A fundamental idea behind both TLMs and flexicurity is that they should encourage 'good' transitions rather than ones that limit future possibilities.

This emphasis on improving the quality of transitional employment states throughout working life is predicated on an understanding of life course trajectories of individual workers, which is central to the WANE project. The life course perspective is generally concerned with examining trajectories in interrelated domains, including family, work and education, and health, and the factors that shape them. These factors include social structures, as well as physical and psychological processes, the effects of historical time and place, and connections between individuals, such as links among family members. Critically, the life course focuses on the importance of earlier events as they create the context for subsequent transitions, and for the decisions and actions taken by individuals as they shape their own lives (Elder, 1994; Marshall and Mueller, 2003). A focus on the life course can help direct attention to the sources of various social and economic resources across an individual's lifetime, and their accumulation and depletion. These resources are acquired from markets, communities, families, state and other institutions, and are used by individuals to shape their own lives, given the biographical, social, economic, and political contexts. Flexicurity, TLMs, and other life course sensitive policies would take a more longitudinal approach than traditional social programs in providing protection against social and economic 'risks.' They would recognize that transitions earlier in life affect the resources and opportunities available later, and that the domains of health, the family, and work and education are interrelated. These policies would focus on providing resources for individuals to make transitions and improving labor force participation over their lifetimes, and preventing labor force rigidity.

Despite the interest in the policy directions of flexicurity and TLM and in the life course as a policy research framework, there are few concrete examples of these policies in operation. It largely remains to be seen whether it is possible to really reconcile flexibility for firms with security for workers, and Schmid's TLMs exist more as a set of principles than actually implemented institutions. Furthermore, even if there are some examples of these policies in Europe, they might be impossible to implement in the context of the strong market orientation of liberal welfare states. One way to explore the potential of these policies is to examine the transitions actually made by employees and firms, as well as the resources and policies that currently support these transitions. By better understanding how transitions are currently made, we gain some insight into how policies might better support them and encourage positive outcomes for both workers and firms. In the remainder of this chapter we examine data on information technology (IT) workers' career trajectories from the WANE project (see Chapter 1 for more detail) to explore these questions and to draw some conclusions about the prospects for these policies in Canada and the UK.

RESEARCH QUESTIONS AND METHODOLOGY

The information technology (IT) industry is particularly useful for studying workers' transitions as they relate to flexicurity and TLM. IT is a fluid sector in which both local and global connections are important and in which firms are subject to the pressures for flexibility in workforces and wages. Even relatively small firms often compete in international markets, within their particular IT niches. The industry is characterized by a lack of formal regulations, very low levels of union membership, and a lack of rigid professional entry requirements. This suggests that the IT labor market will be highly responsive to the pressures to shed or to hire workers and that some workers' careers may be characterized by a fairly high degree of instability and risk. As well, the rapid pace of technological change, including a proliferation of qualifications related to particular software products, means that transitions made in order to upgrade skills may be especially important for workers and firms in this industry. This would include transitions between work and formal learning, as well as transitions made between jobs in order to gain additional experience.

We use evidence from the IT industry to provide some insight into the potential for TLM and flexicurity-style programs and policies to provide support to workers and firms across difficult transitions. We do this by investigating the factors that contributed to successful work transitions, including the maintenance of employment, regaining employment, and changing jobs. We are interested in the various resources that appear to have been important in these transitions and the strategies in which they were used, in order to understand the types of policies that might support similar transitions. In other words, we are interested in finding out 'what matters' for successful transitions. We do this by analysing the life course trajectories of older IT workers using data from the WANE study. Although the study collected data from six countries, this chapter is based on a detailed analysis of a study group of 41 men and women, aged 40 and over, in 15 case study companies in Canada and the UK, as detailed in Tables 9.1 and 9.2. These two countries were selected for policy-related and practical reasons. Flexicurity and TLM policy frameworks have attracted growing interest in both Canada and the UK in recent years, although their applicability remains contentious. Second, our aim was to build a picture of individual life courses in the context of the firm, the IT industry and the national labor markets and, being based in Canada and the UK, these were the countries with which we were most familiar.

Although there are some similarities between these two countries, there are, of course, important differences in their IT industries and labor forces. We cannot thoroughly compare them here, nor do our data allow us to identify much in the way of country effects in our analysis. However, note that geography, and the participation in different trading relationships (the EU and the North American Free Trade Agreement) are very likely to result in differences in these countries' IT industries. Although small

Table 9.1   Study group characteristics: Firms

	Canada	UK
Firm size		
Micro (1–4 employees)	2	0
Small (5–49 employees)	7	3
Medium (50–249 employees)	0	3
Firm niche		
Software development and services	5	6
IT consultancy	4	0
Ownership		
Sole or joint owner-manager(s)	8	3
Multiple owner-managers or consortium	1	2
Public company (listed on stock exchange)	0	1
Location		
Business or science park		
In high-tech corridor	1	3
Outside high-tech corridor	1	0
Rural/suburban base close to or within high-tech corridor	2	2
City base within high-tech corridor	5	1
Company founded		
Within last 5 years	1	1
5–10 years ago	5	3
11 years ago or longer	3	3

and medium-sized enterprises predominate in the IT industry in both of these countries, unlike some of the other WANE study countries (Duerden Comeau, 2004), the Canadian industry may have been affected by the importance of several large telecommunications firms in the 1980s and 1990s, while the UK industry may have a more diverse history (de Hoog et al., 2004; Downie et al., 2004).

Our selected study group was limited to workers age 40 and over who had completed both interviews and the survey components of the WANE study. Many of these workers had been in the IT industry through its growth in the 1990s, the downturn of the 2000s, and the subsequent semi-recovery. This study group includes only 'survivors' in IT, by which we mean that those who remained in the industry. Although 40 and older is not generally thought of as 'older,' the young age structure of the IT

Table 9.2   Study group characteristics: individuals

	Canada			UK		
	Male	Female	Total	Male	Female	Total
Age						
40–49	12	5	17	7	3	10
50–59	2	1	3	9	1	10
60–65	0	0	0	1	0	1
Total	14	6	20	17	4	21
Occupational group*						
Entrepreneur or senior executive[a]	5	3	8	7	1	8
Technical manager[b]	2	0	2	5	1	6
Technical professional[c]	6	3	9	3	1	4
IT-related professional[d]	1	0	1	2	1	3
Highest educational level						
Postgraduate degree (Masters or PhD)	3	1	4	5	2	7
Undergraduate degree	5	1	6	8	0	8
College or further education qualification	4	4	8	1	1	2
Secondary school qualification	2	0	2	2	1	3
Other formal qualification	0	0	0	1	0	1
IT certifications						
IT certifications (proprietary or other) in addition to above qualifications	3	4	7	3	1	4
Contractual arrangement						
Full-time permanent	13	4	17	16	4	20
Part-time permanent	0	1	1	1	0	1
Full-time fixed-term contract	1	1	2	0	0	0
Part-time fixed-term contract	0	0	0	0	0	0
Membership of:						
Trade union	0	1	1	0	0	0
Company-based employee association	0	0	0	0	0	0
Professional association	2	0	2	4	0	4

Table 9.2   (continued)

	Canada			UK		
	Male	Female	Total	Male	Female	Total
Income, family & personal background						
Annual individual income						
Under £40 000 GBP [< $79 999 CAD]	7	5	12	4	3	7
£40–59 999 [$80 000– 99 999 CAD]	2	0	2	6	1	7
£60–79 999 [$100 000– 149 999CAD]	1	1	2	4	0	4
£80 000 or over [>$150 000 CAD]	4	0	4	3	0	3
Member of minority group	1	0	1	1	0	1
English as first language	12	6	18	17	4	21
English as second language	2	0	2	0	0	0
Children and/or step-children	11	4	15	14	4	18

Notes:
a.   Chief executive officer, president, owner-manager, managing director, chairman
b.   Director of engineering, IT manager, production manager, IT support manager
c.   Software developer, programmer, analyst, engineer, designer, technician
d.   Staff manager, sales executive, marketing development manager

industry, reflected in the WANE sample, makes this appropriate for our purpose.

It was our desire to roughly balance the Canadian and UK study groups in terms of size and composition. The Canadian WANE sample of firms and workers was larger than the UK sample; the final study group therefore included all IT workers 40 and older from the UK WANE sample. This amounted to 21 workers aged 40 and over employed by six UK firms, three of which were small (5–49 employees) and three medium (50–249 employees). All of the Canadian firms with four or more employees, and all of the Canadian firms with women aged 40 and older, were included. The result was 20 Canadian individuals, clustered within nine Canadian firms, seven of which were small and two micro (1–4 employees).

Because of the non-random sampling in the WANE project, differences in the size of firms, their ages, and their IT niches may or may not reflect systematic differences between the two countries' IT industries. Taken together, however, they present an interesting sample of firms with diverse histories, working in different parts of the IT industry, with a variety of ownership and management structures. UK firms were located in a number of mainly high-tech corridors in England, and Canadian firms were located in one of three cities, one of which is known as a high-tech centre. The activities in which these firms were engaged included the production of software for use in various industries, including manufacturing, logistics, finance and petrochemical industries. Some of them produced off-the-shelf software products and others were more heavily involved in the design and implementation of customized systems, often working closely with client firms. Four of the Canadian firms were consultancies providing a variety of IT services to clients. The five remaining Canadian firms and all of the UK firms were in software development and/or services. Only one firm was publicly-listed (UK); the remainder were sole- or jointly-owned (eight in Canada, three in the UK) or had multiple owner-managers (one in Canada, two in the UK). The two sets of firms were also similar in terms of their length of operation, with the majority having been in existence for five years or longer.

The final study group of IT workers consisted of 17 men and four women in the UK, and 14 men and six women in Canada. The combined age span was 40 years to 63 years: 66 percent were in their 40s, 32 percent in their 50s and only 2 percent (one UK respondent) in their 60s. The Canadian individuals tended to be younger than their UK counterparts, and were predominantly in their 40s. The small number of older women in both study groups was indicative of the poor representation of females in the IT industry as a whole, and their higher exit rates (Panteli et al., 2001; Duerden Comeau, 2004; Platman and Taylor, 2004; Stephan and Levin, 2005). As Table 9.2 shows, these individuals fell into four professional categories: entrepreneurs, technical managers, technical professionals, and IT-related professionals. There were similar numbers of entrepreneurs and senior executives in both study groups, although slightly more technical managers and slightly fewer technical professionals in the UK.

The study group was highly educated in the main, with 61 percent of the total being educated to degree or postgraduate degree level, although the Canadian group was somewhat less-educated. Most were full-time permanent workers: only one UK and one Canadian worker were part-time and only two of the Canadian individuals were on fixed-term contracts. However, it should be noted that some of the consultants[2] working at the Canadian consultancies indicated in the survey that they were permanent employees despite their formal contract status. Unsurprisingly, given their varying positions, the salaries of these workers also varied widely. Taking the sample as a whole, the salaries were about evenly distributed from the lowest category (under £20 000 [CAN $39 000]) to the highest (£80 000 [CAN $150 000][3] or over), although more of the lowest-income earners were Canadian.

None of the sample were members of company associations, and the only trade union member was only so because she had kept up membership from a previous career. Four UK individuals reported being members of professional associations, but none of these were specific to the information technology profession; however two Canadians did belong to an IT-specific professional organization. Only two individuals (one in each country) identified themselves as members of racial minority groups. English was a first language for all workers in the UK and all but two workers in Canada. The majority reported having had some caring responsibilities over their careers, with most having children or step-children.

Analysis

Our approach here is largely qualitative and exploratory. The relatively small and non-random sample makes generalizations to populations impossible, but does allow us to look at the employment transitions of these workers in a rather more complete way, that complements the more statistical methods which had been deployed generally in the past in relation to transitional labor markets (for example Bothfeld and O'Reilly, 2000). We used three main sources of data for the analysis: online survey responses, transcribed interviews and reports of case study firms. The online survey was designed to capture life course trajectories and transitions in four key domains: school-to-work; work-to-work; family and care; and future intentions, including retirement. It also collected data on age, marital status, income, gender, ethnicity, disability, health and a number of other characteristics. The second source of information was the interview with respondents. These were confidential explorations of individual biographies, work histories and family narratives and were designed to complement the survey by exploring work and family issues in depth. Finally, we drew on case study reports of individual firms, compiled by WANE researchers. These combined available firm documents, policies, and other records provided by firms with information from interviews with CEOs, owners, or executives to create reports that were used for our analyses.

There were two major stages to our analysis. The first was to use these three sources of data to construct a 'life course grid' for each individual, as a way of mapping their lives in a systematic way. Similar grids have been used to collect life course interview data (Parry et al., 1999), but here we use them as a device for ordering pre-collected interview, survey, and case study data. The grid consisted of a time-ordered spreadsheet with dates running vertically and domains or various types of transitions running horizontally. This allowed notes about the experience and quality of various transitions to be included in each cell, and for experiences in each domain to be viewed simultaneously and related to each other. The grid evolved as the analysis proceeded, and in its final iteration included information about individual transitions in work, including the types of firms, aspects of their jobs, their job and income satisfaction; reasons for career changes; education and training; health, marital and family events; and other major life course transitions such as geographic mobility. Columns also recorded individuals' experiences during the IT sector's expansion in the 1990s and contraction during the early 2000s, and additional rows were used to record their expectations for future job changes or retirement. These data came both from the interviews, which provided a narrative account of respondents' experiences, and from survey responses, which collected detailed information on the timing of various transitions and jobs, self-rated health, retirement plans, and feelings about the future.

In addition to the columns indicating individual transitions and experiences, there were columns that pertained to the firms at which these employees worked, with information taken from background documents about the company and the company case study reports. Expansions or layoffs, changes of ownership, and changes in product focus were extracted from the company case study documents and listed parallel to the individuals' histories.

These data sources were mined in order to fill in each cell in the grid as comprehensively as possible. However, these were retrospective accounts and so it was impossible to check for information which had been missed in the survey or by the interviewers. Nevertheless, it has been possible using these three data sources to build up fairly complete pictures of the major transitions in the lives of these individuals and firms. In parallel with grid completion, separate documents were created for each individual, containing quotes, examples and fuller summaries from the transcribed interviews.

The second stage of analysis involved the creation of meta-analytical grids, allowing us to compare one case against the next in terms of their exposure to and entry into IT, critical work transitions, career influences, care giving and family support, child-rearing, and future intentions. Four separate grids were created, one each for Canadian men and women, and UK men and women. These were compared, with attention to the research questions presented above and to the common patterns experienced by individuals as well as to cases that stood out as unusual, and which therefore might yield new information about these transitions.

FINDINGS

As described above, the 41 men and women in our study group were in a variety of jobs at the time of the surveys in interviews. Some were CEOs, presidents, or owners of their own firms, some were consultants or other independent contractors, and some were IT technicians or programmers working for others. They also varied widely in terms of the paths they had taken to arrive at their current positions. Some had begun IT careers directly out of a postsecondary program in their early 20s, while others had begun in IT later in life, often after careers in other industries such as manufacturing or printing. Some of these respondents had seen relatively few employment transitions over the years, sometimes only one major job change, while others had much more turbulent employment careers. However, all of the respondents indicated some periods of insecurity or disruptions associated with their employment. Even those IT firms with long histories had gone through rounds of restructuring and ownership changes that were profoundly destabilizing for employees, often including temporary lay-offs and cuts in hours. Entrepreneurs and executives also often spoke of periods in which their firms and their own employment were in danger of collapse.

Figure 9.1 characterizes the career trajectory of one male worker from our UK study group, who had been an IT worker, a contractor, and an entrepreneur over his IT career. His experiences were far from atypical and include several short layoffs due to the collapse and restructuring of firms. The vertical axis gives an impression of the general valence of transitions for this man. More positive transitions were subjectively identified by increased security, income, or general happiness, as indicated in the interviews and in the survey data. The slight downward slope after age 47, the time of the interview, indicates his lack of confidence for the future, and his concern for his ability to find another job, should he need to.

The result for this man and many others in the study group was that their futures in the IT industry were unclear. For some, pressure to retrain to maintain their skills, and the relative insecurity of work with small IT firms, made continuing in IT unattractive. At the same time, it is clear that periodic career transitions are necessary in this industry, both for individuals and firms. Transitions were important for gaining various kinds of experience or training, and were often felt to be keys to future success.

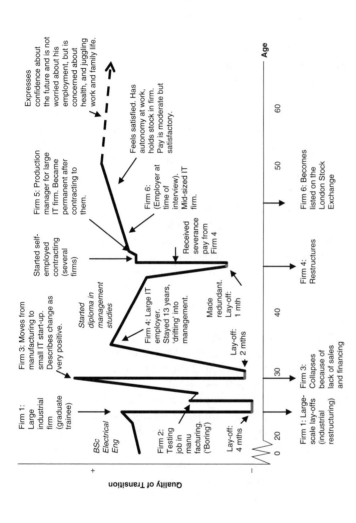

Notes: This trajectory is drawn from interview and survey data and is intended to illustrate the types of career transitions made by IT workers, and how they are related to firm transitions. 'Quality of transition' refers to the researchers' assessment of whether a particular transition increased or decreased the employee's income, security, autonomy, or happiness, as indicated in the interview data.

Figure 9.1 Stylized career trajectory, IT employee (UK case 4405104)

The WANE data also illustrated the importance of flexibility among firms. Many had grown and contracted with the IT industry, and had gone through several different incarnations. This seemed to be a fundamental aspect of small enterprises in the IT industry, which often rely on finding sources of capital, which could be unreliable and difficult to secure.

The respondents in our sample responded to these challenges in a number of ways. Some employees found themselves made redundant and needed to find other jobs. Others left their companies to strike out on their own as consultants or entrepreneurs. For some, the entrance to IT was itself a very important transition strategy, and often a response to the decline of another industry.

Respondents' situations also varied widely in terms of their general satisfaction with their work and the sufficiency of their incomes. As we have indicated, some had quite high incomes, and many of these workers were relatively satisfied with their current situations. Others were much less satisfied, with both their incomes and their working lives in general. It was not the case that those with low incomes and fairly low satisfaction were all employees or technical workers. A few were owners of their own small firms, and some managers were also among those earning relatively little. As might be expected, the study group also varied in terms of their optimism about the future. Some were quite anxious about the futures of their own firms and the industry, or were concerned about their own chances to find employment, should their current jobs end. Others were more sanguine about their own chances on the labor market, and about their firms and the industry.

Although respondents varied in these respects, they shared one common characteristic in our eyes—they had all 'survived' as IT workers. They had, with varying degrees of success, navigated the rough waters of IT employment by making choices and transitions with the help of various resources, in the context of their previous work and family life courses. Below, we examine the factors that were important for these workers to make various transitions in the labor market, especially work transitions that have led, in retrospect, to continued incomes, to better income security, or to more satisfaction. We ask 'what matters?' for these IT workers' employment transitions, and find strong evidence that skills, timing, family resources, gender, networks and alternative organizations all matter, as do chance and luck.

Skills Matter

As one would expect, we found evidence that the skills and experience that IT employees can offer to employers matter for their ability to make career transitions. Certainly the employees themselves thought so; only nine of the 41 study group members indicated in the survey that they were 'not at all concerned' about their ability to maintain their IT-related skills. These IT workers were also unconcerned about their ability to be competitive, should they lose their jobs. For the majority of the study group, though, both of these issues were at least 'somewhat' of a concern.

Respondents unconcerned about their ability to maintain their skills included not only most of the group whose careers had moved from technical aspects of IT to management or IT entrepreneur roles but also some who were currently analysts or programmers. Of the technical IT workers confident about maintaining their skills level, most had university degrees, while those technical workers concerned about their futures tended to have shorter college diplomas or training related to a specific set of products, such as Microsoft software.

It should also be noted that there was little evidence in our study group of opportunities to retrain across working life. Relatively few of them (five UK, five Canadian) reported having had any computing courses in the past 12 months. Rather, by far the most common means of updating skills was through on-the-job learning, as well as self-teaching at work and in home-time.

We might speculate that those in the sample with university degrees in computing had a somewhat different set of skills than those with other training backgrounds, and perhaps a more general foundation upon which more specific skills could be built. Even for those with degrees that were in other fields, such as business or psychology, this may have provided them with skills or credentials that set them on a better career trajectory. Unsurprisingly, nearly all of the 25 people in Table 9.1 who had university degrees had also acquired them at the beginning of working careers, whereas it was much more likely that those with shorter IT-related educations had returned later in life. This suggests one of the ways in which the timing of employment-related transitions may matter to their outcomes.

Timing Matters

There were a number of ways in which the timing of transitions mattered for their perceived success, with timing being defined in terms of the stage in the individual's own work career, the life course of the firm or the industry, and other life course transitions including marriage and childbearing, as well as age.

For these respondents, the transition into IT work was an important turning point, experienced at a variety of ages and life course stages. Some joined IT employment directly from post-secondary programs, which varied from college degrees to postgraduate degrees, into their first jobs. Although the data here do not allow us to determine whether early entrants to IT work do tend to have more successful careers than later entrants,[4] there was some evidence that this might be the case. A large proportion of early entrants who were interviewed in their 40s and 50s reported being satisfied with their work and optimistic about their future, although this experience was not universal. On the other hand, there were several later entrants to IT who were in less satisfactory situations.

The interview data suggested several possible reasons that those who entered IT work earlier in their lives may have done better. One is that more of the early entrants were those with university degrees, either in computing or a related field, as discussed above. In comparison, a number of those who had come to IT after other careers did so through college or other, shorter, education programs. There are several factors that might partially explain why our earlier entrants were more likely to have higher education. An obvious one is the relative difficulty of financing and organizing a return to education later in life, and therefore a preference for shorter programs. One Canadian man, who had begun IT after being a librarian, explicitly mentioned that his wife would not have been willing to support the two of them and their children on her income, for longer than a two-year program.

There may also be some country effect. Canadians in our group were much more likely to have two-year college degrees, suggesting that there may be some national differences in IT training systems. The firms in the UK study group also tended to be linked to universities, often started by former university faculty members, and this might lead to more employees with degrees. Cohort and period effects could also be at play, in which those who began in IT work right out of school, many in the 1970s, entered an industry for which a university degree was required, and for which other programs were not yet available.

Indeed, for those who entered the industry with little or no training in IT, the transition could be difficult, and this could be exacerbated by perceptions of age. The story of one UK late entrant is telling. At the age of 38, he switched from a lengthy first career in the British armed forces to a relatively junior role as a computer operator. He was recruited by a mid-sized firm in one of the UK's high-tech corridors. He described the transition as a shock: he had no formal IT qualifications and had to learn new skills and working methods on-the-job. His colleagues had degrees, unlike himself, and he had difficulty with his much younger supervisor, whom he describes as 'an 18-year-old listening to heavy metal music' (4404422, late 50s). He was later promoted to systems support engineer but he had 'felt himself shrivel' in these computing roles. At the time of our fieldwork, the company recognized his people-handling skills and appointed him staff and facilities manager, a role he relished. However, the researchers remained in contact after the fieldwork had ended and discovered that he had been made redundant and was working for a supermarket chain, stacking shelves.

Besides a higher education, some of the early entrants in both the UK and Canada may have benefited from joining an industry at a time of expansion. For some of these entrants, their first jobs were at large IT firms or utilities that provided additional training and a ladder for promotion.

> So in 11 years there, I actually had 14 different positions and I did everything in IT. I was loading tape drives, tapes at one point, then I got into installing . . . software into rolling out PCs or, you know, you name it. Got into UNIX, got into database management, so I had a little bit of everything. I was not a specialist in anything, but I could do everything.
>
> (1107081, man, early 40s, Canada)

Some of the respondents mentioned the importance of timing, in terms of knowing when to leave a firm and being able to take advantage of fate's hand by controlling the timing of transitions. Several of the interviews indicated the importance of moving to avoid being dragged down with a declining firm. There were many examples of individuals repositioning themselves in a way that saved their careers from possible misfortune, including quick-witted decisions to abandon firms that were on the slide or to leave roles which were heading for redundancy.

In the UK group this is illustrated by one break-away enterprise whose origins lay in a large firm's IT department. Early knowledge of that firm's imminent collapse had led the IT team to re-locate overnight and start trading the next day with a former client, a strategy that maintained their employment. In the Canadian group, one firm's vice president recounted leaving a large IT company at which he had been for about 20 years. Having been responsible for hundreds of people in this large firm, he realized that further career progression would mean even greater responsibilities and time constraints, but perhaps more important was that his pension with the company would have been 'locked in' to a defined benefit plan and no longer transferable. Another man in the Canadian group had also been a senior manager at the same large IT firm, but had stuck it out through rounds of redundancies, until he was laid off himself. Both men were working for smaller firms at the time of the interview, but the former was secure and looking towards early retirement, while the other was living off of his severance and having difficulty securing a stable position.

One respondent, a production manager aged 49, gave a particularly strong indication of the importance of timing, as well as luck, in career transitions. He had been laid off three times before he reached his 40th birthday, yet these experiences had appeared to equip him with industry and firm-specific sensors which he had used to his advantage in deciding to join his current firm. Explaining his decision to leave his last job before being made redundant, he said:

> the company I was at was not looking like a good long term prospect for me. It's still around, it's still doing very well but as it is now I wouldn't have a job there. . . . I do know people, one in particular who was made redundant exactly the same time . . . who was, I guess, probably then about as old as I am now, and had a hell of a time finding anything. Ended up contracting part time stuff, working in Tesco's [supermarket chain], you know, sort of anything to keep going.
>
> (4405104, man, later 40s, UK)

A Canadian man reported being able to take advantage of his employer's leave policy to take a college course and to avoid redundancy.

> Also at that time what was the push that did it, was the [employer] at the time was talking about outsourcing their department, centralizing everything. And in fact, that's when I decided time to take the jump. So I took a leave of absence for four months, went to [college], and did well, and then officially resigned my position . . . and that summer, sure enough, my department was centralized – swallowed . . . so to speak.
>
> (1191133, man, late 40s, Canada)

The timing of job transitions in relation to the trajectories of firms appears to have been important for a number of our study group members. For others, the relationship between job transitions and family events and transitions appears to have been key.

Family Matters

As described above, the WANE data included information on family transitions as well as employment transitions and, as expected, they could be seen to interact and to influence each other in the lives of our study group. For the IT workers in the study group family events such as childcare or the illnesses of family members, were issues that needed to be reconciled with employment. On the other hand family members, and especially spouses, provided a resource of support, allowing IT workers to make critical employment transitions. Some career trajectories were more directly embedded in family strategies. There were two UK and two Canadian firms in which husbands and wives worked together. In each of these cases one or both of the married partners held an ownership stake or a senior position in the firm. This was a strategy that some said allowed them to coordinate work and family life. On the other hand, it also increased their dependence on the firm's success, and risk associated with its failure.

For those who were able to control the timing of employment transitions, this was often possible only through the support of family members, principally spouses. The interviews illustrated several ways in which individual career transitions were made in the context of family resources and care giving obligations. The availability of spouses allowed some to retrain for career transitions and others to begin the risky transition to consulting or entrepreneurship.

An advantage some had was the ability to coordinate the timing of work and family transitions. Respondents at one UK start-up firm reported having a 'baby boom' among the owner/employees as the firm became more stable. One founder of a Canadian firm describes the ability of some entrepreneurs to mesh the timing of childbearing transitions with transitions in their companies.

> we were lucky. [Business partner] and I both were just barely married, our wives both worked, and they made good money so, you know, we could work for a couple of years at two thousand dollars a month . . . and not have to struggle all that much. And around the time that we were ready to start having kids; we both had kids within a year of each other or so. Around that time you know we were, the company was making money and we could see growth and good potential.
>
> (1191042, man, age unknown, Canada)

This contrasts strongly with the case of one of their employees, who had started his job at the same time that his first child was born and his parents were ill.

> **I**: So new baby, new job, lots of . . . tension.
>
> **R**: And recovering from kind of a burnout from the year before. Yeah there was a lot going on . . . and two dying parents. One was gone already; my mother was about a year away from it. It was a little wild.
>
> **I**: How did you do it?
>
> **R**: Well the environment was a bit tough at first partly because I was very new and I was dealing with all of what I just described. You know I guess, I dealt with it partly because I have a wife who is unflappable.
>
> (1191081, man, early 40s, Canada)

This man's wife left her own job at this time, and had not returned at the time of the interview. Thus, as much as it was important for some to have the support of their spouses' incomes during critical transitions, for others it seems to have been equally important that their spouses, mainly women, were not working, but instead cared for their children full-time.

Gender Matters

It is important to note that there were strong gender differences in IT career trajectories that could be identified, despite the relatively few women in the study group. As was shown in Table 9.2, women in the study groups were working in a variety of roles in these firms, both technical and administrative. Women were more likely to have entered IT work later in life, as there was only one in the study group who had begun an IT career directly out of school in her 20s. Most of them had begun their working careers in other roles, such as teaching, accountancy, or administrative or secretarial work, before making their transition to IT.

The most striking aspect of the lives of the women in the study group is that there was considerably more evidence of the influence of family life on working careers than in men's stories. Several women reported putting their own working careers second to childcare. One woman in the UK explained this in terms of the central position her growing children held in her life:

> they are still the most important part of my life; they would always take precedence over my career, you know. Obviously as they're getting older they have less reliance on you so it's not so important but, you know, my family life when I go home, I don't want to be thinking about work when I get home, or trying to learn new stuff, and I just don't want to be doing that.
>
> (4402094, woman, early 40s, UK)

Several women described making important work transitions in order to care for others. This Canadian woman decided to work part-time in order to take care of her daughter and her son, who has special needs.

> being totally and brutally honest, my husband's career comes first because he stands a much better chance of getting anywhere. I hit the glass ceiling (laughs) and it hurt. I want to go back to university, I want to actually study education and start working with special ed kids. I've been tutoring and for literacy work and working with my son's class now and I just love dealing with them so I think that's an area that I'd like to look at further. And, you know, if IT fits in, great (laughs). But it's not, it's not a huge part of my life, or it's not, I've learned not to let it take over.
>
> (1109042, woman, early 40s, Canada)

Another woman, a Canadian consultant/owner, left to start her own consulting company after having to commute to a remote site for eight months. Her husband's shift work meant that they had to rely on their parents to care for their children, which they found untenable. However, she did not find balancing childcare and work any easier as a consultant.

> No, because like I said my husband works shift-work and then, you know, owning a company means you're never stop working, really. You're doing stuff . . . .but [I] have my laptop and I sit in the same room with my family. So they think I'm there with them but you know I'm still kind of working . . . But you've got to do what you have to do. I am the major bread winner in the family so you know I pay the mortgage and got to do it. And you know my daughter's grown up now she's 21, she just moved out so I don't have to worry about her now.
> (1113003, woman, early 40s, Canada)

As described above, care giving is a key factor influencing the career paths of some of these women. Spousal income, as in the case of the woman who chose to work part-time, was naturally a critical component of these decisions. For another Canadian woman, a co-owner of an IT firm, the firm itself is part of a family strategy, as she and her husband run it out of their house. They had no children, and the distinction between their work and home lives seemed to be virtually non-existent.

Networks Matter

One of the factors that clearly distinguished those who had successfully made various employment transitions, or who felt secure in their abilities to survive future shocks, was the presence of networks. Professional networks, in the form of current and past colleagues and IT-connected family members had been critical at various stages in the careers of many. One Canadian man described finding his current position through contacts made at his children's hockey games. Another, older, respondent in the UK had benefited from 'reverse-patronage,' where a younger IT entrepreneur with whom he had worked years earlier had offered him his current position. Relatively few of our respondents reported that they had found their current positions through advertisements, employment agencies, or headhunting agencies. Rather, it was far more common to see that networks and pre-existing relationships played a key role in facilitating transitions.

Some of the small firms in our study group were really held together by the strength of relationships between their members. Several firms had gone through reorganizations and had reformed around the same core group of employees and managers. The strength of personal networks was recognized as important not only for individuals but also for their firms. One of the respondents had been asked to continue working at his firm because of his extensive industry networks in the high tech geographical cluster in which the firm was located. He described himself as having 'a door opening role' and being 'an ambassador-at-large,' helping the firm to reposition itself in a highly competitive market.

Two of our firms provided particularly good examples of the importance of networks for career survival and are also examples of innovative responses to an uncertain industry. One UK firm, described above, was formed on the spot by six IT employees of a larger firm that was about to close down. In danger of losing their jobs, these six employees took their knowledge of the work and their former employer's major client, and had been able to maintain their own employment. The firm had operated as a consortium, in which each of the six had an equal share, for over a decade and the owner-employees had settled into roles within the company that best suited them. Similarly, one Canadian firm was founded by a number of independent IT contractors in order to pool resources and to allow them to contract with larger clients. This 'body shop' consultancy helped match client firms and contractors, who would often work at a single client firm for months or years. The contracting firm improved contractors' networks and helped them find work and provided administrative services, in exchange for a percentage of the contract. Both of these innovative firms provided flexibility in terms of working time and allowed employees some degree of control over their working lives. The owner/employees of the consortium company all had a fair amount of latitude with respect to taking time off to deal with care giving or other tasks, and were able to adjust their work roles to fit their family situations. The contracting arrangement at the 'body shop' firm meant that employees were able to occasionally turn down work in favor of other activities. These firms reflected, to some degree, the idea of the 'lifestyle company,' a term suggested to us by an employee of another UK firm to indicate a company in which the general goal is to maintain steady employment, sufficient income, and a comfortable degree of work–life balance for staff and management, rather than only pursuing profit or growth.

Chance (or Risk) Matters

Ultimately, the IT industry as experienced by these workers was an unstable one for owners/managers, contractors, and employees alike. Many or all of them were currently experiencing some uncertainty about the futures of their firms. For many small firms, the problems faced stemmed from difficulty securing ongoing capital financing. Some were having problems creating new products with which to compete in a fast-moving industry. Changing technology meant that some firms, as well as many individuals, had to re-tool to work with or produce new products.

These factors affecting the working lives of IT workers are perhaps more accurately presented as aspects of the economic or social-structural context in which they work than as 'chance.' However, from the perspective of the individuals, these and other events were among the uncontrollable aspects of their environment. One UK entrepreneur reflected on the role of good luck rather than pre-determined goals in deciding outcomes in IT:

> I'm sort of minded to think of pin-ball machines or something, you know. You'd like to get the ball from the plunger round the circuit and down into one of the high scoring pockets at the bottom. But in reality there are lots of bumpers and mushrooms and things in the way. And, and you know, you can give the whole machine a heave with your hips every so often but on the whole, gravity does most of the work and, you know, your ability to influence exactly what happens is not as great as, you know, management textbooks might like you to believe.
>
> (4405272, man, early 40s, UK)

However, he also referred to the experience he had gained running three previous IT ventures which had equipped him with a sense of the industry:

> . . . if you've had 15 years' business experience that makes a big difference because it means you've already had some corners knocked off, you've already survived some crises, you've already maxed out your credit cards, you know, once, where it concentrates the mind admirably. . .

DISCUSSION

Clearly, there are other things that 'matter' to successful career transitions, and other resources that provide support in times of employment insecurity. Income and savings are probably the most obvious, providing the freedom to leave a job or to retrain, or to leave the labor market entirely. We also take it as given that education matters, and that having saleable skills can make a crucial difference in the outcomes of employment transitions, and whether workers are able to navigate a risky labor market. However, our intention here is to use the WANE data to explore other factors that affect transitions, and which speak to the possibility of programs and policies that would balance flexibility and security for employees and firms. By examining the resources and factors that did help these workers make successful transitions, we hoped to identify how programs might offer further support.

The data used here do not allow us to generalize to a population, but they do give us a glimpse into the types of experiences and resources that were important in allowing these IT workers to maintain employment in the industry. Generally, these results seem to reaffirm the validity of the ideals of the flexicurity and TLM enterprises. For workers, this means that policies should be designed to support workers by providing security for transitions across the life course. The findings here support the idea that transitions in the labor market are often affected by transitions or conditions in other aspects of life, particularly in the realm of the family. Policies that recognize the interconnectedness of these domains, and that strategies are often made in the context of all family resources, including time and income sources, might be important.

We also find that it was important for these workers to have control over the timing of some labor force transitions, including being able to leave a firm or industry when things appear to be in decline, rather than waiting to be made redundant. Policies that improve workers' ability to control the timing of labor market transitions might be able to improve outcomes. Although workers require security, especially of income, the other side of this security is the flexibility for workers to make the transitions that they feel will improve their situations.

Flexicurity is also concerned with providing flexibility for the firm, and balancing security with workers with firms' need to be flexible and respond to market conditions. Many of these small and medium-sized enterprises had been faced with situations in which they needed to reduce their costs by shedding workers, although they were often hired back once conditions improved, or the firm had reorganized in a slightly different form. The expansion and contraction of these firms seemed to be particularly rapid in the IT industry, perhaps because of the pace of technology change and the culture of the 'start up' company, but this might be the case for small and medium-sized firms in general. As some of the entrepreneurs pointed out, failing in start-up ventures was seen as an important part of learning how to operate in the industry and developing a product.

What directions, then, might flexicurity or TLM policies take to assist these IT firms and employees? One aspect that became clear through our analysis of the interview and web survey data was that there was very little use of traditional income security programs, job-finding programs, or retraining programs, among workers in either country. Although many of the respondents had experienced unemployment, mainly for short periods, none of them mentioned receiving employment benefits of any kind, although this may be influenced by stigma associated with these programs.

In addition to the lack of formally-provided training opportunities, this suggests that there seems to be scope for a much greater role to be played by professional organizations, including government agencies and labor market intermediaries, in providing local but sector-specific labor market information. Our study group individuals often relied on their own networks or personal experience to gauge when a career move might be necessary, and what form the move might take. Support might take the form of a new type of broker or representative organization to support and guide individuals in niche sectors and occupations, and which would be capable of understanding and passing on vital trends in changing roles, positions and skills sets. These sorts of supports may help improve people's sense of current and future security, and would allow them to approach periods of uncertainty and risk-taking with more confidence.

The importance of networks for maintaining employment suggests that institutions that foster and promote these networks may be helpful. As well, the two innovatively organized firms in our sample, the six-person consortium in the UK and the Canadian 'body shop' consultancies, provide concrete examples of organizational responses by individuals that have served to maintain their income security and employability in an uncertain environment. In some ways these organizations were able to provide individuals with both enhanced security of income, and increased flexibility, in terms of control over their working lives. Although these sorts of innovative organizations are not likely to replace many traditional firms, they might provide some guide to the implementation of Schmid's 'flexibly coordinated' and locally controlled transitional labor markets. Networks of semi-independent contractors or consultants might be one way to maintain employment for workers made redundant, or who need to increase their control over their working lives.

As the flexicurity and TLM programs continue to be developed into specific policy suggestions, these will certainly be country-specific and shaped by pre-existing welfare states. In the UK and Canada, countries with minimalist welfare states and an emphasis on market-mediated transitions, these policies could take the form of institutions that focus on providing individuals and firms with information or other resources that would improve their ability to make successful transitions, rather than guaranteed incomes or other supports. Although the findings presented here are exploratory, they do suggest that these life course perspectives on employment policies may be important, even if their precise forms may be difficult to imagine.

ACKNOWLEDGEMENT

The authors wish to thank Gale Cassidy for her excellent assistance with the WANE data. Previous versions of this chapter were presented at the third annual Population, Work and Family Consortium (PWFC) meetings in Ottawa, Canada in December 2007 and the annual meetings of the Society for the Advancement of Socio-Economics (SASE) in San José, Costa Rica in July 2008.

NOTES

1. The EU-15 refers to the 15 countries in the European Union before the addition of several former Eastern bloc countries in May 2004.
2. 'Consultants' include those whose jobs involved doing various IT-related work on a project-specific or contract basis. The consultants in our sample were employed by 'consultancies,' firms whose major business was to do bespoke programming or systems analysis for client firms. Some consultancies employed these workers on a permanent basis, others sub-contracted work to them, as independent operators. Many of these 'consultants' spent much of their working time on-site at the client firms. In the WANE study, they are identified as employees of the consultancy firm, rather than of the client firm. All of these consultancy firms were Canadian.
3. The categorizations of income in the UK and Canadian versions of the surveys were slightly different.
4. Because the study group does not include those who left IT employment, we cannot separate these effects from the fact that those who remained in IT may be better educated, or more successful, for example.

REFERENCES

Bothfeld, S. and J. O'Reilly (2000), 'Moving up or moving out? Transitions through part-time work in Britain and Germany', in J. O'Reilly, I. Cebrián and M. Lallement (eds), *Working Time Changes: Social Integration through Working Time Transitions in Europe*, Cheltenham, UK and Northampton, MA, USA: Edward Elgar, pp. 132–72.
Cooke, M. (2006), 'Policy changes and the labour force participation of older workers: evidence from six countries', *Canadian Journal on Aging*, **25** (4), 387–499.
Council of the European Union (2007), 'Towards common principles of flexicurity: draft council resolutions', Council of the European Union Working Party on Social Questions.
de Hoog, A., K. Platman, P. Taylor and A. Vogel (2004), *Workforce Ageing and Information Technology Employment in Germany, the Netherlands, and the United Kingdom, WANE International Report No. 3*, London, ON: The University of Western Ontario, Workforce Ageing in the New Economy.
Downie, R., H. Dryburgh, J. McMullin and G. Ranson (2004), *A Profile of Information Technology Employment in Canada, WANE International Report No.1*, London, ON: The University of Western Ontario, Workforce Ageing in the New Economy.
Duerden Comeau, T. (2004), *Cross-national Comparison of Information Technology Employment, WANE International Report No. 5*, London, ON: The University of Western Ontario, Workforce Aging in the New Economy.

Elder, G.H., Jr. (1994), 'Time, human agency, and social change: perspectives on the life course', *Social Psychological Quarterly*, **57**(1), 4–15.

Esping-Andersen, G. (1999), *Social Foundations of Postindustrial Economies*, Oxford, New York: Oxford University Press.

European Commission Employment and Social Affairs (2006), 'Labour market policy: Expenditure and participants', in *European Social Statistics*, Luxembourg: Office for Official Publications of the European Communities.

European Commission (2007), *Communication from the Commission to the European Parliament, the Council, the European Economic and Social Committee and the Committee of the Regions – Towards Common Principles of Flexicurity: More and better jobs through flexibility and security*, COM/2007/0359 final, Brussels, 22 June 2009 at http://eurlex.europa.eu/LexUriServ/LexUriServ.do?ur i=COM:2007:0359:FIN:EN:HTML.

European Expert Group on Flexicurity (2007), 'Flexicurity pathways: turning hurdles into stepping stones', report by the European Expert Group on Flexicurity, Brussels.

Evans, P.M. (2002), 'Downloading the welfare state, Canadian style', in G.S. Goldberg and M.G. Rosenthal (eds), *Diminishing Welfare: A Cross-national Study of Social Provision*, Westport, CT: Auburn House, pp. 75–102.

Marshall, V.W. and M.M. Mueller (2003), 'Theoretical roots of the life-course perspective', in W. R. Heinz and V.W. Marshall (eds), *Social Dynamics of the Life Course: Transitions, Institutions, and Interrelations*, Hawthorne, NY: Aldine de Gruyter, pp. 3–32.

Maxwell, J. (1995), 'The role of the state in a knowledge-based economy', in P. Grady, R. Howse and J. Maxwell (eds), *Reforming Social Security*, Kingston, ON: Queen's University, School of Policy Studies, Government and Competitiveness.

Organisation for Economic Co-operation and Development (OECD) (2000), *'Reforms for an Ageing Society*, Paris: OECD.

Panteli, N., J. Stack and R. Harvie (2001), 'Gendered patterns in computing work in the late 1990s', *New Technology, Work and Employment*, **16** (1), 3–17.

Parry, O., C. Thomson and G. Fowkes (1999), 'Life course data collection: qualitative interviewing using the life grid', *Sociological Research Online*, **4** (2) accessed at www.socresonline.org.uk/4/2/parry.html.

Pierson, P. (1994), *Dismantling the Welfare State? Reagan, Thatcher and the Politics of Retrenchment*, Cambridge: Cambridge University Press.

Platman, K. (2004), '"Portfolio careers" and the search for flexibility in later life', *Work, Employment and Society*, **18** (3), 573–99.

Platman, K., and P. Taylor (2004), 'Workforce ageing in the new economy: a comparative study of information technology employment', Workforce Aging in the New Economy working papers, Cambridge: University of Cambridge.

Policy Research Initiative (2005), *Encouraging Choice in Work and Retirement: Project Report*, Ottawa: Policy Research Initiative.

Schmid, G. (2001), 'Enhancing gender equality through transitional labour markets', *Transfer: European Review of Labour and Research*, **17** (7), 227–43.

Schmid, G. (2002), 'Towards a theory of transitional labour markets', in G. Schmid and B. Gazier (eds), *The Dynamics of Full Employment: Social Integration through Transitional Labour Markets*, Cheltenham, UK and Northampton, MA, USA: Edward Elgar, pp. 151–95.

Schmid, G. (2006), 'Social risk management through transitional labour markets', *Socio-Economic Review*, **4** (1), 1–33.

Schmid, G. and B. Gazier (2002), 'The dynamics of full employment: an introductory overview', in G. Schmid and B. Gazier (eds.), *The Dynamics of Full Employment: Social Integration through Transitional Labour Markets*, Cheltenham, UK, Northampton, MA, USA: Edward Elgar, pp. 1–20.

Stephan, P.E. and S.G. Levin (2005), 'Leaving careers in IT: gender differences in retention', *Journal of Technology Transfer*, **30** (4), 383–96.

Tros, F. (2004), 'Towards 'flexicurity' in policies for the older workers in EU-countries', paper presented at the Industrial Relations in Europe Conference (IREC), Utrecht, accessed 22 June 2009 at www.tilburguniversity.nl/faculties/law/research/reflect/publications/papers/fxp2004-9-tros_irec_utrecht.pdf.

Wilthagen, T. (2002), 'The Flexibility-Security nexus: new approaches to regulating employment and labour markets', paper presented at the British Journal of Industrial Relations Conference, Cumberland Lodge, The Great Park, Windsor, UK.

10. Work and the life course in a New Economy field

Victor W. Marshall and Julie Ann McMullin

In this chapter we draw selective insights from the preceding chapters to discuss life course issues of work and aging in the New Economy field of information technology. We consider lives as they unfold in time and we also consider the social structures which provide the opportunities and constraints that shape individual biographies. The life course perspective is one of the key resources guiding the work of WANE investigators, the others being explicit attention to gender issues and to framing the issues in a global perspective. People age as they work, and they work as they age. Thus, one of the major research areas in life course studies has been work, aging and the life course, largely pursued from a social psychological perspective. However, the age distribution of a firm's employees can be a major feature of the firm's social structure, one that can become a focus of managerial attention and a basis of patterned social relations within the firm. As we have noted in our introductory chapter, the transformations that have produced the new global economy have coincided in time with the demographic changes that have led to workforce aging. While the chapters in this volume for the most part focus on either social psychological issues or social structural issues, they at least implicitly, and often explicitly, deal with the relationships of individual lives to social structure. Thus, as we also noted in Chapter 1, in the global economy, viewed as a high risk society, tensions arise as workers and owners struggle for both personal and firm survival.

Individuals are simultaneously embedded within different structures, for example, within family structures and workplace structures; but these structures in turn are embedded within larger structures. Thus, the information technology firm is embedded within structural features of the information technology sector, which in turn is embedded within the sphere of production as structured at regional, national and global levels.[1]

Our strategy in this chapter is to draw selectively on findings of the preceding chapters, to make linkages among the chapters, and to comment on some theoretical and methodological aspects of life course analysis to complement the discussion of these in Chapter 1. We begin by focusing on Chapters 2 to 5, dealing with the application of the life course perspective to understand work and careers, then turn to knowledge and training issues raised in Chapters 6 and 7, followed by the two issues of work stress, and public policy, as found in Chapters 8 to 9. We close with some brief comments on theoretical and methodological issues.

MAKING CAREERS IN CHANGING STRUCTURES

In Chapter 2, Marshall, Morgan and Haviland develop the notion of occupational career, contrasting careers with jobs. Changes in the structure of occupations and work organizations associated with the rise of the new global economy have had profound consequences for the relationships that individual have with work over time. Chapters 2 to 5 deal explicitly with these consequences, which have import both for individual workers and the companies that employ them, and these consequences and their policy implications have been further developed in the later chapters.

By definition, all of the individual workers who became respondents in the WANE case study research have jobs. Depending on how one defines career, all of them may be thought to be experiencing careers, albeit careers with great diversity in the extent to which they are 'orderly' in Wilensky's (1961: 522) definition: 'a succession of related jobs, arranged in a hierarchy of prestige, through which persons move in an ordered (more-or-less predictable) sequence.' As Marshall, Morgan and Haviland note, an organization that links jobs in this way, offering an internal labor market, security of position and prospects of advancement, provides careers for its employees. Career can thus be thought of as both a property of the social structure of the firm and an individual biographical experience. The WANE project sought to capture both the structural and biographical (experiential) dimensions of work by studying individuals within the context of firms. Career is one of the analytical features that is differentially available in firms, and thus variably open to be experienced by individual workers.

Marshall, Morgan and Haviland employ survey data from the US, Australian, Canadian, and English case studies to examine career mobility within firms and extending beyond individual firms. There is limited mobility within firms, and this finding is consistent with the picture drawn by other authors in this volume, notably Ranson (Chapter 4), and Brooke (Chapter 5). However, when asked to report job mobility over all of their working life, over three-quarters of US respondents reported at least some upward mobility, another 8 percent reported lateral mobility, and 8 percent reported either downward or no mobility. The pattern was similar in the other study countries, with English and Canadian IT workers reporting more upward mobility and Australians about the same amount.

When respondents were asked to assess several aspects of careers, the similarities across countries were also quite high. About two-thirds of respondents agreed with the statement, 'My chances for career development are good' while the proportion agreeing that 'My chances for promotion are good' was just over 40 percent (highest in the US at 42.9 percent). These data suggest that many IT workers do not assess career progression in terms of promotion within the firm. In fact, two-thirds of respondents agreed with the statement, 'I believe that I have opportunities within the IT field, given my education, skills and experience.'

These issues are further developed in Chapter 3 by Haviland, Morgan, and Marshall, but attention turns to the structural level of firm practices that are used to reward employees in companies that depart greatly from the internal labor market format and do not offer careers in the traditional sense of progress and advancement in the internal labor market of the firm. A 'career development' scale was developed to identify highest and lowest career-development firms, which were compared and contrasted in a qualitative comparative case study analysis. This approach identified management strategies that promote a sense of career satisfaction despite the general lack of opportunity to progress through the ranks in a traditional upward mobility within-firm career. Six strategies characterized high commitment firms: creating a sense of ownership, pursuing cautious growth in order to maintain lifestyle, providing protection for employees, firm-based training and development, promotion of teamwork and regular team meetings, and overt demonstrations of commitment to maintaining employment security.[2] Low-commitment firms did not have distinctive features but rather a relative absence of the positive characteristics. In terms of the life course perspective, the chapter shows how actors (in this case firm owners and management) work to create social structures that will shape the real and perceived life course opportunities for employees.

In Chapter 4, Ranson looks systematically at male career transitions in this male-dominated sector, focusing the analysis on men aged 30–40 who were interviewed as part of the WANE case studies conducted in Canada, Australia, and the US. A key analytical feature of this chapter is that it places the individual worker in a temporal context within firms that are themselves in a temporal context, that is, the history of the firm, and not just its current situation, is important in shaping the careers and career strategies of workers within the firm. Firms are viewed in relation to individuals who try to create careers in five different ways: as non-permanent stopping places, as launch-pads for careers, as places to stabilize or build careers, as places to rescue or revitalize careers, and as entrepreneurial opportunities.

For employees hired in 2000 or later, the firm history seemed to be unrelated to the role of the firm in affecting individual employees. That is to say, a given firm could provide multiple functions supportive of different career strategies of its employees including (especially for some of the longer-established firms) the ability to sustain stable single-employer careers (see Chapter 2 for the contrast between firm-based and field-based careers). In contrast, a focused analysis of 12 men who had remained with the same case study firms since joining prior to 2000 found them to have had stable, long-term relationships with the firms. These men, and the firms in which they worked, survived the technology boom and bust, establishing a track record for survival. The careers of these men were not characterized by advancement up a conventional career ladder but rather by their having the opportunity to participate in building and growing the firm. Half of these men were owners or managers and their individual success was closely tied to that of the firm.

Theoretically, Chapter 4 provides a basis to address the question of how to understand careers and career trajectories – a crucial life course consideration in studies of work and organizations. This study shows that even in the IT sector, some individuals are able to make careers within the single organization, even a small company. The concept of 'boundaryless career' does not cover all cases of IT sector employment, and needs theoretical elaboration. Boundaries linked to individual competence and to social networks can be as important as firm boundaries. Patterns of careers go beyond those found within the firm (and with greater variability than that examined in Chapter 2). Ranson tentatively suggests one pattern of careers in IT, given the frequent temporal ordering of launching, stabilizing and building careers, and the move to entrepreneurship which might simultaneously describe organizational and individual trajectories.

As is evident in several chapters in this volume, one of the major components of globalization has been the individualization of working relationships. In Chapter 5, Brooke highlights this phenomenon by focusing on negotiation over wages. As she puts it, 'Remuneration . . . is embedded within labor processes, defined as the way work is performed and rewarded in IT firms.' Her chapter further refines the analysis by attending to how age and gender structure processes of distribution of the wage in small and medium-sized IT enterprises. She establishes a typology distinguishing 'high-end, high growth firms' from 'small, fragile firms,' and uses this typology to organize an examination of one case study firm of each type in Australia, Canada, and the United States.

The different high-end, high growth firms used a variety of remuneration practices but all of them tended to place older workers at a disadvantage or, as Brooke explains, 'the labor processes presented systematic forms of risk to older workers, which influenced the value of their remuneration.' In addition, women's remuneration was on the whole lower because they were less likely to be in technical roles in the firms. The impact of globalization was evident in the fact that, in all three countries under study, performance-based wages 'were stringently calibrated to enhancing global competitiveness' and this too disadvantaged older workers as well as women (who, for example, were less able or inclined to put in extra time in a billable-hours system).

In the other type of firm, the small, fragile firms, a distinct set of remuneration practices was found. Owners and CEOs could see themselves as 'in the same boat' with employees, with their compensation highly at risk, often variable depending on work flow, and with the companies making use of temporary contracts for some of their employees. Such conditions of uncertainly led to employment of younger workers, who expect lower compensation than older workers. Job flexibility could be a 'chip', to trade off against the wage, in highly informal negotiation processes, and informal profit-sharing (real or anticipated) reduced the gulf between owners and employees. In summary, in firms falling into either typology, the individualization of employment relationships resulted in those who were least marketable having the lowest negotiating power. Stable, high-end firms had standardized remuneration structures with incentives providing individualization based on performance. Low-end firms linked wages to profits and profits were uncertain and sometimes declining; the fate of the business was also the fate of the worker.

One of the reasons that IT sector wage negotiation is individualized is that unionization rates in the IT sector for all WANE study countries are generally low, and minuscule in the small and medium-sized companies that are the subject of WANE research. Most employees surveyed in the WANE case study sites (86.4 percent) are defined as permanent employees, although the sampling strategy in some countries, such as the United States, minimized or excluded contract workers.

Together with Chapter 1, Chapters 2 to 5 introduce a number of concepts that are explicitly embedded in the life course perspective or, in conjunction with life course concepts, provide analytical tools that help to apply the perspective to work and aging: the distinction between job and career, between objective and subjective career, flexible work regimes contrasted with internal labor markets, 'boundaryless careers', human and social capital, the 'individualization of labor', the age structure of the firm, risk, exchange theory. No single chapter embraces all these concepts but taken together they constitute a conceptual took kit to enrich the life course perspective for application to work and life course issues.

KNOWLEDGE AND TRAINING

The global economy is in many respects a knowledge economy and nowhere is this more likely to be true than in the information technology sector. Because of the rapid pace of technological change in IT, the acquisition and maintenance of high skills levels are particularly problematic and require flexibility. In Chapter 6, Adams and Demaiter address the question of how workers attain high skill levels. Paradoxically, formal university degree specialization in IT and computer-related skills is low. As an example, Adams and Demaiter note that in Canada only half of IT workers have a university degree in a field such as computer science or computer, software or systems engineering. This is not to say that IT workers are poorly educated. In all WANE study countries, about four out of five respondents to the web survey report a postsecondary credential of some kind. Between one-third and one-half report a bachelor's degree while many have more advanced degrees (the US is exceptional in that the vast majority of IT workers in the WANE study are university-trained). If the university credential is not directly related to IT work, how then are skills attained? Perhaps surprisingly, they are not often attained through professional associations or even through technical certifications such as that offered by Microsoft and Oracle.

Adams and Demaiter argue that the university degree provides a signal that they are capable of learning, rather than a signal of what they have learned that suits them for IT work. While the data do not allow for a strong generalization, they find some indication that those with higher formal education are more likely to pursue informal skills acquisition. How, then, are the technical skills acquired? WANE respondents report acquiring their skills through self-learning, previous work experience, and on-the-job training, in effect exemplifying the 'self-programmable worker' described by Castells (2000). We saw also in Chapter 3 that those firms that to offer in-house training opportunities are likely to have workers who are more satisfied with their careers in IT.

Charness and Fox hypothesize in Chapter 7 that older workers would in general be less likely to participate in training, and if they did participate, to do so with less intensity, than younger workers; however, they were expected to participate more in management training than do younger workers. They found instead that age was unrelated to reporting having had training in the previous years (and that only 26 percent of respondents said they had training in the previous year). They also found neither gender differences on this variable, nor differences in manager/non-manager status. They did, however, find a slight trend for more intense training with advancing age, in the minority of workers who did report training; and they found that those who supervised others were somewhat more likely to report having received management training, regardless of age. Another interesting finding is that not having had training in the past year was more often reported by those of any age who scored low on a measure of self-efficacy. This suggests that attempts to motivate older and younger employees should recognize the need to promote self-efficacy in their workers.

The fact that only 26 percent of respondents reported having had training in the previous year should be viewed in the context of Shuey and Spiegel's finding (in Chapter 8) that 62 percent of web survey respondents reported that they felt pressure to continually learn new skills, and that nearly a third reported that they had worried 'quite a bit' or 'a great deal' about failing to keep their IT knowledge and skills current. These findings are interpreted by Shuey and Spiegel as a major source of stress, one which is best seen not as a point-in-time stressor but as having a 'cumulative negative effect on stress levels, with workers growing increasingly tired of the never-ending process of skill upgrading over time.' In Chapter 9, Cooke and Platman argue that among older IT workers in the Canadian and English case studies, maintenance of skills is considered important but there are few structured opportunities to upgrade skills.

Taken together, and in relation to the data in Chapter 3 concerning training's role in high-performance firms, these chapters underline the importance of continuing education and skills upgrading as the IT workforce ages, as well as the challenges of providing such training.

STRESS OUTCOMES AND POLICY SOLUTIONS

Chapters 8 and 9 address two important issues that have not been addressed in earlier chapters. Two chapters address first, the health implications of working in a high-risk, flexible work regime, and second, the role of public policy in relation to the IT employment sector.

In Chapter 8, Shuey and Spiegel document the tremendous work pressures in the IT sector. Their description is no surprise given the widespread knowledge that IT is an intense industrial sector, but their grounding the description in terms of both the firm level and the changing economic climate with its ups and downs for IT reflects the importance of relating 'personal troubles' to 'public issues,' or 'biography; and 'history' (Mills, 1959). As we write (March 2009), we are acutely aware of current distress in the IT sector associated with the current global economic crisis, affecting both large companies and the smaller and medium-sized enterprises that have been our focus.[3]

In terms of the life course perspective, the demands placed upon IT workers by the fast pace of work is exacerbated by their 'linked lives' as they strive to avoid having work interfere with their family life. The dilemma Shuey and Spiegel describe is reminiscent of Broadhead's description, in *The Private Lives and Professional Identity of Medical Students*, of the struggle of medical students to maintain a life independent of their medical training. Broadhead (1983: 58) invokes the concept of 'inundation', crediting it to Barney Glaser: 'As a process, inundation refers to an individual's life being flooded and dominated by a substantively narrow set of concerns and rounds of activities. It involves the absorption and encapsulation of an individual's general range of identities, interests, and activities into a far more substantively focused order of events and concerns usually pivoting around a single, all-informing identity.' IT industry work has the capacity to flood out everything else, and the qualitative data in Chapter 8 graphically illustrate resistance to the forces of inundation, particularly in relation to age-related transitions such as getting married or having children. This dilemma is well-recognized by employees and by management and Shuey and Spiegel describe the differences in the nature of stress between owners and managers on the one hand and other employees. They also outline several individual and company-level adaptation strategies to reduce work stress.

Shuey and Spiegel conclude Chapter 8 by noting something they found less of than they had anticipated: stress due to job insecurity. They suggest that this might reflect the culture of IT work in the New Economy, which by its nature requires, recruits and retains workers who 'embrace industry norms of flexibility and risk, rapid industry change and job turnover.' This returns us to the analysis in Chapter 2, of 'making a life in IT.' In that chapter, Marshall, Morgan and Haviland argue that the frame in which workers would view their lives is often not the individual job in the current firm, but rather the broader frame of the IT industrial sector. Yet we can only wonder as to how much stress these workers and the owners of 'our' small and medium-size IT firms are experiencing in the much more precarious environment of 2009.

Chapter 9 turns to the policy realm, providing a framework that might be helpful as public policy initiatives come to grips with that question. The life course perspective has frequently been used, especially by European scholars, to understand how public policies can shape the life courses of individuals. However, there are a few examples of explicit attempts by the public sector to use the life course perspective to develop public policies (for a systematic review, focusing on Canadian attempts to do so, see Marshall, 2009).

In Chapter 9, Cooke and Platman draw on WANE data from the UK and Canadian case studies to discuss how the life course perspective can be used to develop public policy. In particular, they argue that 'we need to understand how employees currently navigate insecure employment, and how policies might be formulated to provide better security,' and so they 'explore the strategies and resources that helped IT workers make key transitions in employment and to maintain their employability in a turbulent industry.' As they point out, the IT sector provides an ideal basis on which to think about the relationship between flexibility and security in the new global economy, because it is a 'fluid sector in which both local and global connections are important and in which firms are subject to the pressures for flexibility in workforces and wages.' As well, they note, transitions in this sector provide the opportunity to upgrade skills, and are at times deliberately undertaken for just that purpose.

Examining the careers of 'older' workers (age 40-plus), Cooke and Platman find that skill is important to ensure successful transitions, but that most respondents had little opportunity to retrain across the life course. They argue that the experiences of living with chance and risk in the IT sector reaffirm the importance of flexicurity and transitional labor force management approaches that seek to enhance security during transitions and to give workers more control over the timing of labor force transitions. Such approaches, however, are intended to simultaneously provide flexibility with security to both employers and firms. Cooke and Platman's recommendations need not be repeated here except to underline their concern for new organizational strategies, public and private, than can fine-tune programmatic responses to local-level needs.

Some of the other chapters in this volume can also be drawn upon to inform public policy development. Chapter 2 focuses explicitly on IT in the context of the 'risk society', which is the context for the flexicurity and transitional labor market policy developments examined by Cooke and Platman. Chapter 4, on male career transitions in IT, Chapter 5 on negotiating the wage, Chapter 6 on skill, flexibility and credentials, and Chapter 7 on formal training, all point to importance of gender, age, and the intersection of gender and age, as differentially affecting the life chances of IT workers.

THEORETICAL AND METHODOLOGICAL ISSUES

In Chapter 1, we provided a general overview of the theoretical and methodological perspectives and principles that guided the WANE project. We wish to highlight a few points that can best be discussed in the context of the intervening empirical chapters.

The WANE study design included a highly structured web-based survey of employees, and extensive qualitative data from interviews with individual employees, key informant interviews with owners, CEOs and management, and the development of a qualitative description of each case study firm that supplemented these data with archival sources. Multiple methods allow for triangulation that has generalizations generated from one data source to be checked against generalizations from another. This approach has been used in several of the preceding chapters. However, multiple methods can be used in other ways, such as Brooke's use of the survey data in Chapter 5 to establish earnings patterns used to distinguish wage levels, a crucial part of her analysis, and Haviland, Morgan and Marshall's use in Chapter 3 of quantitative survey data to develop an index to place firms in a typology that was then used to guide subsequent qualitative analyses. In the latter case, this process inductively generated a list of characteristics that distinguished firms in the two extreme types, and additional nuances were added to the argument, using a kind of deviant or anomalous case analysis (Pearce, 2002) that examined case studies that did not precisely fit into the polar types.

WANE researchers have explicitly attempted to move beyond univariate thinking, to take into account the intersection of different social forces, such as gender, age, class and place (McMullin, 2000, 2004; Marshall and Clarke 2007). A given feature, such as age, will not necessarily be associated with social behavior in the same way under different social conditions. For example, Adams and Demaiter report in Chapter 6 that the relationship between age and feeling pressured to continually learn new skills differed by place and gender. Younger workers in Canada and England reported more pressure than older workers, but the reverse pattern was found in the US and Australia. In Australia and Canada, men were more likely to report such pressure than women, but in the US, women were more likely to report such pressure, and there was no gender difference among respondents in England. Such intersecting patterns beg for more research, and larger, more representative data files than the WANE project had, but the WANE findings at the least sensitize us to avoid simplistic pictures.[4]

As noted in Chapter 1, in the life course perspective, place matters. The IT firms and employees studied through the WANE project come from various regions in four different countries. These countries have many similarities: for example all are OECD members and are advanced industrial democracies; the age structure of the countries is comparable, and they are quite similar in their welfare state characteristics. Esping-Andersen (1990: 27) notes that 'The archetypical examples of (the "liberal welfare state") model are the United States, Canada and Australia,' and England is not far removed from that classification, being less 'liberal'. However, the countries also differ in many ways that are touched on in the preceding chapters, including the educational systems and experiences of their workforces, and the governmental regulation and policy domains. While the WANE study design does not provide a basis to strongly demonstrate differences among IT workers and companies in the four study countries, we do find suggestions that IT work and its consequences for IT workers varies by country. Shuey and Spiegel present dramatic evidence of this in Chapter 8, when they report substantial differences by country in the extent to which IT workers reported that their work has a negative impact on their health. The percentage reporting this ranged from a high of 50 percent in the US to a low of 26 percent in Australia.

The WANE project was explicitly informed by a methodological approach for case study analysis outlined by Marshall (1999), which involves a strategic selection of cases for comparison based on the theoretical interest at hand. Thus, the various chapters include different subsets of case studies from the complete set, and these subsets reflect the judgment of the investigators to the most suitable cases to investigate their particular topic. The sampling is theoretical and in no way based on any intent to generalize to any population as to the frequency or systematic occurrence of the phenomena under investigation. This approach is consistent with the overall ways in which the selection of all WANE case studies was made – not as a random or otherwise representative sample of some population of all small and medium-sized IT enterprises in the study countries, but rather as a compromise between availability, ease of entry, convenience, and the need to represent a range of different types of IT firms.

With the above caveats in mind, we hope that the case studies we conducted in small and medium-sized IT firms in four countries, and the analyses we fashioned from these data, have something useful to say to people practically or scientifically interested in work and life course issues. To designate something as a 'case' is to imply that it is a case, or exemplar, of something (Marshall 1999). Introducing the edited volume by himself and Howard Becker, Charles Ragin (1992: 6) notes that at the workshop that gave rise to the book, 'Becker wanted to make researchers continually ask the question, "what is this a case of?" The less sure that researchers are of their answers, the better their research may be. . . . The question should be asked again and again, and researchers should treat any answer to the question as tentative and specific to the evidence and issues at hand.' While never claiming anything close to statistical representativeness, the authors in this book, all WANE research team members, claim that the case studies, and the analysis developed from them, provide insights as to a number of structural features of small and medium-sized firms in the IT sector, and the implications of these features for the unfolding biographies of people who are employed by these firms. The cases, and the analyses, may, *very carefully*, be taken as cases of something 'larger.' This could possibly provide insights into structural and biographical properties and behavior in other occupational domains or economic sectors characterized by globalization and substantial individualization, flexibility, and risk in working relations. More broadly and, perhaps more carefully, the cases and the analyses built upon them might be seen as exemplars of relationship dynamics at the individual–formal organization level or beyond. We hope that this is 'the case.'

NOTES

1. The family is not a central axis of analysis in this set of studies from the WANE project, yet we have seen that one cannot focus on work without also attending to the family Because another book (McMullin, forthcoming) based on the WANE project addresses family and gender issues, we do not focus on these in this concluding chapter. An individual's nuclear family is embedded within larger kinship structures but also within state-level social welfare systems, for example, that can enable or constrain action.
2. On the importance of this point when people do lose their jobs, see Mendenhall et al. (2008).
3. For example, according to the Raleigh *News and Observer* of 16 December 2008, the number of IT job vacancies in North Carolina (the site of most of the US WANE case studies) was down nearly 50 percent from a year earlier. Since the fall of 2008, numerous North Carolina IT companies, large and small, have laid off workers (Ranii, 2008).
4. In research not based on the WANE project, McMullin and Cairney (2004) focused on intersections of age, class, and gender in relation to self-esteem – a construct similar to the efficacy construct used by Charness and Fox in Chapter 7, with results that seem relevant to readiness to engage in training. They found that from middle age on, but not earlier, men and women from lower social classes experience the lowest levels of self-esteem and in all age groups, women have lower levels of self-esteem than men.

REFERENCES

Broadhead, R.S. (1983), *The Private Lives and Professional Identity of Medical Students*, New Brunswick, NJ and London: Transaction Books.

Castells, M. (2000), 'The information age: economy, society and culture', *The Rise of the Network Society*, vol 1, 2nd edn, Oxford: Blackwell Publishers.

Esping-Andersen, G. (1990), *The Three Worlds of Welfare Capitalism*, Princeton, NJ: Princeton University Press.

Marshall, Victor W. (1999), 'Reasoning with case studies: issues of an aging workforce', *Journal of Aging Studies*, **13** (4): 377–89.

Marshall, V.W. (2009), 'Theory informing public policy: the life course perspective as a policy tool', in Vern L. Bengtson, Daphna Gans, Norella M. Putney, and

Merril Silverstein (eds), *Handbook of Theories of Aging*, 2nd edn, New York: Springer, pp. 573–93.

Marshall, V.W. and P. Clarke (2007), 'Theories of aging: social', in James Birren (ed.), *Encyclopedia of Gerontology*, 2nd edn, Amsterdam: Elsevier, pp. 621–30.

McMullin, J.A. (2000), 'Diversity and the state of sociological aging theory', *The Gerontologist*, **40** (5), 517–30.

McMullin, J.A. (2004), *Understanding Social Inequality: Intersections of Class, Age, Gender, Ethnicity, and Race in Canada*, Don Mills, ON: Oxford University Press.

McMullin J.A. (ed.) (forthcoming), *Gender, Age and Work in the New Economy: The Case of Information Technology Firms*, Kelowna, BC: University of British Columbia Press.

McMullin, J.A. and J. Cairney (2004), 'Self-esteem and the intersection of age, class, and gender', *Journal of Aging Studies*, **18**, 75–90.

Mendenhall, R., A. Kalil, L.J. Spindel and C.M.D. Hart (2008), 'Job loss at mid-life: managers and executives face the "new risk economy"', *Social Forces*, **87** (1), 185–209.

Mills, C. Wright (1959), *The Sociological Imagination*, New York: Grove Press.

Pearce, L.D. (2002), 'Integrating survey and ethnographic methods for systematic anomalous case analysis', *Sociological Methodology*, **32** (1), 103–32.

Ragin, C.C. (1992), 'Introduction: Cases of "What is a case?"', in C.C. Ragin and H.S. Becker (eds), *What is a Case? Exploring the Foundations of Social Inquiry*, Cambridge: Cambridge University Press, pp. 1–17.

Ranii, D. (2008), 'Job prospects for IT workers grow dimmer across state', *News and Observer*, Raleigh NC, 16 December, pp. 7b, 10b.

Wilensky, H.L. (1961), 'Orderly careers and social participation: the impact of work history on social integration in the middle mass', *American Sociological Review*, **26** (4), 521–39.

Index